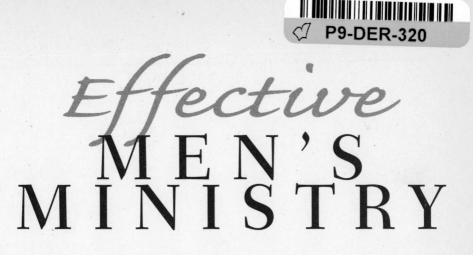

Effective
MEN'S
MINISTRY

Effective MEN'S MINISTRY

The Indispensable Toolkit for Your Church

Foreword by Patrick Morley

Author of *The Man in the Mirror*

PHIL DOWNER, EDITOR

GRAND RAPIDS, MICHIGAN 49530

ZONDERVAN™

Effective Men's Ministry
Copyright © 2001 by the National Coalition of Men's Ministries

Requests for information should be addressed to:

Zondervan, *Grand Rapids, Michigan 49530*

Library of Congress Cataloging-in-Publication Data

Effective men's ministry : Phil Downer, editor.
    p. cm.
    ISBN 0-310-23636-3 (pbk.)
    1. Men—Religious life. 2. Mentoring in church work. I. Downer, Phil, 1947–
BV4528.2 .E44 2001
259'.081—dc21   2001026164

Illustrations by Jill Rozek
Interior design by Todd Sprague

Printed in the United States of America

04 05 06 /❖ DC/ 10 9 8 7 6 5 4

CONTENTS

ACKNOWLEDGMENTS

Our thanks to the authors for sharing so much of their wisdom and experience, to Chip MacGregor for both the idea and the rewrite, and to Dave Lindstedt for his fine editing.

Great appreciation is also due to those who have made NCMM and DNA life-changing tools in the hands of our Lord to make disciples.

—Phil Downer

BUILDING THE LIVES OF MEN

| *Pat Morley* |

T he book you hold in your hands is worth its weight in diamonds. I personally know each of the authors to be a man of deep wisdom, insight, and passion for Christ. Their commitment to reaching men staggers my imagination. These spiritual giants represent a handful of the most gifted disciple-makers alive today. Their single interest is to help you reach and disciple the men of your church.

No man fails on purpose. No man wakes up in the morning and says, "Well, I think I'll see what I can do to ruin my life today." But many men do fail. This book is a profound effort to assist leaders and would-be-leaders who seek to help such men.

IT'S TRENCH WORK

If you are a woman picking up this book, you are holding the answer to these questions: Why is my husband not on fire for the mission of our family and the church? Why is our Sunday school not compelling enough for my husband's interest? What can be done to have a more Christ-focused family? How can I help our church be the vibrant life- and community-changing instrument of God we all want? If you are a woman, I implore you to read this book, to get your husband to read this book, and to give one to your elders and pastor to read.

If you are a man holding this book, read it for the answers to these questions: How can I face my work with new purpose and courage? How can I lead my family with new vision and tenderness? How can I be a part of a life-changing and world-changing group of men to whom God will one day say, "Well done, good and faithful servant"?

Perhaps you are a pastor. If not, I hope you will pass this book along to your pastor when you are finished. Any man who ever became a pastor did so because he wanted to nurture a flock and grow a church. Few, however, expect the resistance they find. It's like the young basketball player who did such a terrific job in practice that his coach put him on the starting team. Ten minutes into the season opener, however, his performance was downright terrible. The coach called him over to the sideline and said, "What's going on? You're not moving the ball or scoring."

"Coach," he said, "I'd be doing great if it weren't for all those tall guys out there waving their arms in my face!"

This book will help you identify effective ways to minister to your men—even if you've got a lot of arms waving in your face.

You already know it's not easy. As one of our leaders put it, "A man is a hard thing to reach!" Men's ministry is trench work. But few ministries have as much potential to revive our families, churches, and communities. When one man turns to Jesus Christ, it breaks a chain of bondage to sin and broken relationships. One changed man can set an entire family lineage for many generations to come on a whole new course of joy, peace, and reconciliation. I know of nothing in this life quite so intoxicating as watching a man come to faith and repentance.

YOUR SYSTEM

In the business world, we have the saying, "Your system is perfectly designed to produce the result you're getting." If you manufacture cars and every third car rolls off the assembly line missing a front right fender, then your system is perfectly designed to produce that result.

The same principle applies to our ministries. If we have men in our churches who don't "get it" spiritually, we can assume it's because our ministry system is perfectly designed to produce the result we're getting. This book is about redesigning your system to produce men who love God, serve the Lord, and provide spiritual leadership to their families.

Building an effective men's ministry boils down to managing momentum. It's about overcoming the inertia in men and keeping them moving. I would like to give you a system to create, capture, and sustain momentum, which you can use to process the terrific ideas you are about to read in this book. The system is represented by figure 1.

Understand Your Purpose

Notice the circle at the center of the diagram. A dynamic men's ministry begins with a clear understanding of your purpose for the men in your church, around which everything else revolves. The first step is to write down what you're trying to accomplish and why. Then you will have a tool to filter out what you don't need to do. For example, if your purpose statement is, "To reach and equip the men of our church to

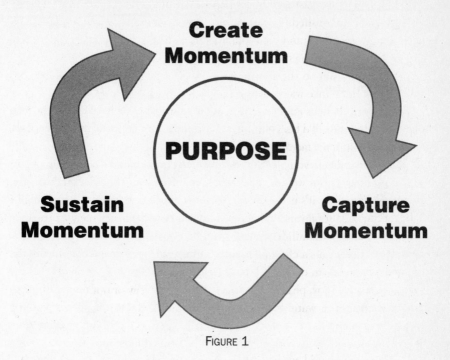

FIGURE 1

be spiritual leaders for their families, church, work, and community," you probably wouldn't focus on service projects. Instead, you would focus on discipleship groups.

Create Momentum

The first challenge in having a dynamic men's ministry is overcoming the inertia in men. When NASA launches the space shuttle from Cape Canaveral, they strap it to a booster that contains 500,000 gallons of liquid fuel, all of which burns off in 8.5 minutes. Then the shuttle literally coasts another 4 million miles. Why is that? You need only as much energy as is required to put a stationary object in motion. But it takes a lot of energy to overcome inertia. You are about to read a host of ideas proven to get men's ministry off the ground.

Capture Momentum

It is crucial to capture momentum once you've create it. The first error is to attempt too little. You wouldn't go to the expense of cooling your house to a comfortable 72 degrees in sweltering summer heat and then leave all the doors and windows open. You would try to capture what you had created.

The second error is to attempt too much. If you say to men who have attended the first men's ministry event of their lives, "Next week we are going to begin a three-year inductive study of the Bible in the Hebrew language"—well, you get the idea. Give your men a definite next step that they can visualize themselves taking. Don't try to shift them from first gear to fourth gear. Offer them a second gear—small group studies that last three, four, maybe six weeks in length.

Sustain Momentum

The greatest challenge in reaching men through your church is keeping the men involved after the novelty wears off. Capturing momentum is crucial but not enough. You need to sustain the momentum for the long haul. Sustaining momentum is really about offering as wide a variety of compelling men's growth and discipleship opportunities as possible. The more you offer, the better. Give men—whether on the fringe, in the mainstream, or leading the charge—every chance to hook into something.

In this book, you will read numerous ideas on how to engage men for the long haul: Bible studies, book studies, men's workbooks, issues-oriented small groups, accountability groups, prayer groups, early morning leadership development with the pastor, and ongoing ministry projects such as mentoring teens.

Finally, notice in the figure the arrow going up from "sustain momentum" to "create momentum." The principle of the parable of the sower is always working against the command to make disciples. We will experience drop-off at every step. That's why it's important to periodically create additional momentum.

MEN ARE WORTH IT

This book is a project of the National Coalition of Men's Ministries (NCMM), and each of the authors is an NCMM member. Founded in 1996, NCMM's vision is "a disciple-making ministry to men in every church." We want to accomplish this by serving you and equipping your church to have a more effective ministry to men. We exist to serve you. Over 200,000 churches already have representation in NCMM through their denominational leaders. Learn more about how NCMM can help you by visiting our website (www.ncmm.org).

Working with men isn't easy. It takes a long time to make a disciple. But there is power and hope in the gospel. In fact, the gospel is the only place men will find hope. So, yes, it's worth it.

Start small. "Do not despise this small beginning, for the eyes of the Lord rejoice to see the work begin" (Zech. 4:10 LB). Start with however many men God gives you—two, four, six, or eight. Remain faithful to those men.

Don't lose heart. If you'll commit to working with the men of your church, I can offer this promise: God may not give you the church you wanted, but he will give you the church the world needs to see. And that will glorify our great and holy Lord.

Perhaps you feel as if it's too late for you. It's never too late. A Chinese proverb says, "The best time to plant a tree was twenty years ago. The second best time is now."

PART ONE

DEVELOPING
THE PLAN

1

MODERN MAN IN CONTEMPORARY CULTURE

Dan Erickson and Dan Schaffer

As the family goes, so goes the nation." This simple statement reflects the truth that the family is the essential building block of all human society. The question is not, Will we have families? but, What will our families be like? For better or worse, the family is the primary means by which values are taught, morality is established, and sense of identity is formed.

Our government invests billions of dollars each year in the future of our nation through programs that primarily affect children outside the home; meanwhile, the family unit is under attack and is, in many cases, fragmented and without purpose. Studies have shown that one of the main reasons for the breakdown of our families is a lack of proper leadership in the home, especially by husbands and fathers. We might well amend our initial statement to read, "As the father goes, so goes the family, and so goes the nation."

If the church is to be an effective witness and influence in our nation, we must focus our attention on the condition of the family and its leadership. In other words, we must turn our efforts to the development of effective husbands and fathers. This is the greatest opportunity and challenge facing the church in the twenty-first century, because government social programs will never be able to capture men's hearts and mentor them into becoming responsible leaders of their homes.

Unfortunately, most local churches do not know how to train men to be productive leaders. In many congregations, the normal process is for a man to get saved and then be rushed into a ministry position before he is ready. To be effective, however, he must first be trained to lead himself and his family before he can successfully lead the church. The church has a responsibility to teach men how to be spiritual leaders.

THE STATE OF OUR NATION'S MEN

Men in our society—including Christian men and pastors—are caught in a web of deception about their masculinity. As counselor Alexander Mitserlisch postulates, "Society has torn the soul of the male, and into this tear the demons have fled—the demons of insecurity, selfishness and despair. Consequently, men do not know who they are as men. Rather, they define themselves by what they do, who they know, or by what they own."

Many men today feel isolated. Studies have shown that most men over thirty do not have close friends. They have colleagues and work associates, golf partners, and maybe a "couples" friend or two, with whom the bond is really between the wives. If they say that they do have a best friend, often it turns out to be a childhood buddy they talk to occasionally or visit every few years.

In a 1993 survey, Dr. Gary Rossberg identified the following influences on men in our society:[1]

Major Pressures	*Major Challenges*
1. Career and Success	1. The search for significance
2. Finances	2. The desire to be in charge or take control
3. Relationships	3. The tendency to withdraw or be passive
4. Sexual Temptation	4. A competitive spirit

Regrettably, for most men in our culture, male friendship is a relic of the past. One man spoke for many when he said, "I haven't made a new friend in twenty-five years." This estrangement of men in our culture results in part from a societal stan-

---

[1] *Vibrant Men's Ministry Resource Kit* (Denver: Promise Keepers, 1996), 9.

dard that discourages true friendships between men. We've been taught to protect ourselves by keeping our adult relationships within certain "safe" parameters. A close companionship between two males who are not relatives is often seen as suspicious or unhealthy. Society has convinced us that a relationship like that of Jonathan and David in the Old Testament is impossible.

CURRENT BELIEFS AMONG NONCHURCHGOERS

According to George Barna, most men who are not involved with a church believe that the church does not offer any lasting value to their lives. The typical adult male in our society is more likely to spend his Sundays watching sports on TV than attending a church service. A majority of unchurched men believe that participating in church life cannot be justified because the return on their investment of time, attention, and energy is too slim.

Despite the negative feedback, Barna also identified seven key factors that unchurched men said would draw them to the church. These factors define the window of opportunity that lies open to the church and sets the parameters for effective men's ministry.[2]

1. Men are looking for meaning and purpose in life.
2. Men are seeking understanding of who they are and what they are thinking.
3. Men want solutions to their everyday problems and difficulties.
4. Men want to know God—who he is and what he means to them.
5. Men want effective men's ministry that touches them where they are.
6. Men want friendships that are built on trust and that will last.
7. Men want help with family issues, especially training for their children.

If our ministry to men is going to be successful, we must develop a system that will help men to form significant and lasting friendships. Without vital relationships between our men, too many men will continue to feel lonely, isolated, and without hope. When building our ministry, we must focus primarily on establishing relationships, not on developing programs. A successful ministry to men will encompass the following key components of a man's life: identity, friendship, God's calling, discipline, marriage and family skills, and stewardship.

Identity. God has placed into each man a longing to be significant, a need to feel that his life counts. Countless men feel inadequate and insecure, no matter how much talent they possess. A man needs to learn how to find his identity in Christ. And every man needs a sense of purpose. Without a godly purpose in life, a man is left to measure his significance and his success by what he owns, what he achieves, and what

---

[2]George Barna, "The Battle for the Hearts of Men," *New Man* 4, no. 1 (1997): 40–44.

> **Two are better than one because they have a good return for their labor. For if either of them falls, the one will lift up his companion. But woe to the one who falls when there is not another to lift him up.**
>
> Ecclesiastes 4:9 – 10 NASB

he controls. The problem with finding his self-worth in his position, possessions, or power is that if he loses his job, his house, or his influence, a man also loses his self-respect.

Friendship. Most men know a lot of people by name or by acquaintance. Conversations with these individuals are light, brief, and nonthreatening. Even in the church, very few men have close friends. For the most part, men are spiritually fed but relationally bankrupt. Ask a group of men to identify their greatest needs, and most of them would respond with the need for close male friendships. The need for intimate, trusting relationships with other men proves to be a compelling need, regardless of race or culture.

Men are looking for spiritual brothers who will become genuine friends. In spite of many stereotypes, most men desire to draw near to people who will encourage, exhort, and love them. Out of brotherly love grows hope. This is what Jesus means when he says, "By this all men will know that you are My disciples, if you have love for one another" (John 13:35 NASB).

God's calling. Men need to see themselves the way God sees them: full of potential and promise. When a man sees purpose in everything he does, he will live a purposeful life. When he views himself as a faithful servant doing everything as unto the Lord, he is released to live an obedient and productive life in God's perfect and revealed will. God tells us through Paul in Ephesians 1:4, 11 that he chose us for a divine purpose. "Just as He chose us in Him before the foundation of the world . . . also we have obtained an inheritance, having been predestined according to His purpose" (NASB). As we minister to men, we must help them to identify God's purpose for their lives and then equip them to fulfill their godly purpose at home, in the church, and in the world.

Men want to know God, but many don't know how to begin. And those who do begin to seek relationship with their heavenly Father need help to continue their pursuit. As men, we need someone to show us how to seek, find, and hear God. A gifted teacher can explain the principles of prayer, Bible study, and worship, but the typical man learns best by example. Discipleship is better caught than taught. That is why Jesus chose twelve men to be "with Him" (Mark 3:14 NASB). He knew that his greatest impact would come from living side by side with these men day after day. He knew that the more time he could invest in them, the more they would learn from his teaching and modeling. The best method for teaching men how to pray and seek

God is not from behind a microphone; it is spending time with them in a personal relationship.

Discipline. Most men have values and priorities that they keep in their minds, but many have difficulty incorporating those priorities into their daily schedules. Many would say that God and family are their top two priorities, but in reality, God and family are often given less time and commitment than work and other pursuits. Consequently, many men feel guilty every time they are faced with the issue of their values and priorities.

Men need to know how to excel in the basics of the Christian life. Like a newborn baby, who must be taught by his parents how to walk, eat, read, and write, a man must be taught the fundamentals of the faith in order to live a purposeful and productive life in Christ. To grow into maturity and productive service for the Lord, each man must be given the necessary tools for Bible reading, prayer, Scripture memorization, witnessing, and discipling others. And he must learn how to incorporate what he learns about the Word of God into his everyday life.

These habits and skills don't come about by accident but only by a concerted effort by the leaders of the church. God intends that men develop under the helpful influence of mature believers. Hebrews 13:7 says, "Remember those who led you, who spoke the word of God to you; and considering the result of their conduct, imitate their faith" (NASB).

Marriage and family skills. Most men have never been taught how to be godly men, husbands, or fathers. Many boys grow up with a poor or nonexistent relationship with their fathers, resulting in deep wounds and resentments. Often these past experiences are carried over to their own families, thereby perpetuating the cycle of poor fathering, wounding, and resentment in the next generation.

Many men have given up the role of spiritual leader of the home because of pride and embarrassment, and now they feel that any sudden change in their role would be viewed as hypocritical or superspiritual. Men need to know that it's okay to repent and be humble in front of their families. Men need to set a standard of

---

Keys That Reveal a Man's Commitments and True Values

1. *His goals.* What he wants most in life.
2. *His thoughts.* What he thinks about most of the time.
3. *His finances.* How he spends his money.
4. *His pursuits.* How he spends his leisure time.
5. *His friends.* The people with whom he associates.
6. *His attention.* Who and what he admires and appreciates.
7. *His humor.* What amuses him.

—A. W. Tozer

righteousness in their homes and live in moral obedience to the Bible. And they need other men to help reinforce their stand. Men need to see models of loving fathers, and they must learn to model spirituality through love and consistency in their personal behavior. Husbands and fathers need to commit like Joshua did when he said, "As for me and my house, we will serve the LORD" (Josh. 24:15 NASB).

Stewardship. Men today need to learn how to give God the firstfruits of their lives—not only their finances but their time, talent, and energy. God deserves our best, but too often he gets the leftovers of our time and attention. We give our best at work and play but give little time and effort in preparation for our service to the Lord. The teaching of stewardship skills will allow our men to sharpen their God-given gifts and talents so they can be used in excellence for the Lord.

CREATING A MALE-FRIENDLY ENVIRONMENT

At Promise Keepers and other men's ministry gatherings across the United States, thousands of men have flocked to stadiums and arenas to praise and worship Jesus Christ. With their hands uplifted and voices joined in singing and cheering, at times the crescendo of sound is almost deafening. Yet why do many of these same men sit passively and quietly in the church pew each Sunday, barely raising their voices, much less their hands and arms, in worship? We believe it's because these stadium gatherings have succeeded in creating a masculine context, or male-friendly environment, that is often lacking in the local church. If we want to be effective with our local men's ministries, we must create a climate that allows men to feel safe and at home in the church.

Despite the obvious need for developing men as leaders in their homes and local churches, studies have shown that few men will change based on hearing or obtaining information such as what they might receive in a typical church service. The majority of men will make needed changes in their lives only after they have experienced intimate relationships with God and other Christian men. Sadly, the same studies have also shown that the average man in the church has few or no close Christian friends. Unfortunately, men tend to isolate themselves from close and meaningful relationships. As we seek to establish a male-friendly environment, to break through this isolation and reach the men in our churches, we must understand six unique traits of the masculine context.

1. Men equate personal distance with safety and security.
2. Men communicate through questions.
3. Most men are goal or challenge oriented.
4. Men tend to focus and compartmentalize.
5. Men choose rules over relationships.
6. Men are hesitant to express emotion.

Keep in mind that these are general principles. Most men would recognize these tendencies within themselves, but there is room for differences based on individual temperament and culture, so we must avoid stereotyping. The goal of understanding the male context is to help your men's ministry work *with* your men, not against them.

Personal distance equals safety. In general, men equate personal distance with safety and security; closeness or intimacy is perceived as a threat. Men are accustomed to being guarded and competitive in their relationships with other men, so uniting around a common purpose within the church can be difficult for them. Men will seldom be transparent in a large church gathering. They are more likely to share openly in a men's small group or a face-to-face encounter. To overcome men's tendencies to preserve their personal distance, the men who lead your small groups will need to model a masculine openness and intimacy and demonstrate the benefits of healthy male relationships.

Key questions:

1. Who are some men in your church who have healthy male relationships and could help to initiate relationships with other men?
2. How can you challenge your men to take the first step in beginning a close relationship with another man? Do they understand the benefits?
3. What can your men's core group do to encourage and promote men's small groups in your church?
4. How can you equip and encourage the men in your church to become men's small group leaders?

Communicating through questions. Because men are motivated to solve problems and "get to the bottom line," they communicate primarily by asking a series of questions. You can tell you have a man's interest and attention when he starts asking questions. An effective strategy when communicating with the men in your church is to ask open-ended questions that cause them to think through an issue and respond. The focus of leadership, then, should be on listening to their responses.

Key questions:

1. What kinds of open-ended questions are you asking your men? Prefacing inquiries with "What do you think about," "How do you feel about," or "Why do you think that" will draw men into conversation and deeper interaction.
2. How are the men in your congregation responding?
3. What specifically do you want the men to do in your men's ministry? How will your leaders communicate this to them?

Creating goals and challenges. The typical male views most situations as a challenge to be met or an obstacle to be conquered. Men enjoy meeting goals because it gives them a sense of accomplishment and satisfaction. The men in your church need to be challenged with clearly defined goals that are big enough to stretch their faith but possible for them to achieve with God's help. The goals of your men's ministry should be broken down into small steps, so that the response of your men will be, "I can do that!"

Key questions:

1. What are the goals of your men's ministry?
2. How do your goals demonstrate your dependence on Christ to accomplish them?
3. What are your men doing that indicates they understand the goals of your men's ministry? How are you motivating the men to achieve these goals?
4. How are you challenging your men to participate in and take ownership of your men's ministry?

Opening the compartments. Most men have tunnel vision. They tend to compartmentalize their lives and manage one thing at a time in order to reach their goals. When you define the goals for your men's ministry, give your men one or two specific steps they can focus on and achieve. Emphasize one goal at a time. Multiple points of focus will seem overwhelming to most of the men in your group.

Key questions:

1. What clearly defined steps have you given your men so that they can see how to accomplish the goals you have set before them?
2. Who are you accountable to for carrying out these steps?
3. How do the goals of your men's ministry relate to the overall goal of becoming godly men, husbands, and fathers?

Rules versus relationships. To maintain logic, sequence, and order in their circumstances, men tend to emphasize rules and principles. Although this brings order out of chaos, it also creates distance from other people. Because most men place a higher value on rules and principles than on relationships, the men's ministry activities in your church should be structured to include elements of both. To satisfy the desire for order, make sure to clearly define the topic, time, place, and format of your men's meetings. Structure creates stability, which in turn creates the proper environment for men to relate to one another. To encourage men to move into meaningful relationships, create times for personal sharing, prayer for individual needs, application of Scripture, and other opportunities for interaction.

Key questions:

1. How can you plan your men's ministry activities to help your men focus on relating to each other?

2. How much time are the men in your gatherings given for personal sharing, praying for one another, and applying God's Word to their lives?
3. What structure needs to be in place to create stability for the men in your church?

Unlocking emotions. Most men do not easily express their emotions unless they feel it is safe to do so. Men will limit how they express their emotions to what they think is acceptable for males. Men hesitate to share the way they feel, for both internal and external reasons, including how they were raised, cultural limitations, and the masculine propensity for equating distance with safety. The men in your church will seldom share openly unless the environment is a safe place to express their emotions. Most often, this will be in a men's small group or on a one-to-one basis.

Men also need time to figure out why they feel the way they do. If they don't have adequate opportunity to process their feelings, they will usually revert to a "fight or flight" response and become angry or run from the situation. Men will avoid most situations that don't offer them a sense of control.

Key questions:

1. Where do the men in your church feel free to express their emotions?
2. Who will your men be accountable to when dealing with their feelings?
3. How will you encourage your small group leaders to share their own feelings, listen when other men in the group are upset, follow through to seek understanding, and deal with issues through confession, forgiveness, and appropriate action?

ISOLATED PASTORS

The sad reality in many churches is that the pastor is as isolated from other men as his laymen are—if not more so. Most pastors will admit that they do not have one good, solid friend. The thought of letting their guard down in favor of genuine transparency threatens the comfort zone of many pastors. They might think that if others really knew about their failures, thoughts, and struggles, they would be disqualified from ministry. Nothing could be further from the truth. Most men want to see their pastors as normal human beings who face the challenges we all face every day. Unfortunately, some pastors shy away from initiating men's ministry because they feel as though they haven't figured it out for themselves yet.

Another reason why many pastors hesitate to get involved in the development of a men's ministry program is because they already have too much to do. The thought of yet another program on the schedule does not appeal to most pastors. Effective men's ministry, however, is not a program; it's a transformational environment built on vital relationships, which inevitably brings positive changes within the church.

God is calling men—including pastors—to discover their place in his purpose. And he's choosing to work within the context of the local church. God is calling all men to pursue him, and he is calling his pastors to allow the Holy Spirit to shape, recover, and rebuild anything in their manhood that needs to be reconditioned after the heavenly Father's design. Spiritually mature men know how to discern, pray, and walk in the Spirit to minister to the needs of their churches and communities. When they become engaged in the Lord's work, their hearts are motivated to offer their time, talents, and treasures as expressions of their love for God.

God desires to mold pastors who will model biblical manhood for their men. Transformed pastors are foundational to God's cause and are the beginning of men's ministry in the church. Pastors inevitably multiply what is true in their own lives. Therefore, the starting place for effective men's ministry is with pastors who will submit themselves to the process of becoming Christlike.

2

WHAT IS MEN'S MINISTRY?

Steve Sonderman

One night in June 1944, General Dwight Eisenhower walked the beaches of England, deep in thought. Occasionally he stopped and stared across the dark waters of the English Channel toward the coast of France, where the Nazi armies had built a military fortress. The next dawn would see hundreds of Allied ships and thousands of soldiers storm that coast, and Eisenhower knew that for many of those soldiers, it would be their last morning.

As he walked along, he came across an American private, standing by himself, also staring across the ocean. The general asked him what he was thinking. "Home," came the reply. Then the supreme commander of the allied forces suggested they walk together, that perhaps they would draw confidence from each other's company. So the two men walked on—one older, one younger; one experienced in the ways of war, the other inexperienced; but each man drawing strength from the other.

That is exactly what many men need today—others to walk with them, offering wisdom and encouragement, particularly in difficult times. Men in our world are in turmoil. The pressures of our modern age are draining away the joy of life and leaving people too exhausted to experience the abundant life God has promised. They are physically tired, emotionally drained, overwhelmed by debt, and trying to cope with damaged relationships. What a man needs is a brother to draw close, minister

> **The things which you have heard from me in the presence of many witnesses, entrust these to faithful men who will be able to teach others also.**
>
> 2 Timothy 2:2 NASB

to him, and help him mature. He needs somebody to demonstrate to him another way to live, modeling a godly marriage, biblical parenthood, and the love of Christ. He needs someone who will take the time to assist him in his spiritual walk and help him find the new life Christ promised.

The purpose of men's ministry is to do just that. A healthy men's ministry will create a framework of vital relationships among men, within a distinctly masculine context, that will intentionally reconcile men to God and to each other. Through these relationships, men will be able to minister to the needs of the body of Christ and the community, under the authority and direction of the Word of God and the leaders of the local church. A vibrant and vital ministry to men will be founded on biblical truth and prayer, inspired by Christ-centered worship, and guided by a well-defined vision and clear goals. In the process, the men in your congregation will be equipped with the resources and training to become effective, godly leaders in their homes, the church, and the community and will proactively apply their spiritual gifts to influence the world (both locally and abroad) for Jesus Christ.

When a men's ministry is led by a group of men who submit to God's Word, pray diligently and deliberately, respond in obedience, and worship freely, they will model righteous living for other men and teach them how to transform society through the power of God's love.

One of the best ways to introduce the Word of God into the lives of men is through small groups designed especially for men. Within the context of a small group, men can become rooted in the Scriptures, develop their prayer lives, and learn to worship God in spirit and truth. Of course, not all men are ready for the relational commitment of a small group, and so to be effective, a men's ministry must create a variety of entry points that will draw men at every stage into vital relationships with other men. A ministry that is not based on building genuine friendships between men will not prosper or persevere.

We must also create and foster a uniquely male environment based on an understanding of how men learn, relate, and communicate. We must call men out of isolation into affirming, accountable relationships with other men, so that they can genuinely open up, be honest with each other, and become free to be the men God has called them to be.

Guided by a clear set of goals and a well-defined vision, we must equip the men in our congregations with the necessary resources and training to effectively implement biblical principles in their lives and encourage them to keep their commitments to God, their families, their friends, their work, and their community.

Above all, our men's ministries must call men to deeper intimacy with God, genuine accountability with other brothers in Christ, purity of heart, servant leadership, honoring of women, mentoring of the next generation, commitment to church leadership and the mission of the church, and unashamed witness to the Lord Jesus Christ.

UNLEASHING GOD'S GIFTING OF MEN

A well-implemented ministry to men will identify, develop, and release the unique gifts of men into the life and service of the church. It will call men out of their spiritual passivity and equip them for godly influence at home, at church, and in society. Rather than adding an extra burden to church leadership, men's ministry trains men who can in turn train others.

Men's ministry intentionally draws men to God and to each other. It reconciles sinful men with God through the life and work of Jesus Christ, and it encourages and equips men to live in peace with each other and to reconcile their differences. It develops a group of bridge builders who are committed to link the body of Christ together by lovingly and prayerfully crossing racial, cultural, and denominational barriers in the church and society.

By strengthening the lay leadership in the church, men's ministry serves the needs of the congregation and community. Pastors are freed to shepherd the flock, pray, teach, and network with other pastors to identify needs in the local community, whereupon they can lead their men to minister to those needs.

LAYING A SOLID FOUNDATION

Every builder knows that the foundation is the critical part of any building. If the foundation is not strong enough to bear the weight of the structure, the walls will ultimately crack, floors will buckle, doors will stick, and the life of the building will be drastically reduced. Only the most unscrupulous contractor would intentionally lay an inadequate foundation.

The implications for men's ministry are obvious: take great care to lay a proper foundation in the bedrock of prayer, the Word of God, and worship. The personal readiness of church leadership in these areas and the vision they cast for the church will affect everything that follows.

Start with prayer. In Mark 11:17, Jesus says, "My house shall be called a house of prayer for all the nations" (NASB). The Lord knew that prayer is the only answer to our daily confrontations with the enemy. Prayer must be the number one activity of men's ministry in the local church. In the Gospels, we continually see Jesus praying. He prayed among the hypocrites in the temple, in crowds, on hillsides with his disciples, in a crowded upper room, and alone on the mountains outside Jerusalem. Many times he spent the entire night praying. At the lowest point in his life, he asked his disciples to spend time with him in prayer. Prayer was more than a part of Christ's life; it was the foundation of his life.

Prayer is the ultimate indicator of our level of trust in our heavenly Father. Prayer is not optional; it must be the first and last order of business in the lives of men. Men in the local church must embrace the daily practice of prayer, because an absence of prayer leads to an absence of power. Where prayer is a daily, persistent practice, there will be a continual display of God's power in the lives of men in the church.

There is no true spiritual growth apart from a devotional habit of daily prayer. Consistency in prayer is *prima facie* evidence of a true spiritual commitment. The first and decisive battle in building a foundation of prayer is the conflict that arises when men covenant to be alone with God each day. Immediately, Satan begins to fill their paths with distracting hindrances. Job responsibilities increase, special projects arise, schedules overflow, and fatigue sets in. Prayer does not come naturally to men; it must be cultivated. Nevertheless, persistence in prayer pays off.

Daily, systematic prayer taps into the practical power of God—which is not merely theoretical—and adds strength and depth to the foundation of prayer in a local church. Men with very little prayer experience who pray in the presence of other men will catch the spirit of prayer and become great intercessors. Prayer must be taught, modeled, and practiced, and persistence in prayer must be encouraged if the foundation of our ministry to the world is to stand the test of time.

Anchor in the Word of God. God's Word is his central revelation of truth to the church. God's Word offers answers to the deepest longings of our souls, and in its pages, God will be found by all who truly seek him. As leaders in our local congregations, we must be both students and teachers of the Word. Our goal is to create a hunger for the Word of God in the hearts of men. Then we must teach them to read, study, meditate on, and obey God's absolute truth and include God's Word in every aspect of their lives.

Freedom in worship. The essence of a man's worship determines everything about his life. In worship, we come honestly before God and give attention to his desires and his ways. Worship pours substance into a man's soul, strength into his life's foundations, unshakable stability into his marriage, steadfastness into his relationships, and trustworthiness into his work and business practices.

Redeeming worship is centered on the Lord's Table. Before he went to the cross, Jesus established communion as a regular practice of the church. The redeeming power of the blood of Christ not only saves our souls, it is the foundation of every redemptive, recovering, and renewing work of God.

Worship is the means by which a man is summoned into God's divine presence, asked to remove his shoes, shown God's heart of compassion for mankind, and called to take on the role of leadership (see Ex. 3:1–10). Sometimes worship is meeting with God alone and waiting in his holy presence. Empowering worship emerges from our quest for God and opens us to the fullness of his Holy Spirit. Men who worship become men of spiritual power, because they are filled with the mightiness of Jesus. A man maintains a life of power when he spends time in God's presence, praising him.

THE FRAMEWORK OF EFFECTIVE MEN'S MINISTRY

Every effective men's ministry must provide a variety of entry points that will facilitate the involvement of men in the church. This is not a new strategy. Jesus did the same thing, from preaching to the multitudes, to sending out the seventy disciples, to spending concentrated and quality time with his twelve closest disciples— even setting aside special time with three: Peter, James, and John.

An exciting element of this strategy is that every man can be involved at various levels, depending on his spiritual interest and the time he has available.

Familiarize yourself with the funnel diagram (fig. 2), which illustrates a strategy for attracting men into the life and ministry of the church. As a man progresses down the funnel, he will be drawn into closer and more committed relationships with other men and will grow in his biblical knowledge and understanding. The goal of the funnel is to provide a transformational environment in which a man can learn how to convert biblical truth into action that serves and honors his commitment to Jesus Christ, family, friends, church, and community.

Because men will be attracted by different aspects of our men's ministries, we must create a variety of gateways by which a man can enter into the fellowship of the church and become involved in vital relationships with other men. We have defined five major entry points on our funnel model of men's ministry: conferences, special events, equipping seminars, congregational gatherings, and small groups.

Some of these events are designed to be larger than others. For example, a catalytic event such as a men's conference will normally be much larger than a seminar or a small group. But each entry point meets a particular need and creates a unique opportunity for men to participate at various levels of involvement. A successful men's ministry will utilize all five types of events and entry points. Let's take a closer look at each type of event.

Men's Conferences

These intercongregational and local church events act as a catalyst to motivate men and ignite local men's ministry. Examples of this type of event include denominational men's conferences, parachurch men's conferences, and men's retreats.

When your men return from a catalytic event, they will often be inspired and motivated to do something for God. Some of them will have made a commitment to Jesus Christ and to significant people in their lives. Many will want to become more closely involved in men's ministry in your church.

Biblical Information Given

Relational Commitment Required

Men's Conferences

Men's Special Events

Men's Equipping Seminars

Men's Congregational Gatherings

Men's Small Groups

Men Who Make & Keep Commitments That Last a Lifetime To:

JESUS CHRIST
FAMILY
FRIENDS
CHURCH
COMMUNITY

FIGURE 2

Key questions:

1. When revival happens, what will you do with all the new men?
2. How do you plan to channel a sudden influx of inspired men into your church?
3. What types of ministry activities will your church provide to strengthen men's relationships with one another and with God?

Knowing the answers to these questions will help you better prepare for training events that can significantly impact your men's ministry.

Special Events

Special events focus on nonthreatening activities that allow men to become acquainted with each other. Events are organized by a local church to provide an entry point for men on the periphery of the congregation or for men from the community. Examples of men's special events include barbecues, softball games, fishing trips, basketball tournaments, and men's breakfasts.

Special events are a good way to publicize your church's men's ministry. The men in your community will enjoy these activities, and they are a good place for your men to bring their unchurched friends.

Key questions:

1. Follow-up after special events is crucial. What further opportunities to become involved will your church offer a newcomer?
2. Are your men prepared to help a newcomer through that process?
3. A guiding principle for special events is this: one man will come because another man asks him. How will you encourage your men to invite their friends and acquaintances to your men's special events?
4. Which neutral location works best for hosting special events?

Equipping Seminars

Equipping seminars and training sessions offer men an opportunity to grow personally and develop leadership skills. Such things as fatherhood seminars, community involvement seminars, marriage workshops, and financial seminars are other good entry points for men on the periphery of the church.

Most of the men in your church know what they *should* be doing. Men's seminars encourage them and show them *how* to do it. The men, their families, and your church will all benefit.

Key questions:

1. Have you surveyed the men in your church to discover what types of seminars will address their needs?
2. When the seminar is over, what are some ongoing men's activities in your church that would strengthen a man in his relationship with God and others?
3. Your men's ministry will grow only as fast as its leadership does. What men's leadership workshops, small group leaders' training sessions, and discipleship opportunities will your church provide for your men?

Congregational Gatherings

Congregational gatherings invite all the men of the congregation together for biblical teaching, fellowship, and prayer. They challenge Christian men to interact with and build up one another as they pursue godliness. Effective men's gatherings include monthly breakfasts, retreats, and "Men's Day" programs.

Your men need a place where they are encouraged in their walk with God and can develop friendships with other Christian brothers. A gathering at your church or a retreat will begin to do that and will also give your men a taste of what can happen in a men's small group.

Key questions:

1. How will you plan your men's congregational gatherings to have a healthy balance of time for fellowship, prayer, and scriptural teaching and application?
2. What are some ways that you can strategically use congregational gatherings to encourage your men to become involved in men's small groups?
3. When and where is the best time and place for the majority of men in your church to gather together?

Small Groups

Men's small groups offer a man the greatest potential for spiritual growth, because he chooses to become a member of a team committed to mutual support, self-disclosure, and honoring Jesus Christ in their relationships. These groups usually involve four to seven men who meet on a weekly or other regular basis.

Men's small groups are vital to the spiritual health of the guys in your congregation. If your church is just starting or has few men attending, men's small groups are where you should begin your men's ministry. Note the importance of men's small groups as a link to personal ministry in the funnel strategy.

Key questions:

1. How will you encourage and promote men's small groups in your church?
2. Who are some relationally strong and spiritually mature men who could serve as men's small group leaders in your church?
3. How will you train your small group leaders, and when?

THE ESSENTIALS OF MEN'S MINISTRY

No two men's ministries are the same. However, certain principles are common to every effective men's ministry. If you want your men's ministry to work, don't overlook the following essential guidelines.

1. *Focus on relationships, not programs.* Men generally don't talk easily about their faith and feelings. Consequently, it's critically important for your men's ministry to provide a male-friendly environment focused on encouraging relationships, not just programs. Try to develop a place were men can feel relaxed and secure. Remember, men don't like to be forced into relationships. Genuine friendship is a natural process that men will initiate and control.

2. *Communicate clear goals.* Men need to know who they are and where they're headed. Develop a clear purpose statement with measurable goals that focus your men on relating to God and one another. Goals should be easily understood by everyone, measurable, attainable, based on the ministry's statement of purpose, and agreed to by all participants.

3. *Target men's ministry exclusively for men.* Most men simply do not communicate to the same depth about spiritual or emotional issues when women are present. Effective men's ministries structure their activities in ways that allow men time to talk with other men, without women present.

4. *Get your pastor's support and support your pastor.* Men must honor and respect their pastor by seeking his counsel on and approval of any men's ministry activities. Brainstorm ways to encourage your pastor and to assist him in his ministry and work. Your pastor's support is essential to the men's ministry in your church. Without his active participation, your men's ministry will not be successful. After all, he is the key leader of the church.

5. *Build a ministry leadership team with a core group of men.* The majority of men's ministries begin with a group of laymen praying for other men in the church, based on a mutual desire to help men deal with issues of conviction, integrity, and action. A pastor's investment of himself in these "leading laymen" will greatly aid their progress. A core group of men in your church will be the heart of an effective men's ministry. The core group does not exist to exclude other men but rather to pray for, direct, and serve the entire men's ministry.

6. *Avoid implementing too much too soon.* Inspired leaders sometimes try to make a men's program "happen" without first taking enough time to build relationships and communicate vision and purpose to their men. Most effective men's ministries take three to five years to develop. Give your men plenty of time, and don't give up. Even Jesus took three years to develop his relationships with his twelve disciples.

7. *Minister with flexibility and variety.* Successful men's ministries offer a variety of entry points that provide men with the opportunity to grow spiritually and relationally. Men in your church are at different stages of spiritual maturity, so try to offer a variety of men's activities from all five levels of the men's ministry funnel.

GETTING STARTED

Gathering a core group of committed men to pray for the men of the church and for God's leading is foundational to men's ministry. The pastor's leadership and participation are of the utmost importance. In addition to meeting regularly to pray and seek unity in planning the men's ministry, the core group should develop personal relationships with one another that will serve as a model for other men in the church.

The men you select to participate in this core group are often already involved in another ministry in the church. Because most ministries usually need more men, a core group member could view the men's ministry as a way to get additional men involved in his individual ministry. There's a greater need, however, to forego personal ministry goals until the men's ministry begins to produce spiritually maturing men. One day, with God's help, there will be enough men of faith available to supply all areas of ministry within the church. In the meantime, the core group should agree to focus on building up the men's ministry first.

Your men's ministry must have a clear focus that will encourage relationships between men in your church. A purpose statement defines your ministry and becomes the guiding point that helps direct it. This statement should be both qualitative and quantitative. A qualitative statement might read something like this: "Westside Assembly's men's program is dedicated to building men into Christlike leaders for their families, friends, church, and community." A quantitative statement will include numerical goals; for instance: "Bethel Temple is committed to having thirty men in small groups by the end of the year."

Before you write your statement of purpose, answer the following questions.

1. What are your goals?
2. Why do you want to achieve those particular goals?
3. How will you accomplish these goals?
4. How will you know when your goals have been achieved?

Using your answers from these questions, create a one- or two-sentence purpose statement for your men's ministry. Don't be discouraged if it takes several meetings, over a period of time, to develop your statement. This is the normal process. It is best to take the time to carefully think through each word of your statement, because what you agree upon will guide your ministry for years to come.

In light of the purpose statement you develop, plan a yearly calendar of events, incorporating each element of the funnel model.

1. What kinds of men's conferences will you attend or organize?
2. What men's special events will you sponsor? Space these meals, retreats, and recreational activities throughout the year.
3. What training would most benefit the men of your church? Take into account their spiritual needs, spiritual experience, ages, employment, families, gifts, and so on. Schedule essential training events throughout the year.
4. What men's congregational meetings are essential during the year? A quarterly men's breakfast or a seasonal dinner might be a good way to set the tone for the year.
5. What small group options do the men in your congregation need? What time should your men meet? What type of focus should be included? How can the opportunities to be involved be communicated?

A List of Warnings

Don't start without pastoral support.

Don't start without prayer.

Don't start without key people; form a leadership team.

Don't start without preparation; plan each event carefully.

Don't try to do too much too fast.

Don't create events for everyone; design them for men only.

Don't limit events by age.

Don't be boring and disorganized; make it exciting!

Don't start without input from a variety of other men.

Don't make decisions without a proper plan.

Don't try to develop a plan without prayer.

Don't do the same things at every event; use variety.

Don't neglect small groups; focus on relationships.

Don't neglect the discipleship process; build godly men.

Don't reinvent the wheel; use developed resources.

Don't be a one-man show; release others to ministry.

Don't think too small; think big!

Don't wait for next year; begin now!

3

VISION THAT DRIVES MINISTRY

| *Vince D'Acchioli* |

During the early 1970s, my wife and I had been married only a short time when we decided to go looking for a van to pull our ski boat. We found the perfect one: bright orange with mag wheels and dual chrome side pipes—the coolest. After considering how to finance our purchase, we discovered that we were thirty dollars a month short. I wanted that van so badly I could taste it, but in those days, thirty dollars was like two hundred today, and we couldn't afford it.

At the time, I was not a Christian, and my lifestyle reflected it. One of my vices was a four-pack-a-day cigarette habit, which I had tried many times to overcome, with no success. As I was pondering how to squeeze an extra thirty dollars out of our budget, it occurred to me that at twenty-five cents a pack (which was the cost of cigarettes in those days), my habit amounted to exactly one dollar a day—or thirty dollars per month.

I said to my wife, "Cindy, if I quit smoking, we can afford that van." When she responded favorably, I quickly added, "Let's do it." Unfortunately, then came the catch. With great wisdom, Cindy said, "Hold it. Time out. You quit smoking first, and then we'll go buy the car." I was so close!

I desperately wanted that van. In fact, the vision was so strong that I put down a four-pack-a-day habit that Sunday night and did not pick up another cigarette from that day on. Oh, the power of vision!

Perhaps the most important lesson I learned from that situation is that the quality of our vision equals the character of our goals. Vision is a powerful tool—both positively and negatively. The Columbine High School shootings were carried out by two young men with vision. And they were passionate about their vision. Passionate enough to end the lives of fifteen promising young people. We must understand that the power of vision is not related to any particular set of values. It cuts both ways. The quality of our vision will always determine the character of our goals and, ultimately, our behavior.

DEFINING OUR VISION

Pablo Picasso once said, "If only we could pull out our brain and use only our eyes." This seems a ridiculous notion, but it illustrates the reality that the same brain that helps us interpret our original vision often draws us off course. It happens everywhere: at work, at home, even in the church.

While speaking once to a group of local pastors, I asked them the following question: "Pastor, what is your product? In other words, if the church were a factory, what would its product be?" I could tell that some of them were a bit intimidated by my use of business terminology, so I explained that my question was not meant to address them personally but rather to address the broader aspect of the church.

Many of these men had difficulty articulating a response. After a few moments, I posed a second question, "What is Chrysler's product?" The immediate response was, "Cars." I then suggested that although it is true that Chrysler makes cars, cars are really not their product. As confusion began to break out among the audience, I continued, "Chrysler's product is really transportation. They manufacture cars to satisfy a wide range of transportation needs."

When the pastors seemed to accept this notion, I restated my first question. "So, using this illustration, what is your product?" After several minutes, someone responded, "The product of the local church is Christlike people." What a great answer. We should be producing people who truly reflect Jesus. However, Christlike people in the context of the church are like cars at Chrysler—a means to the ultimate end.

You see, I believe that the product of the church ought to be a godly world. It follows, then, that the product of my local church in Colorado Springs ought to be the godly city of Colorado Springs. I wanted these pastors to see the big picture. Just as Chrysler fulfills its purpose to satisfy and provide transportation needs every time they manufacture a car, we as the church need to recognize that the purpose of building up Christlike people is to produce godliness in a hurting world.

I continued with a challenging question. "Most of us would agree that Chrysler is doing a pretty good job in delivering a quality product. Now, tell me, how do you think the church is doing?" The silence was deafening. I completed my discussion with the following illustration.

"Let's assume that Chrysler went out and purchased the best raw materials available, then dumped all of this rubber, metal, glass, and plastic into a box on the factory floor and called it a car. Obviously, we would never identify this box of parts as a car, because it could never provide transportation. Now think about the average man sitting in church receiving the greatest raw material the world has ever known. Not since Jesus walked the planet have we been equipped with such extraordinary wisdom and knowledge. To think that this man will walk out of the building as a Christlike individual is as ludicrous as believing that a box of parts is a car."

Building a Means to an End

To build a car out of a pile of parts, Chrysler employs a strategy that I believe we as the body of Christ need to consider and employ. First, they go to the drawing board and ask themselves some tough questions. What is the finished product supposed to do? What should it look like? How will it operate, and what features will be needed to ensure quality transportation? In short, they define the vision.

Next, they design an assembly line. You can't put the tire on until the wheel is in place. You need to build the frame before the engine goes in. In the academic community, we know that you do not teach advanced calculus to a first grader; yet somehow we have forgotten that concept in the church when trying to develop Christlike people. At Chrysler, the work is done part by part. In the church, it should be done precept upon precept.

It is commonly known in the business world that your product is only as good as your ability to measure or evaluate it. In continuing their process, Chrysler does not stop at the assembly line. They do not want to take any chances. Before one of their cars is allowed to leave the factory, it undergoes a thorough inspection, according to a thorough checklist of criteria. Only then is the car released to be sold.

I believe that a large part of the body of Christ is not doing a very good job of defining, designing, producing, and evaluating its product. Many churches struggle to understand what their product should be. Others have not yet discovered how to put the assembly line together. Still more churches, which are working hard and using the precept-upon-precept approach, ultimately have limited success because they are not measuring their results.

The Chrysler illustration suggests at least three major points that must be considered if we are to build a successful ministry to men. First, we need to catch the vision. What is our true product? What does it look like? Second, we need to put the assembly line in place. Finally, we need not only to understand what the end product should look like but also to find accurate ways of measuring its effectiveness. In other words, is it doing what it was designed to do?

BUILDING BY THE BOOK

In the mid-1980s, while on the secular speaking circuit, I met a woman by the name of Betsy Sanders. Betsy, in her late thirties at the time, had worked her way up from the position of sales associate to executive vice president for Nordstrom's Department Stores. Betsy told a story at an event I attended that so caught my attention that I asked her if she would come to my company and share it with our executive team. She agreed, and this is the story she told.

One day a group of executives from Nordstrom's invited a number of top executives from JCPenney's to a luncheon. They were all seated around a large table enjoying their meal when one of the executives from JCPenney asked, "To what do you attribute your tremendous success? Nordstrom's has become a model that people all over the world are studying." In other words, What is your secret?

The way I remember Betsy telling it, one of the executives from Nordstrom's left the room to retrieve a large book from an adjacent room. He brought the book over to the Penney's executive, opened it, and laid it in front of him. The book, written one hundred years ago, was the original operations manual for JCPenney.

He simply said, "We do everything that it says in that book."

What an odd moment that must have been. You see, what he was really saying was, You lost your first love. You had the vision, and somewhere along the way, you let it slip away. This, sadly, is what happens to many organizations, churches, marriages, and yes, individuals too.

In the business world, I had some limited experiences with mergers and acquisitions. I have seen very few examples of two organizations that came together and were better off than they were apart. It has little to do with what it looks like on paper. It always looks good there. The problem, in my view, lies with management's inability to surface a new and greater vision that eclipses the individual visions of the competing companies.

I believe this same thing often happens in a marriage. Two people with different visions fail to see God's new and better vision for them as a couple, resulting in a competition of visions at a lower level.

I can't prove this, but I believe that the reason most teaching today in our churches is not very effective is that it does not have a context or vision to submit itself to. A lot of good information without a vision is just that—a lot of good information.

We must revisit the original vision, develop a passion for its fulfillment, and design effective processes to insure quality results.

If the church of Jesus Christ is ever to be an effective agent in our culture, it must return to the original vision: building Christlike people. Vision begins at the top. It will not happen through grassroots efforts. And we must also understand the critical role of men in the overall process.

MEN: THE KEY TO A HEALTHY CHURCH

In almost seven years of putting on men's events in hundreds of churches, I am convinced that meaningful ministry to men cannot evolve from a grassroots effort. For too long now, we have ignored the senior pastor and asked lay leaders to move the mountain.

I do believe that pancake breakfasts, camping trips, men's conferences, and the like can easily be run by lay leaders. However, that's not ministry to men; it's men's ministry—and there is a big difference. I have yet to see a truly effective ministry to men in which the senior pastor was not fully involved and in charge. I don't mean to take anything away from the talented lay leaders across the country who are doing an incredible job in men's ministry. But what I would prefer to focus on here is ministry to men.

Ministry to men, as I've defined it, is the process of bringing men into meaningful relationship with God and developing them into fully devoted followers of Christ who are capable of making a difference in their world. To achieve this objective, we need to move away from the "event" mentality of recent years to a more intentional, pastor-led ministry to men. Even in large churches, where there are several levels of management, I believe that ministry to men should flow directly from the senior pastor. This sends a very strong message to the whole church about priorities.

Toward that end, I am offering the following suggestions for senior pastors who want to enter into a new dimension of ministry to men. This four-stage process will guide you and give you ideas for establishing a structure for ministry to men in your church.

Stage 1: Significance

Consider God's order here on planet Earth. It flows from God the Father to Jesus the Son, to the man as the spiritual head of the family, to his wife, and ultimately, to their children. Where in that hierarchy is the first place where the church can make an impact? Obviously, it's with the man, but if you look at most churches today, you'd probably agree that we have our ministry priorities out of order. We spend much more time on programs for our youth and on women's ministries than we do on ministry to men. I am convinced that we need to move ministry to men up the priority scale in our churches. If you agree, here are some ways to move forward.

Prayerfully consider two or three men (in larger churches it might be as many as eight or ten) who you believe possess sufficient maturity and desire to be involved with ministry to men. Call each man and ask him if he would consider helping you manage the most important ministry in the church. Invite those who agree to your office for an interview.

Conduct the interviews as if you were hiring an executive staff member. Communicating a high level of importance will stimulate your leadership candidates.

Share your passion for ministry to men and explain how you believe this ministry will impact the church. After you have presented a compelling vision, ask each man if he will join the core group of leaders.

Once you have your core group in place, ask this group of men to prayerfully make a list of ten to twenty (depending on the size of your church) other men who they believe carry a passion for ministry to men and have a sufficient level of spiritual maturity to serve in supporting roles. Make your own list as well, then agree with your core team on the men you will invite to join the next level.

Use the same interview process as before. Remember, the main purpose is to plant the vision. Let these men sense your passion as their pastor. When this process has been completed, you will have a small core group of men whom you can begin calling upon for help and a second group of men ready to assist in carrying out the day-to-day management of your new ministry. Together you may want to come up with a name, like Men's Ministry Council, to formalize the group's identity.

Stage 2: Strategy

The next step in establishing your ministry to men is to plan your strategy. Schedule a series of meetings with your whole group to discuss your goals and objectives. At this stage, I suggest that you answer the following questions.

1. What are the unique needs of the men in your congregation and community?
2. What will a successful ministry to men look like?
3. How will you measure success? Remember, you can expect what you inspect.
4. What are some obstacles that men face in their spiritual development?
5. What are some challenges or weaknesses that your church faces in addressing men's needs?
6. Which specific topics do men need to understand in order to grow spiritually?
7. How can you best design a systematic, precept-upon-precept approach for teaching your men?

Stage 3: Structure

Every effective organization requires management. Who will be responsible for implementing each step of your ministry to men? Assign specific responsibilities to each man on your team, without abdicating your personal involvement as the senior pastor at the highest level of ministry. Administrative responsibilities, if properly delegated, will help you remain free to shepherd your men.

Here are a few ideas to help you begin to structure an effective ministry to men.

- Schedule a Saturday morning men's meeting once a month, during which you as the senior pastor bring an important, targeted message. Build your messages on a precept-upon-precept approach.
- Organize an annual men's council or core group retreat, during which you pour yourself into your leaders in a more intimate environment. Reenergize them with the vision. Discuss any necessary course corrections.
- Schedule an annual getaway retreat for all the men of your church.
- Create a focused, curriculum-driven Sunday school class for men.
- Bring in a nationally known speaker or schedule a major men's event once a year that fits into your curriculum. Make sure it fits the vision, and don't allow it to become an "oh, by the way" event. You must attend, or the men in your congregation won't.
- Following the principle of the funnel diagram discussed in chapter 2, schedule some fun activities for men, such as athletic events, campouts, breakfasts, or barbecues to attract seekers and unchurched friends.
- List specific expectations for each event. Who do you want to attract, and what do you want to accomplish?
- Initiate a men's small group program to build increased intimacy among your men.

Stage 4: Schedule

Now it's time to move from development to implementation. Commit all your plans to the church calendar. I recommend scheduling teaching times, seminars, events, and other gatherings for at least one year. I suggest that you publish a nice-looking calendar and introduce it on a Sunday morning as part of a message or series of messages to introduce your new ministry to the entire congregation. It is time to share the vision in a churchwide context. Communicating your intentions clearly to the congregation is crucial. They need to know your heart and buy in to the vision. If properly communicated, a renewed focus on ministry to men could revolutionize your whole church.

CATCHING THE VISION

Recently I was invited by a church in Florida to conduct a planning session for putting together an effective ministry to men. I met in the pastor's living room with about fifteen or twenty men from the core men's leadership team. After I had finished a one-hour introduction and overview, one of the men, obviously very frustrated, said, "That sounds great, but you don't understand; we have tried everything and still cannot get the men to turn out for ministry events."

I stopped the meeting and asked all the men a question. "Tell me, why are you guys here? Why did you come to this meeting?" After a few quips aimed at the pastor's arm-twisting ability, the men got serious. "I came because the pastor made me feel as though I could contribute," one man replied. "I feel what we are doing is important," another man added. After several similar responses, I asked the men to consider the common theme they were expressing. "You guys are here because you have a vision," I explained. "But you must transfer that same dynamic to the other men. They won't come just because you are putting on a great event. They need to catch the vision and see the need."

Our lives do not change simply because we attend an event, hear a good sermon, or read a great book. It would be nice if it worked that way, but the evidence suggests that much more is needed to bring meaningful changes to a person's life. I believe there are six stages we all must go through before real change can take place: event, awareness, decision, commitment, process, and change. (See fig. 3.)

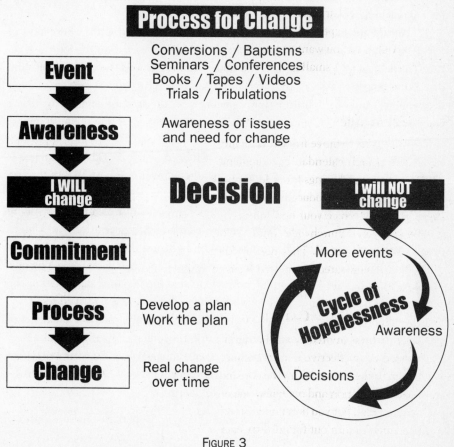

FIGURE 3

Event. An event can be anything from attending a Promise Keepers rally to reading a book, hearing a sermon, or participating in a wedding. Most of us men want the event to produce the desired result, quickly and painlessly. Our attitude is "let's get it over with." Unfortunately, it doesn't work that way. The best an event can do is to raise awareness.

Awareness. Awareness occurs as the result of an event. I discover at a men's retreat or Men On Target seminar that I need to get closer to God, pray with my wife more often, or whatever it is. This realization then leads to a decision.

Decision. I attend an event, my awareness is raised, and I decide to do something about it. A good example of this occurs every New Year's Eve, which is an *event.* I have an *awareness* that I'm a little overweight and out of shape, so I make a *decision* to go on a diet and work out more often—starting tomorrow. New Year's Day arrives. The guys are all over to watch the Bowl games, and my wife has made chili and garlic bread. I say to myself, "I think I'll start that diet tomorrow." Then tomorrow comes and something else gets in the way. Six months later, I still can't see my shoes past my bulging belly. Nothing has changed.

I call these first three stages the cycle of hopelessness, which is where most of us live. In order to break out of this cycle, we must press forward to the fourth stage.

Commitment. Commitment is the bridge that transforms the old man into the new. According to Webster's, the root word *commit* means in part "to carry into action deliberately," and one definition for *commitment* is "the state of being obligated or emotionally impelled." Commitment is what is needed to enter into the most important and difficult stage: process.

Process. Process is a behavioral change achieved over a period of time. Here is where most men struggle, because process requires a level of intentionality that we are unwilling to enter into. For the most part, men are very impatient with anything that requires process. We do not want to work for results if it means experiencing long-term discomfort. We have truly become a "microwave generation," seeking to accelerate the process through steroids, rapid-weight-loss diets, and get-rich-quick schemes. We often look for similar quick fixes to aid in our behavioral development. What many of us fail to understand, however, is that God is more interested in the process—the habits we form and the way we live—than in any perceived results.

Developing a plan and then working that plan are the essential elements of process. Process is the only way to bring about lasting and meaningful change.

Change. The desired result of process is a real change over time in our level of maturity. In order to maintain consistency in our processes, we need accountable relationships. These relationships fall into four categories.

1. *Discipleship and mentoring relationships.* The purpose of these relationships is spiritual growth and development.

2. *Fellowship and social relationships.* The purpose of these relationships is to meet other Christians, build friendships, and establish prayer support.
3. *Study and information relationships.* These Bible study or other structured learning systems are designed to build knowledge.
4. *Accountability and encourager relationships.* These relationships meet our needs for prayer support, advice, encouragement, and accountability.

CHIPPING AWAY AT THE MARBLE

As we evaluate our efforts to develop ministry to men, we must commit ourselves to stick with the process until we have achieved meaningful and lasting change in line with our vision.

Michelangelo, the immensely talented painter and sculptor, was asked once how he was able to carve such magnificent masterpieces. He replied that he was able to see the beauty of the statue he was about to create even before the marble was cultivated in the rock quarry. Then he added, "I simply have to chip away what does not belong." Whether that's a four-pack-a-day cigarette habit, a scattershot array of men's events, or any other thing—maybe even good things—you will find it much easier to chip them away once you have caught the vision. Ask God to reveal his vision for you and your church right now. Your ministry will never be the same.

4

GETTING THINGS RIGHT—THE FIRST TIME

Gary G. Bateman

Every summer, my family vacations at Horn Creek Ranch, a Christian family camp in the Sangre de Christo Mountains of Colorado. My sister and her family attend as well, and we have a great time with all the activities and friends at the camp. On the last day of camp, before we forlornly go "down the mountain" and back to the hustle and bustle of the city, we line up in front of an old buckboard wagon for a family picture.

One summer, Jason, my second oldest, was in the army. He was in and out of Bosnia, and none of us knew whether he would be able to get leave and be at the camp with the rest of us. At the last minute, he made it—all the way from Europe to be with his family at camp. The snapshot from that summer is special. It hangs on a wall in every home represented in that picture.

Photographs tell us a lot about ourselves. They give us the "real" picture. Snapshots tell it like it is, not like we think it is or want it to be. And our annual family photos do more than bring back great memories—we can use them as a gauge to show how we have all changed. They're good for recording information. They remind us of what our likes and dislikes were. Photographs can even serve as guides to help us make things right again.

A good assessment is like a good snapshot. It tells us what our men's ministry is like—where it's strong, where it's weak, and where it has changed. To be successful in our ministry, a good assessment is critical. It offers us a starting point, from which we can begin our journey toward a brighter future.

THE INFORMATION GAP

Nehemiah faced the same difficulty many of us face—he received some bad news, and he responded with mourning and prayer. As he prayed day and night, God began growing a vision in Nehemiah's heart. Nehemiah wanted to remove the reproach on the name of the Lord, by rebuilding the walls and the gates of Jerusalem, so he prayed through the needs and prepared to meet the king with his requests. Nehemiah knew there would be roadblocks; he would need letters of safe passage, permission to cut timber, authority to lead the people, and so on. He also estimated the time he would need for travel and construction. By God's grace, the king granted these requests, and Nehemiah was off to Jerusalem.

It was there that Nehemiah faced an information gap—the distance between a general knowledge of needs and the specific knowledge needed before action can begin. Nehemiah knew what he needed to rebuild the walls and the gates. He knew he had to gain the trust of the people. But he also knew he would need to do some scouting and find out the exact state of affairs in Jerusalem before he could begin any action. Specifically, Nehemiah needed to understand the leaders, the people of Jerusalem, and the nations surrounding them. Many questions had to be answered before he could move forward, so Nehemiah took three days assessing every aspect of the circumstances that surrounded him. After taking stock of the situation, he shared the vision, called people to action, and led them into an undertaking, with remarkable results.

How we handle an information gap is crucial to planning a ministry. If we ignore it, we tend to push forward into the planning phase and then wonder why people don't respond like we thought they would. If we focus on it, it's too easy to slip into "paralysis by analysis"—feeling overwhelmed and accomplishing little. But if we can get an accurate assessment of our situation, we'll discover fruit that would otherwise have been left unharvested. Good assessment leads to effective ministry by providing a working understanding of who we are.

MISSION ACCOMPLISHED!

Simply put, assessment is the gathering of information to give us a clear picture of our situation. It is descriptive, and as Webster points out, it "is used to determine roughly the size, extent, or nature of something . . . serving as a guide to our actions." Assessment is essential in any undertaking, whether it's a new ministry or one that has been in existence for years. Good assessment, like Nehemiah's, takes stock of the situation, examines what we want to accomplish, assesses the various aspects, and checks the available resources. Once the plans for the wall are complete, work can begin.

Assessment is at the heart of every decision we make. Assessment

describes the who and what of ministry

offers clear understanding of the status of an existing ministry

guides our actions for the future of the ministry

defines a precise starting point for ministry

establishes the nature of an existing ministry

When we prepare to pull into traffic, we assess how fast the cars are coming, how much space we need, the acceleration rate of our vehicle, and so on. When buying a house, we take a little more time, look at many more details, and compare our options. We may consider such things as cost, neighborhood, location, quality of construction, schools, and many other factors before making a decision. If we get faulty information, we may make faulty decisions. In ministry, assessment is simply the task of taking stock early in the process in order to plan for later success. Launching a ministry without first assessing the situation is like pulling the trigger without aiming. We'll hit something, but will it be the bull's-eye?

The purpose of assessment is to gain the best possible understanding of your situation and the surrounding factors that impact it. Assessment is a process that employs a number of tools and methods to gather quality information about your group, which in turn will allow you to make informed decisions about the future. It defines your location and helps you select the best route to the vision of the future of your ministry to men.

There is an adage that says, "If a thing is worth doing, it is worth doing right." And if you don't have time to do it right the first time, you're never going to find time to do it over. Quality assessment helps prevent the need to undo things. The crowds of Jesus' day were struggling to understand the concept of discipleship. He was making some serious demands on their lives and wanted to illustrate what these demands were like, so he asked them a question. "If you want to build a tower, don't you sit down and estimate the cost of the tower before you begin? Of course you do! If you begin to build and then realize that you don't have the resources to complete the task, others will mock you." Jesus was encouraging them to take stock of themselves to see whether they had the desire to complete the discipleship to which he called them. His illustration of the builder cautioned them to examine their true desires, to assess themselves and see if they had what it would take to be his follower. He wanted them to count the cost, lest they be ridiculed when they couldn't complete what they began.

DESCRIPTION PRECEDES PRESCRIPTION

Assessment has two sides. The first side is descriptive in nature. It shows exactly what we are like right now. When we assess our ministry to men, we in effect take a snapshot of the men, the church, the leadership, and any resources available.

The other side of assessment assigns value to that description. This aspect is prescriptive in nature, looking for ideas and answers to improve the situation. To prescribe before adequate description takes place is putting the cart before the horse. This temptation to proceed too quickly is frequently fueled by false assumptions, inaccurate or incomplete information, or simply wanting to get started.

In the second and third chapters of Revelation, Jesus takes a close look at seven churches. He gives an accurate assessment of each church before he corrects them. In each case, we see both the description and the value statements of assessment. Many of the comments of the apostle Paul that relate to the practices of his audiences were assessment oriented. He continuously describes situations such as the condition of the pagan world around him or the state of a man's heart. He describes before he prescribes—that's assessment!

The number one benefit of conducting an accurate assessment of the men in your church is that you come to understand the men, their needs, and their interests in a realistic light. By gathering the correct and complete information about your men, your ministry, and your church, you are able to avoid several pitfalls: you won't base your decisions on false impressions, you won't assume everyone is exactly like you, and you won't plan something just because the person demanding it yells the loudest.

Sometimes we may be seeking to meet an important need in men's lives, but it could be the wrong starting point for our target audience. Just because something meets my needs doesn't mean that it will meet yours. Sometimes simply gaining men's attention and establishing a relationship is the best thing we can do.

I was once involved in a weekend effectiveness consultation with a church staff and board. We were discussing the Individual Needs portion of a report, and I could see that the men weren't on board. After addressing the apparent discomfort, one of the men spoke up. "We've done exactly what you're talking about. We understand that the financial pressures families face are tough. One of the leading causes of divorce is related to money issues, so we set up a financial planning seminar to help out—but it bombed! Why should we try this stuff again?"

What had happened seemed simple from an outsider's perspective. The leaders understood the financial pressures families face and addressed an important need. The congregation didn't respond to the seminar, leading the staff to conclude that seminars weren't for their church. Had they assessed the situation accurately, they would have discovered, before the financial planning seminar, what we were now looking at together: the results of a congregational survey showed that the congregation desired help in another area.

As we probed the problem further, the reasons for the "seminar bomb" became clear to them. To put it simply, the people of the church had financial planning needs, but they didn't see the church as the place to go to have those needs met. What the people were more interested in was getting help from the church in building relationships with unchurched people. There are times when a financial planning seminar is a great tool to build bridges, but not in this church and not at that time. The results of the survey were clear, and the leaders were able to realize they did the right thing in planning a seminar, but they had chosen the wrong subject. Having an accurate assessment would have saved them a lot of frustration. Armed with this new information about their church, planning for the next seminar went forward with enthusiasm and much success.

Gathering incomplete, inaccurate, or misleading information may lead us to make wrong decisions. When we make assumptions about our situation based on general information, we run into trouble. Avoid these pitfalls by checking out the findings in your context. Make an accurate assessment of your situation and erase those false assumptions.

WORKING WITH MEN

In our information age, we can easily be overwhelmed with assessment and its ramifications. So my goal is to keep it simple—make assessment work for you instead of you working for assessment. Identify steps that you and your core team can apply in order to minister to men, then establish a safe, creative environment that will challenge the men and meet their needs.

Begin by assessing the leadership and infrastructure group. Take a look at the mission and vision of your church, its organization, and the niche that a ministry to men would fulfill. What is your purpose, how are you organized, and what resources do you have?

Second, seek to understand the men in your church. What are their interests, needs, levels of current involvement, and availability? Physical and spiritual demographics can build a profile of your target audience and answer the question, To whom am I seeking to minister? How and where they are currently involved builds a profile that will help you understand possible avenues of ministry. Limitations and other barriers can be brought to the surface, thereby heading off any false sense of expectation as you plan. Find out the personal challenges or needs of your men and measure their interests to allow for the development of ministry facets focused on those challenges and interests.

As you investigate the men in your church, remember that you are dealing with a broad spectrum of involvement and potential involvement. Surveying the men that are currently involved in ministry may give a particular viewpoint that probably will not represent the other men in your church.

For churches just beginning a ministry to men, this information will guide you toward a clear statement of vision as well as show you where the men are most likely to become involved. For churches with any significant level of a ministry to men, this data will help you evaluate the effectiveness of your ministry, why some things work and some don't, and what adjustments might be made to improve or capitalize on a particular facet of ministry.

The third area for assessment is the target or outreach group. The church whose ministry to men is seeking to reach out will want to understand the "neighbor" they want to reach. A neighbor is a person with whom the men of the church have some contact. It could be someone in the neighborhood, the workplace, the athletic club, other civic organizations, or the community at large. This assessment needs to be done by a simpler, less intrusive questionnaire. It needs to get right to the point but produce the information needed for quality planning. There are various organizations that will provide community demographic profiles at reasonable costs. Such data will benefit both the men's ministry and the church as a whole. Your chamber of commerce is also a source for community profiles, as are public libraries that have Census Bureau information available.

TYPES OF ASSESSMENT

Recently I read that the average size of men's shoes is a size ten. I went out immediately and bought three pairs of size ten shoes. Not satisfied with the fit, I went back to the shoe store and demanded my money back. The clerk asked why I had purchased three pairs that were far from a good fit, and I told him that I suspected the manufacturer had a problem at the plant. He assured me these were bona fide size ten shoes, and suggested I have my feet remeasured. "Remeasured?" I asked. "But I never had them measured. I simply found out that the average shoe size is a ten. And I'm pretty average, so I bought the tens!" The clerk politely measured my feet and recommended I try on a size eight. They fit perfectly.

The moral to my story: one size does not fit all! Accurate assessment would have saved me embarrassment, effort, and some valuable time. So it is with our ministries.

There are three types of valuable information we should gather: global information, local information, and individual information.

Global information is that which deals with the broader issues. For example, in a series of questions asked of more than 60,000 individuals by the Institute for Church Development, we found that men were less interested than women in having the church assist them with family needs. Men were less apt to seek help from the church than women, except in the area of how to become a Christian or how to understand theology and the Bible. Women, on the other hand, were much more likely to seek help from the church on attitude or emotional issues. That is good information, but be wary of applying global information to your local church. What's true of most people may not be true of your congregation.

Some sources of good global information include magazines, organizations like the Barna Research Group, or Gallup Poll results. Some denominations have good records available to their churches. All this information is valuable for shaping the big-picture aspects of your ministry.

Local information is that which you find by asking the people to whom you minister. Create a questionnaire on a topic and hand it out at a meeting to discover what people think. Get various groups of people together to brainstorm on problems, then ask them for potential solutions. Asking four or five questions that target one issue can pinpoint valuable information. For example, ask your men if they would attend a retreat, what time of year it should be, what starting times they would prefer, how long it should last, and what topics they'd like to see covered. A more comprehensive survey can gather broader information about the men, so a short questionnaire is best when used as a follow-up to a good congregational survey of all the men. The survey will help you build the profiles needed for strategic planning, while the questionnaire is more tactical in nature. Focus groups can help gather very specific information, so consider putting together small groups of men who can speak directly to the issue you are studying.

I once helped a church that was planning to build a new sanctuary, based on global information—the well-known fact that the average American gives only 4 percent of his income to the church. But in assessing local information, we discovered that their average parishioner was giving 12 percent of his income to the church, well above the national average. To ask the parishioners for more may have been a bit of a stretch. This example demonstrates just how crucial it is to "know thyself." As you begin a new ministry or seek to develop plans for improving an existing ministry, make sure you are receiving good local information.

Individual information is the most valuable information for those in charge of a men's ministry. Use personal interviews, informal conversation, and small groups to gather the individual information you need. Spiritual gift indicators, personality profile tools, skill and interest assessments, and talent tests all collect personal data for the purpose of getting an individual into a place of service or ministry suitable to them. These questions are private in nature and personal in application, therefore they may need to be administered in a more private, comfortable setting. Small groups and discipling or mentoring relationships are excellent contexts for discovering and applying individual information.

Global information can aim you in the right direction, but local information will define your situation and better prepare you for planning. Individual information focuses on your specific congregation and will help you to know your men. Each individual is uniquely created by God and is most fruitful when involved in a ministry designed to best bring out his giftedness. Your ministry should be assessing, casting vision, and setting goals in these various areas. Smaller churches will use more simplified formats but cannot overlook the needs at the various levels of involvement. Churches with an established, prolific ministry to men will have all of these aspects going on at once, in one form or another.

CONSIDER THE BENEFITS

A comprehensive assessment of your men will provide accurate information so that you can best meet their needs. This is essential, whether you are just beginning a ministry to men in your church or have a well-organized and ongoing ministry. The simple act of taking a congregational survey will also educate both leaders and participants. Issues are raised that an individual may not have previously considered. This in turn widens everyone's perspective. For others, the bar is raised on topics of which they are already aware.

For participants in a survey, being exposed to the broader picture may increase their expectations and their desire to be involved. The busy day-to-day world of our parishioners doesn't leave much room for another church program unless they see a higher purpose and benefit for involvement. In addition, men who may feel on the fringe and are not assimilated into church life can find an opportunity to become involved in a ministry that is purposeful for their lives.

When a comprehensive assessment is complete, the planning process takes on a new approach. With accurate information, leaders have data that will allow them to focus their application. Men in different age groups or life cycles (or many other variables) have different needs—it's clear that one size does *not* fit all! By focusing our efforts on tailor-made opportunities for specific need groups, we motivate men to become involved. Large rally events may fit most groups, but as the men return to the church, they need a place to land—one designed for their interests, needs, and availability.

As I work with church leadership teams, the need for an accurate starting point continues to rise to the top of each church's priority list. As description precedes prescription, so assessment precedes planning. If you call a AAA office and ask them for assistance in planning a trip, they will ask two questions: Where are you going? and What is your starting point? Those are the same questions we need to ask ourselves when starting a men's ministry.

Where you are going? What is your destination, your goal, your vision for your ministry to men? Where do you want them to go? Jesus said, "Follow Me, and I will make you fishers of men" (Matt. 4:19 NASB). He knew where he wanted his disciples to go with their lives. Has that been established in your ministry yet?

What is your starting point? That is the assessment role in ministry. If you use assessment wisely, you'll know where you are starting from, and you'll have some excellent information to help you know where you want to go.

Five Steps to Successful Assessment

1. *Link your assessment to your mission.* The men's ministry should be a microcosm of the church and therefore needs a purpose statement that reflects the overall goal of your church. A good assessment will identify your church body's areas of need and will measure the extent to which your ministries are fulfilling your mission statement.

2. *Link your assessment to your planning.* Since description precedes prescription, take the time to assess your situation carefully, then follow your assessment with strategic planning. A good assessment will help you know what plans and programs your men's ministry needs to create.

3. *Link your assessment to evaluation.* When you assess your church, you are able to evaluate the quality and effectiveness of each aspect of your men's ministry. To gauge your success, ask yourself how well you are accomplishing your goals.

4. *Link your assessment to adjustments.* Churches can be like governments, refusing to kill a program no matter how outdated or ineffective. A good assessment should help you know how best to use church resources and give you a context for making helpful changes in your men's ministry.

5. *Link your assessment to prayer.* Everything we do in ministry begins with prayer, which reveals God's will, purpose, and method. The Bible won't address all the details of running a men's ministry in the twenty-first century, but by remaining close to God through prayer, we can listen to his wisdom and direction. A good assessment establishes an excellent prayer list and identifies both the strengths and the concerns of your ministry.

Twenty Questions to Ask Your Men

Demographic Questions
1. What is your age?
2. What is your marital status?
3. What are the ages of your children?
4. What is your vocation?

Church Involvement Questions
5. Where and how often do you attend worship services?
6. Where and how often do you attend Sunday school?
7. Where and how often do you attend a small group?
8. Where and how often do you attend a mentoring group?
9. What men's activities have you attended in the past year?
10. When is the best time for you to attend a men's activity?
11. What men's activity would you most like to occur?

Interest Questions
12. What does your family enjoy doing in your spare time?
13. What recreational activities do you enjoy?
14. What type of ministry or service would you enjoy doing?
15. What are your hobbies?
16. What special skills do you have?

Personal Questions
17. What marriage or family issues would you like to see addressed?
18. What workplace issues would you like to see addressed?
19. What spiritual issues would you like to see addressed?
20. What preparation do you feel you need so that you can be effective in ministry?

5

THE PASTOR'S ROLE

| *Jack Hayford* |

When our church began to grow, I realized that one of the most important things that needed to happen was the development of a strong ministry for our men. That would mean my role, as pastor, would be that of discipler and model as well as that of the chaplain-leader. Unfortunately, our society has seen an erosion in leadership roles for men. Everywhere you turn, you see people trying to blur the line, emasculate men, and somehow negate the God-given differences between the sexes.

The same emasculating forces that have diminished the perspective of most men on what biblical manhood involves have been pressing upon pastors as well. No pastor has remained completely uninfluenced by our culture's ideas and habits, nor have we remained unmarked by the effects of the invisible spiritual forces that seek to refashion the base of God's character and ways in us.

Because God is committed to "fathering sons" through the ministry of pastors, it is understandable that he will want to work on pastors first. He wants to purify us, because whatever is deficient or distorted in us will become manifest in the men we lead. God is calling us to be reworked and humbled before him with a readiness for renewal in our souls.

Not only are we being called to a new pastoral mind-set, but we are being summoned to a new place of manly honesty before God. If we are to shepherd the next generation of men toward biblical manhood, we must allow God to shape us as men ourselves. Only then will the fruit of our lives replicate men according to God's order, not our own.

God is accomplishing two purposes simultaneously: reviving the church and restoring men. These are separate yet dynamically related works, for if the church is to reach its maximum potential, men must find their places in God's economy. In striving to accomplish this, however, we need to recognize how easily a focus on men can be misinterpreted by society at large or by the women in our congregations. God's divine will in achieving his purpose has obviously been distorted at times, but wherever his terms are applied, a woman's place, worth, and potential will never be reduced. Indeed, it will be maximized, and the fruit will be the release of each woman to her highest possibilities—in life and in Christ.

Our pastoral challenge, then, is to find God's way to develop a breed of holy offspring who know his ways. We need to "father" men by pouring ourselves into them as we open our hearts to share our own struggles in growth. Such shaping of men, by "pastors of promise" who learn to "father" according to that promise, returns to God's foundational plan for the church.

FINDING THE ORIGINAL PATTERN

The New Testament way to realize such promise was set forth in the life of the church long ago. Though contemporary pastoring has too often become defined by a score of other assignments, the original pattern can still be found and applied. At the church's beginning, the pastoral task was essentially wrapped up in two phrases: (1) pour yourself out, as pastor to men, and (2) teach those men to do the same, man to man. This dual assignment is encapsulated in Paul's injunction to Timothy: "You therefore, my son, be strong in the grace that is in Christ Jesus. The things which you have heard from me in the presence of many witnesses, entrust these to faithful men who will be able to teach others also" (2 Tim. 2:1–2 NASB).

Notice how the opening words of this passage establish the nature of the apostle's influence on this young pastor: "You therefore, my son." These words carry a combination of authority and affection. The young man, Timothy, is both commanded and comforted in the same breath: "You are to lead, but I've shown you how, and I know you can do it!"

I can't read those words without sensing what Timothy must have felt—a surge of personal assurance born of Paul's confidence in him. I urge you to join me in hearing the Holy Spirit's whisper to us in those same words. He did not record them simply to report a fact from history. Nor are they intended merely to provide poetic beauty, as though to say, "What a paternal graciousness Paul models to his young charge!" Rather, as surely as Timothy received comfort in Paul's assuring kindness, I believe you and I are to find the same. Paul's words contain both a promise as well as a mandate.

Listen closely to the words, "You therefore, my son." For the God who called us—the ultimate Father himself—is calling again and is assuring adequacy. He is charging us with the same pattern for pursuit in ministry, according to his original plan for fruitfulness in the church. Furthermore, in calling us "sons," he is making a designation not only laden with grace and affection but also filled with the promise of an adequate genetic dynamic for the "fathering" task we are being assigned.

The Holy Spirit is working to restore our focus on our fundamental call. When the original order is in place, all the benefits of the full divine order begin to flow together unto mightiness! At the same time, however, let us remember that the opposite is equally true: a fullness of God's power and truth without a focus on God's priorities in ministry will inevitably result in a dissipation of holy energy and eventually lead to frustration.

Look at the basic, original, and simple but profound pattern for pursuing a biblical pastoral mission. The second part of 2 Timothy 2:2 sets forth a two-step process.

1. Timothy is charged with *committing* the things of God to believing men—men who are openly committed to growing in Christ. This first step is pastor to men.
2. As these men are shaped, they are to *turn and shape others*, with an increasing depth of relationship and breadth of fellowship. This second step is man to man.

Of course, founding a program that "begets sons" will require (1) establishing a pattern and program of discipleship for men, (2) bringing a biblical focus on husbanding and fatherhood, and (3) guiding men into service and ministry as human need and holy purposes direct. The fruit of such a teaching program will be pastors who are fulfilling their "fathering" roles in a practical way.

GOD'S PLAN OF REDEMPTION

God is calling men to rediscover their place in his purpose. As the Holy Spirit moves to redeem a generation of men whose minds and manners have been muddled by the disintegration of the world's order, he is summoning pastors to recover the New Testament order for building men.

Few things are more likely to stir debate or conflict in the church than to assert that men are first in God's human order. Although the Bible is clear that it is to be so, it is nonetheless a puzzling proposition. But whatever may have happened at any time or place in its history, the church was never intended to become an institution that tolerates or justifies male chauvinism, either intentionally or unwittingly. God has never relegated women to an inferior or second place; he simply has given each gender a distinct place. God initiates through men, but contrary to secular or carnal ideas, that assignment never gives men a private privilege or a higher hand of power. The sum of Christ's entire teaching about leadership is that the first shall be last and the last first. The call to prioritize our ministry to men is a mandate to lead each man to a place of humility, responsibility, and servanthood.

As pastors, we are appointed to "father" a new generation of "sons" who see, understand, and live out the truth of true manhood. Answering that appointment requires our being gripped by a conviction and being willing to serve with a tender sensitivity to the balance it demands. The fullest realization of either gender—and of society and the church—will be possible only when men are awakened to and responsibly serve their roles. In the present awakening, pastors must lead men into a divinely ordered alignment. Most men have too little instruction in or understanding of what true biblical manhood entails. The fact is, few pastors have been trained to prioritize discipling men.

Worse yet, given the mood of the world mind today, we are all so pressured to equalize the place of women and men that the place of a man in the divine order becomes confused and thereby minimized. To secure a long-term, transforming renewal and leadership development in the men of our congregations, we must answer two foundational questions: (1) Why are men prioritized by God as they are? and (2) Why are men so reticent to respond to their places in God's plan?

To respond to these questions is not only to answer significant issues that block men's growth but also to confront essential points of bondage that bind men's souls. Each man needs an inner perspective on the complications that Adam's sin has welded into the male psyche.

UNVEILING A KEY PASSAGE

To open the way for discussing a cluster of men's issues, read the passage from 1 Timothy, which reveals a conceptual base for men's ministry that withstands or neutralizes the world's confusion about men and their roles:

> Therefore I want the men in every place to pray, lifting up holy hands, without wrath and dissension. Likewise, I want women to adorn themselves with proper clothing, modestly and discreetly, not with braided hair and gold or pearls or costly garments, but rather by means of good works, as is proper for women making a claim to godliness. A woman must quietly receive instruction with entire submissiveness. But I do not allow a woman to teach or exercise authority over a man, but to remain quiet. For

it was Adam who was first created, and then Eve. And it was not Adam who was deceived, but the woman being deceived, fell into transgression. But women will be preserved through the bearing of children if they continue in faith and love and sanctity with self-restraint.

It is a trustworthy statement: if any man aspires to the office of overseer, it is a fine work he desires to do. An overseer, then, must be above reproach, the husband of one wife, temperate, prudent, respectable, hospitable, able to teach, not addicted to wine or pugnacious, but gentle, peaceable, free from the love of money. He must be one who manages his own household well, keeping his children under control with all dignity (but if a man does not know how to manage his own household, how will he take care of the church of God?), and not a new convert, so that he will not become conceited and fall into the condemnation incurred by the devil. And he must have a good reputation with those outside the church, so that he will not fall into reproach and the snare of the devil.

—1 Timothy 2:8–3:7 NASB

THE STARTING POINT FOR UNDERSTANDING

I am about to describe a biblical way to communicate the truth of "men first" as a God-ordained redemptive means for achieving an eventual full and equal partnership between husbands and wives. My approach refuses to cower to the world spirit in the militant feminist movement. Although I want to affirm the Bible's revelation regarding the woman's original and ultimately proper place, I want to remove the idea that she was ever to be "second." My approach insists that God has indeed positioned the redeemed man first in reference to the believing woman, but we will see this revealed as a redemptive role—not as a privilege, a permanent position, or a right to primacy but as a call to servanthood. To raise a man to this role, I believe the truth of "men first" must be separated from confused ideas of male superiority. God's order did not intend a superior role for men. Contrary to the angry presumption of the feminists, and miles from the dogmatism of traditionalized Bible interpretations, God's agenda has a deeply redemptive purpose. Furthermore, his decree regarding the respective roles of men and women, though to be desired for all humanity, is actually only incumbent upon believers in Christ, for only by his power can the faith and dynamics of these biblical roles be lived to their fullest.

Foundationally, we need to see that God's "men first" decision was not his original purpose as Creator but among his first actions as Redeemer. I am persuaded that the man's role is as basic to the redemptive scheme as "the seed of the woman" is essential to crush the serpent's evil work. These roles are complementary in God's strategy to bring full restoration to mankind; they are part of his means to implement a redemptive remedy aimed at recovering the earlier, pre-Fall equality of man and wife.

Let's see how God's goal in calling men to lead is to release a redemptive dynamic that not only fulfills his Word but also frees and elevates women and enriches and enhances marriages. When men accept their "leading" roles, everything finds its maximum release and realization and brings the fullest fulfillment to women, families, churches, businesses, and the community at large.

A QUEST FOR MALE LEADERSHIP

First Timothy 2 unravels a tangle of problems, from the reason men tend to be less responsive to spiritual things than women are, to answering why a few New Testament texts seem to demean a woman's role. Above all, it addresses a society that is confused about God's Word and the purpose for each gender. The unraveling of the mystery of the male psyche begins with verse 8: "I desire therefore that the men pray everywhere, lifting up holy hands, without wrath and doubting" (NKJV).

These words cannot be properly understood out of context. Although I had often quoted Paul's exhortation to men to pursue open, forthright prayer ("lifting holy hands"), away from angry debate (born of male competitiveness or human self-righteousness) and unbelief (produced by the masculine tendency to discredit one's own spiritual viability because of failure or condemnation), it wasn't until I had been pastoring for more than fifteen years that I noticed the larger context. As the result of a distinct encounter with the Lord, I now saw this appeal, as it flowed through chapter 2 and into chapter 3, as a complete plea for *men!* Illumined by the wisdom of a sound interpretive approach, one thing became exceedingly clear: the key to understanding 1 Timothy 2 is Paul's overriding focus on prompting men to take their responsible roles in spiritual leadership and ministry.

In verses 1–8, Paul is virtually trumpeting: "Men, take your place of leadership in the congregation's prayer life!" Then in chapter 3, verses 1–15, he says, "Men, to be servant leaders in the body of Christ, these growth traits need to show!" Recognizing Paul's strategic approach to men helps us not to miss the key to our text: "Brothers, in order to rise to your role, learn your responsibilities—as a man!"

These insights help us to see how the introduction of women's issues in 1 Timothy 2:9–15 has more to do with building godly men than it does with correcting or criticizing women. God is seeking to help men see the root of their failure to accept leadership responsibility and is calling women to help men answer that call.

The first key to understanding this passage is to remember that the context is very emphatic in expecting men who are growing in God to also learn the responsibilities essential to a growing relationship with their wives. If we contextually translate the Greek noun *aner* as "husband" (which is its foremost use, even though it is also used as a gender-referencing word for "men"), it suggests that what is said about women is addressed specifically to wives, not to women generically.

Applying these keys, a thoughtful analysis reveals that Paul is not reprimanding women; he is working at releasing men! His purpose is to move husbands away from unresponsiveness and neglected responsibility, toward their proper roles as redemptive leaders.

Apparently, then as now, the style and speech of believing women—carried over from habits shaped in a pagan society—tended to discourage their husbands' growth toward leadership. As Paul is seeking to embolden men as prayer leaders and servant leaders, he is concerned that the men learn to accept their full roles and responsibilities. At the same time, he acknowledges that the worldly patterns of role reversal and strained relationships between spouses are working against his God-ordained goal.

Paul is calling both husbands and wives to contrast their behavior with the world's behavior. In short, he says, "Don't take on the characteristics that the world has shaped into your gender. Men, stop your anger and doubt; women, stop using your beauty as a tool to allure or as a key to your appeal."

Verses 11–12 are a plea for the wife to restrain herself in two ways: (1) from being too quick to crowd her husband's initiative in spiritual things and (2) from her inclination to take over and lead in response to her husband's passivity.

WHAT ABOUT "WOMAN, BE QUIET!"?

To free this text to truly speak its fullest message, we must correctly translate the word *quiet* in the context of its usage here. The same word translated as "quiet" in verses 11 and 12, *hesuchia*, is used in verse 2 as "tranquil." Still, I have never found a commentator who drew attention to this fact. In context, *hesuchia* clearly means to call wives to exercise orderly, self-governing spirits. The passage is not a muzzling cease and desist order but something far more gracious and meaningful. Paul is saying to wives here the same thing that Peter says in his first letter: "Ladies, don't depend upon your talk to train your husband in godliness. Gain his release as the man he's meant to be by your walk!" (1 Peter 3:1–6, my paraphrase).

When we stay focused on the apostle's paramount objective in this passage, it all comes together. His priority is to awaken men and women to a dynamic point of spiritual understanding. The power principle at stake is essential to both genders, and the men we teach need to see how crucial their return to responsibility is. Why? Because this is the starting place on the path to recovering God's original design for husbands and wives.

Paul is not diminishing women. Rather, he is trying to say, "Wives, if you'll learn to restrain yourselves from pushing your husband to be spiritual, and if you'll exercise a self-administered graciousness of loving submission, you'll maximize the likelihood that your husband will rise to accept his God-ordained role—and you'll be blessed!"

That blessing is directly linked to a man's rediscovering and reclaiming his role, to restoring male leadership that releases a redemptive recovery rather than leadership that preserves a masculine preeminence.

ADAM'S RESPONSIBILITY

"For Adam was formed first, then Eve. And Adam was not deceived, but the woman being deceived, fell into transgression. Nevertheless she will be saved in childbearing if they continue in faith, love, and holiness, with self-control" (1 Tim. 2:13–15 NKJV).

Why has Adam's being formed first become an issue? And why the mention that Adam was not deceived? Paul is pointing to the issue of the first man's responsibility, because Adam's sore neglect, at his pristine moment of opportunity to protect Eve, became the source of the fall of the race. Furthermore, the redemptive truth disclosed here is pointing the way back, not to a pre-Fall domination of women by men but back to the originally intended dominion shared by man and wife.

The record of Genesis clearly shows that God created the man first so that he would be profoundly impressed with his own distinctiveness, as separate and apart from the animal kingdom; so that he would be profoundly aware of his own need of a partner, seeing no creature was comparable to him; and so that he would be profoundly prepared to tenderly welcome and deeply appreciate the partner he would receive.

The original order was one of complete partnership, neither gender being subordinated to the other. Adam's position in the relationship was not elevated by reason of his being first in the sequence of creation. To see this is to establish a critical starting place for understanding God's purpose. It is no secret that God ordered distinct places for men and women in his creative and redemptive enterprise, but those relationships have largely been clouded by sin, pain, confusion, and human traditions. Paul's words calling us back to the beginning become all the more important when we realize that they are not spoken to reinforce a ranking of the genders but to recall a failed responsibility by the first man, whose neglect of his assigned partnership plunged the first pair into sin.

THE MOST DEVASTATING MOMENT IN HISTORY

"And Adam was not deceived" (1 Tim. 2:14 NKJV).

The most devastating moment in human history was when Adam broke the divinely decreed contract through disobedience. But how often have you heard this staggering indictment against the man (see 1 Tim. 2:14) misconstrued to rail against the woman? Paul is actually distinguishing between the relative degrees of responsibility for the Fall. Adam is identified for his greater failure, not lesser. He was not deceived; he was disobedient (see Rom. 5:12).

Though some would see the words "the woman being deceived, fell into transgression" as charging Eve with primary responsibility for human failure, that is not Paul's point. Instead, verse 14 contrasts Adam's outright, conscious, and calculated rebellion with Eve's very differently motivated (but no less guilty) act of sin. They both sinned, but Adam did it with his eyes wide open. He was consciously disobedient; while Eve succumbed to a carefully crafted stratagem by the serpent; she was deceived.

Romans 5:12 sets the record in categorical terms: "Through one man sin entered into the world, and death through sin, and so death spread to all men" (NASB). So it is that the Scriptures put the entire responsibility for the fall of mankind at Adam's feet, not because he was a greater sinner than Eve was but because his conscious act of disobedience is judged a deeper failure when contrasted with her action born of deception.

I propose that in every male of Adam's fallen race lies some residue of this conscious failure. My proposition is not that man is more deeply sinful or harder to save than is woman, but that men are more deeply engraved with an undiagnosed yet present and abiding sense of having been marked by an order of failure that still haunts their identity as men. In my view, this is a fact of the male psyche, evident in the habits, responses, fears, and attitudes uniquely characteristic of the male of our species.

CONTINUING ON THE PATH OF FAITH

"Nevertheless she will be saved in childbearing if they continue in faith, love, and holiness, with self-control" (1 Tim. 2:15 NKJV).

Critical to understanding the mighty promise and redemptive potential of this verse is to note the grammatical difference in the object of the verb *saved* and the object of the verb *continue*: the first is singular; the second, plural. This oft-overlooked construction reinforces our point. It disallows confusion about the Holy Spirit's intent in this passage, and it may provide the most supportive verification of the interpretation I have offered. Allow me to freely paraphrase and amplify the text of verse 15 to describe this: "As the husband and wife together *continue* on a path of faith (believing that God can flourish their lives) and love (patiently learning to live out their roles under the redemptive order) and holiness with self-control (submitting to the Lord according to his Word), then they will both be rewarded—even unto the possibility of a beginning recovery of what was lost when the first pair fell into sin."

This is redemption's goal under the new covenant in Christ: God not only saving souls but also restoring the blessings of his original, created design. Just as surely as God is returning the hope of eternal life, so he is offering a path to a couple's rediscovery of his originally designed full partnership.

MOVING TOWARD TRIUMPH

Though these concepts are not mandatory to a theology of human salvation, they are essential to grasping the fuller degree of God's desire for practical redemption of the roles of men and women. Even as all believers are "called saints" yet must still grow in the disciplines of that calling, we pastors must "call" men to manhood, and we must back our call with concepts that will enable men to respond with understanding. The issues unveiled in 1 Timothy 2 are designed to pave the way to that triumph. Its insights are to clarify the intent of a man's assignment to lead; namely, that it is a charge—a responsibility for ministry—not a privileged status to exercise from a stance of superiority, and it is redemptive in intent. In other words, a man's "leading role" is given to help restore the earlier equality, not to perpetuate a permanent disparity.

As pastors, our ability to help men find the way to these far-reaching possibilities requires that we review and renew our own paths. We cannot teach the recovery possibilities of the redemptive order without being deepened in them ourselves, and that will call us back to the altar where our marriage vows were made. It is there that the secret unfolds.

PART TWO

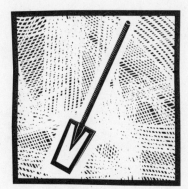

PREPARING
THE GROUND

6

BUILDING A LEADERSHIP TEAM

| *Chip MacGregor* |

G reat teams have great coaches. The championship teams I remember from my growing-up years had at least one thing in common: a head coach who was superbly able to motivate and manage players. Players would come and go, but the man at the top remained the same. The Cowboys had Tom Landry; the Dolphins had Don Shula; UCLA had John Wooden; the Reds had Sparky Anderson; the Steelers had Chuck Noll; the 49ers had Bill Walsh; North Carolina had Dean Smith; the Packers had Vince Lombardi; and Penn State still has Joe Paterno. They were all men who molded other men into winners and shaped an environment in which players worked and won together.

POINT MAN: THE MAN WHO KNOWS WHERE GOD IS GOING

Developing a lasting men's ministry in your church starts with leadership. Nothing in ministry, or all of life for that matter, happens without leadership. Until you have a man willing to lead your men's ministry, you will have a difficult time getting started. In fact, you may want to hold off on starting your ministry until you have your point man in place.

Can you identify the head of your team? Maybe you're it, or perhaps it's another man who is passionate about men's ministry. The men of your church may be looking around at each other, waiting for someone to take the lead. It's time to get the ball rolling. The head man needs a clear vision of where God is going. He must see the incredible harvest that lies before us. He also needs some leadership skills, or at least a willingness to learn.

Of course, just as a head coach will never win a championship without good players, it isn't enough to find one man who can see where God is going. You need to build a leadership team to serve alongside that man. Building a solid team of leaders is the first big step in starting your men's ministry.

Ministry works best in teams. A ministry team will jump-start your outreach to men and position you for future growth. The key to effective ministry is the quality of the ministry team. Teams with solid leadership will move forward and make a difference in the future. Your aim should be to develop three to five men who will form your core leadership team. There are five qualities to look for in the men you desire to lead your ministry: servant spirit, character, godliness, passion, and giftedness.

Servant Spirit

In Mark 10:42–45, Jesus shares with his disciples the key element in spiritual leadership. He tells them that the way to move up is by moving down. In other words, the person best suited to lead is the one who is willing to serve. Our society is obsessed with climbing the ladder, upward mobility, and chasing promotions. Jesus let it be known that those who will lead in the kingdom of God will be obsessed with descending the ladder, scaling down, downward mobility, and spiritual demotions. The man who leads will be a servant to all.

It's easy to find men who will get involved in ministry as long as they can start at the top and don't have to do the ordinary, dirty jobs. They want to be up front teaching or around the table making decisions, not in the back room making coffee or setting up chairs on Saturday night. Sometimes I get the impression that some men feel they are above certain tasks. They import their marketplace philosophy that values position, power, and prestige and believe it will work in the church. It doesn't, and it shouldn't.

Launching a ministry creates an enormous amount of work. Some tasks, such as making calls, compiling surveys, or sending out mailings, are repetitive and menial. But they need to be done. It takes only one guy on your team who thinks he's above this kind of work to breed instant division.

Character

It isn't how you look, where you work, what you have, who you know, or even what you know that counts. It's who you are when no one is looking. It's character that counts. Men of character drive real ministry.

One of my favorite passages on leadership is 1 Samuel 16:7, where God tells Samuel not to look at the outward appearance of a man, the things that most people look at, because God looks at the heart. What a key principle for selecting men to lead your ministry! Also consider the lists that Paul gave to Timothy for selecting elders and deacons (1 Tim. 3:1–13). And 1 Timothy 4:12 makes one of the best measuring tools for choosing leaders. "Let no one look down on your youthfulness, but rather in speech, conduct, love, faith and purity, show yourself an example of those who believe" (NASB). This verse provides five standards by which to gauge a man's character.

1. *Speech.* Does he use his tongue to tear down or build up? Does he lie or speak the truth? Is he sarcastic and cutting or loving and kind?
2. *Conduct.* Is there consistency in his behavior on Sunday and Monday? Does he behave in accordance with what he believes? There is no room on a leadership team for someone who isn't living out his faith in the marketplace.
3. *Love.* Is he interested in the well-being of others? Does he show compassion and tenderness toward others?
4. *Faith.* Is he willing to take wise risks and live on the edge? Is he willing to trust God or does he live purely by human wisdom and strength?
5. *Purity.* Is he seeking to be morally, ethically, and spiritually pure before God? This doesn't mean he's arrived—but is he striving to do right?

Godliness

The greatest gift your leadership team can give the men of your church is personal holiness. There is nothing more important in leading other men to Christ than a vital, authentic relationship with Jesus. Men today want the real thing, not second-hand religion. They want reality, not more ritual. In selecting men to be on your team, start with men you know are in love with Jesus. Look for the following characteristics.

Strong private life. Does this man spend time with Jesus on a regular basis? When I get together with men, I often ask them what they are learning in their daily devotions. A long silence after that question is a good indication that there isn't much happening in that area of their lives. Unless a man drinks from Jesus on a regular basis, he will have nothing to give to others. A man's private relationship with Jesus will directly influence what he does in public with other men.

Obedience. Is he seeking to obey God in all areas of life or is there an area in which he knowingly continues to sin? Is he open to accountability to others for his life and actions?

Worship. Godly men love to worship. They make it a priority to meet regularly with God's people to worship. If a man's hobbies, golf game, or favorite spectator sport regularly cause him to miss Sunday worship, he's making a loud statement about his priorities.

Passion

Every once in a while, when I least expect it, I get a huge bear hug from a fellow named John. After squeezing all the air out of me, he says, "Chip, I just love working with men. I just wish I could do this full-time." John has a passion for ministry. Passion means that you're enthusiastic about what you are doing and can't wait until the next time you get together with your men. It's a love for what you are doing and a thankfulness that God has given you gifts and the incredible privilege of serving him. When I interview a man for a leadership position, I ask a few questions that help me to gauge his passion for ministry, such as, What is your vision for men's ministry? What gets you the most excited about serving? Where do you see yourself fitting in?

From these and other questions, I get a sense of whether he really wants to do ministry or if he is motivated by guilt or a feeling that he should do something just for the sake of doing something.

Giftedness

The final quality I look for in a man for my leadership team is giftedness. Every man is gifted, but I want to make sure that a man's gifts fit his area of responsibility. Our natural tendency is to surround ourselves with men just like us, people we want as friends. Men with different gifts think differently. They might laugh at opposite things. They process experiences and emotions in a variety of ways. It can be death to a ministry if everyone on the team is the same.

Mike Holmgren, the head coach of the Seattle Seahawks, is a great offensive coordinator, but he isn't as strong on defense. To compensate, he surrounds himself with strong defensive minds, men who can build a defense to complement his offensive schemes. In the same way, a leader of men needs to surround himself with men who complement his giftedness. As you pull together a group of men, think through the following areas to get a well-rounded team.

1. *Is there a man with the gift of leadership?* A lot of men end up in leadership positions—even pastors—who do not have the gift of leadership. A leader has the ability to develop a vision and get others to buy into it. They can mobilize others and get them involved in making that vision a reality. Every team needs gifted leaders.

2. *Is there a man with the gift of administration?* A ministry start-up generates endless administrative tasks. Find someone who likes administration to keep ministry details organized and workers on task and on time. Any man with the adventurous spirit of a leader needs a guy like this on the team.

3. *Is there a man with the gift of service?* With so much to get done, every team needs a man who relishes doing the little things, the behind-the-scenes things that make a ministry work.

4. *Is there a man with the gift of mercy?* Sometimes a leadership team full of guys who like to get things done leaves battered people in their wake. You need someone who can care for the men, be a kinder and gentler example to overeager leaders, and shepherd the other leaders as the team develops.

This list is not comprehensive, but these four gifts are keys that keep a team working well. They bring balance to each other. Even with the proper mix, however, it's still possible to get nowhere. These gifts are different enough that the team will need to work hard at working well. Each man must possess a deep willingness to be a team player.

Exercise 1: Identifying Your Leadership Team

1. What are the characteristics of the men you want leading your men's ministry?
2. What types of gifted men do you need to balance out the gifts you have? What are the strengths and weaknesses of your team right now?
3. Who among the men in your church should you ask to be on the team?

RECRUITING YOUR LEADERS

It's one thing to know what kind of men you want, even to set your sights on specific guys. It's another thing to get them involved. If your church is like ours, 20 percent of the people do 80 percent of the work, and all of the key people are pulled in many different directions. When I started doing men's ministry a number of years ago, I vowed that I wouldn't steal leaders from other ministries. I decided instead to develop my own team from among the many men who were on the outside looking in.

Here are steps you can take in recruiting men to be on your leadership team.

1. Pray them out. In Matthew 9:37, Jesus tells the disciples that "the harvest is plentiful, but the workers are few" (NASB). That's true in our day as well. What did Jesus recommend? That they hire a headhunter? No! The first step is to "beseech the Lord of the harvest to send out workers" (v. 38). Effective team building begins with focused prayer.

Whenever I see someone at church who isn't involved but should be, I put his name on a list. I regularly pray through this list, asking God to send these people into the harvest, maybe in men's ministry, maybe somewhere else. I pray that God would bring just the right position for each man, based on his giftedness, passion, and availability. Make a list. Start praying right now for men who can be part of your leadership team.

2. Develop relationships. Ministry happens best through friendships. Do things with your potential leaders to get to know them. Take them out for breakfast or lunch. In these informal settings, you can begin to evaluate them according to the principles discussed above.

3. Meet them one on one. The best way to ask a man to become involved in ministry is one on one. I usually meet a guy for a meal or in his office or mine. I try really hard to connect face to face before I will settle for a phone conversation. My first objective is to share our vision for the ministry. I work to recruit men to a vision, not a program. Once he grasps the big picture, I share more specifically about the area I see him getting involved in. I let him know why I think he is the right person for the job and how he would fit on the team.

4. Share a job description. At this one-on-one meeting, I share a straightforward job description for the specific area in which I would like the potential leader to help. Putting it in writing makes everything as clear as possible, though you might choose to cover this job description orally. A well-written job description will include the following components.

- specific expectations
- specific ministry responsibilities—what he would do
- qualifications necessary for the job
- how much time it will take
- reporting relationships
- term of service
- support he can expect from the men's ministry leadership team and the church

After walking a guy through the job description, I ask him if he has any questions.

5. Ask for a commitment. I finish the conversation by asking my prospective leader to pray about the opportunity and, if he's married, talk to his wife about it before making a commitment. I give him a specific time frame of when I need a response, usually a week to two weeks maximum.

Initially, you are looking for three to five men who will form your main ministry team. If you already have a core team assembled, these same steps can be used to recruit other leaders once your core team has determined how many additional men you need.

Exercise 2: Recruiting Your Leaders

1. Make a list of ten men to pray for. Pray according to Matthew 9:37–38, that God would thrust them into leadership.
2. Decide who will contact each of these men about getting involved in the ministry.
3. Take time to develop job descriptions for the areas where you need leadership.

TRAINING YOUR LEADERS

Fear of failure is a huge roadblock that keeps many men from serving in the church. One key to working with your leadership team is to provide the training the men need to do what you have asked them to do. It's not enough just to recruit them and turn them loose to serve. You overcome a man's fear when you give him the skills, instruction, and resources to do the job properly. Never ask a man to do anything you aren't willing to train him to do. I have found that most of my effective training takes place in short, informal settings. Here's a list of some ways you can train your men.

1. *Train through small groups.* By far the most effective training I have done has been through our Top Gun program. Though training isn't the main purpose of this program, I was able to share basic leadership principles throughout the course of the year and to slowly bring along a number of men based on their giftedness. Like all ministry, leadership development happens best in the context of relationships.

If you are just starting your ministry, it may be hard to wait to begin small groups or monthly men's meetings, but you can't go wrong by taking the first year just to develop your leadership. You will set a solid foundation for whatever course you take in the future. The best way to get started is to gather a group of men around you and meet as a small group. There are plenty of great leadership books that can help you prepare your men.

2. *Train through committee meetings.* The normal give-and-take of a planning meeting almost always opens opportunities to interject good leadership principles. These are quick, little, minute-or-less lessons. During these meetings, I often find myself coaching the men on church procedures—how to reserve rooms, place bulletin announcements, and keep the custodial staff on our side.

3. *Train through books.* Another thing I like to do with my key coordinators is to read a book together. At our monthly meetings, we take time to discuss the book. Some books I have found helpful are *The Master Plan of Evangelism* by Robert Coleman, *Too Busy Not to Pray* by Bill Hybels, and *Hand Me Another Brick* by Chuck Swindoll. Studying books together gives all of the leaders a common understanding of service and ministry, and it keeps them reading, which most men do not like to do. I love to read and often pass on a good book when I finish it.

4. *Train through other resources.* One way you can train your men informally is by providing them with resources. Besides books, you can use periodicals, audiotapes, and videos. You may want to get a subscription to *Discipleship Journal* for each small group leader. Ask your pastor to pass on good articles he comes across. Some video series make great take-home helps that men can view at their convenience.

5. *Train through consulting.* It's often helpful to bring in an outside person to meet with your leadership team. A consultant can evaluate what you're doing and provide objective feedback.

6. *On-the-job training.* Whenever possible, I first work alongside a man before asking him to do a job by himself. Our other leaders do the same. On our special events committee, each member is grooming another man to take his place. These men attend all the meetings and take some responsibilities that will prepare them to lead.

7. *Train through outside seminars and conferences.* If you have men preparing to lead small groups, Serendipity provides excellent regional training sessions. Promise Keepers holds leadership conferences across the country. Your pastor may have more information about training available in your area.

Exercise 3: Training Your Leaders

1. Which character qualities do you want to build into your leaders? (i.e., honesty, integrity, perseverance)
2. Which core competencies do you want to build into your leaders? (i.e., how to lead a small group, how to plan a special event)
3. How will you train your leaders for future ministry?

GIVE AWAY THE MINISTRY

A true leader gets excited when others succeed. He pulls together a group of men, equips them, trains them, and then releases them to minister. Your ministry will develop and grow only as you develop leaders and allow them freedom. As long as you try to do everything yourself, the scope of your men's ministry will be small and its impact limited. Here are three principles for delegating responsibility to the men you coach.

1. *Point them in the right direction.* Planning is an overlooked process, but it is vitally important. Your first task as a leader or leadership team is to decide what you want to do. Creating a vision means deciding where you are going with the ministry and discerning what has to happen for you to get there. You have to know where you want to take your men.

2. *Transfer ownership.* You may be sure where your group should go, but you can't get your men anywhere without help. You need to give your men the authority, freedom, and resources they need to perform as God has gifted them. Biblical delegation starts a man out with small tasks, then moves him on to bigger assignments when he proves himself faithful. I start by putting men in charge of tasks, then move them to projects, and finally to working with people. Since people are our most precious commodity, I want to make sure the guys we choose to lead them are men of character and ability.

Giving away your ministry requires conscious effort. The first step to letting go is to make known what you need and expect. Before I delegate responsibility, I sit down with the prospective leader and answer the following questions: What has to be done? How will it be done? When will it be done? Who will help?

3. *Release your leaders.* In the summer of 1995, I served with Greg Groh of Worldwide Leadership Council at a leadership school in the Middle East. We worked with pastors, evangelists, church planters, and counselors, all of whom were working in difficult situations. As we taught on prayer, discipleship, evangelism, planning worship services, and other issues, we used a phrase that has stuck with me: catch and release. Leadership means helping men to *catch* a vision for using their gifts and then *releasing* them to do it.

Catch and release does not mean "dump and run." Don't give away aspects of the ministry without making progress checks or offering follow-up help. Stay in touch with your leaders. You need to be available to talk through how they are doing. Chances are they won't do the job the way you would. They may not avoid the mistakes you would have seen a mile away. And they may never do their job as well as you could. But that's okay. Ministry isn't about perfection. It's about building up people and developing them into the men God wants them to be. Be available to support and encourage your hardworking men. Each man's needs will be different. Some like a lot of room. They'll run with a job and forget all about you. Others need more of your time in order to stay on track. The wise leader will make the necessary adjustments and watch the ministry take off.

7

ORGANIZING YOUR MEN'S MINISTRY

| Steve Sonderman |

M en's ministry isn't a one-man show. You need a point man to make things happen and a leadership team of men to help him. In all your efforts, though, never lose sight of the fact that God is the head over all you do. You can make your plans and ask God for his rubber-stamp approval, or you can invite him to guide and empower your efforts. I can tell you from experience that the latter approach works a lot better.

BUILDING A PRAYER TEAM

Once you have a gifted leader in place who has a vision, passion, and the character to lead the ministry, your next step is to pray. Prayer is the undergirding for the rest of your ministry. A ministry that will bear lasting fruit must move forward on its knees. Unfortunately, in many churches today, prayer is only given lip service. We talk about it, sing about it, and read about it, but rarely do we do it. The only way that I am willing to do men's ministry is if other men will pray for me and for the ministry on a regular basis. It is vital to start a prayer ministry first. Prayer is where the real work gets done. Service is just gathering up all that God has done through our prayers. Here are four steps to help you start a ministry of prayer at your church.

1. Find a small group of men who will commit to pray regularly for you and the ministry. You can find these men through a number of means. You can make a list of fifteen to twenty men and send them each a letter with a commitment card to return to you if they will accept the challenge. You can run a bulletin announcement letting the men of your church know that you are developing a prayer team.

It isn't necessary to gather to pray. Each man can pray on his own wherever he is. At our church, I asked the men to pray and fast for the ministry every Wednesday at noon. Some of the men had other meetings on Wednesday, so they had to do it another day, but each man committed to set aside a regular time of prayer specifically for our men's ministry.

2. *Send the prayer requests for your ministry out to the men on a regular basis.* I send a prayer card before the first Wednesday of the month so that the men can pray specifically. These cards usually have new requests, both personal and ministry related, as well as answers to prayer.

3. *Get the men together.* During the course of the year, we have a periodic breakfast for the entire prayer team. We get to know one another, and a couple of the men share how things are going. We talk about struggles as well as joys.

4. *Keep the men informed.* I use a monthly newsletter to instruct the men on prayer. I encourage them to read other writings about prayer in order to grow in their prayer lives. One year we read *What God Does When Men Pray* by William Carr Peel. Another year we read *Too Busy Not to Pray* by Bill Hybels. This year, we're reading *Revival Fire* by Wesley Duewel. I also keep them informed by letting them know how God is answering prayer. There's no greater motivation for prayer than to see and hear about answers to prayer.

Exercise 1: Building a Prayer Team

1. Make a list of five men you are going to ask to be on your prayer team.
2. Determine what you are going to ask them to pray for, both personally and for the ministry.
3. How are you going to keep these men growing in prayer and informed of the answers?

INVOLVING YOUR PASTOR

Because I have pastored for twelve years, I fully appreciate the love-hate relationship pastors have with new ministry ideas. Pastors are at once excited and nervous. They're happy that someone else is grabbing hold of a ministry, but where is this thing headed? Pastors look at the big picture and wonder what additional demands they will face to keep one more ministry going. They can also interpret a ministry start-up as a not-so-subtle suggestion that they aren't doing an adequate job of meeting the needs of the congregation. Here are some steps you can take to involve your pastor in the process.

1. *Include your pastor early.* Before you even get started, make an appointment with your pastor to share your vision and ideas. Ask if he has any plans for starting a men's ministry and what they are. Ask him when would be a good time to get something started. Your pastor may ask you to speak to the church board or put you under the supervision of an elder or deacon. If he does the latter, work hard to include that man in your planning in the same way you would include your pastor.

2. *Interview your pastor.* Get together with your pastor when you do your survey. The time I spent with our senior pastor and other associates was highly profitable.

3. *Inform your pastor.* Send your pastor copies of the minutes from your meetings as well as the results of your surveys. Keep him involved in the process by scheduling your planning meetings at times when he is able to attend—if he wants to be there. Ask him if he wants to be present or just to be kept informed. Don't pressure him to attend.

4. *Intercede for your pastor.* You can give your pastor no greater gift than your prayer support. A church in Madison, Wisconsin, has a group of men who meet in the pastor's office each Sunday morning to pray for him before he goes into the pulpit. What an encouragement! Call your pastor and ask him how you can pray for him and his family.

5. *Invite your pastor.* Invite your pastor to the events you sponsor. Ask him to speak at some of your events as well. Pastors enjoy the opportunity to get out with the guys and talk with them, hang out with them, and bring teaching. Don't take it personally, though, if your pastor doesn't show up for every event. He could easily be at meetings every evening of his life if he said yes to everything. He does have a family, and he needs his down time too!

6. *Encourage your pastor.* Make sure the men of your church encourage your pastor in the work he is already doing. Drop him a note or give him a call to let him know how much he means to you and the church. For a pastor, there is no greater feeling than knowing that the men of the church are standing with him.

DEVELOPING A GAME PLAN

As I travel the country and talk to leaders of men's ministries, I always ask the same question: What is your purpose statement for your ministry? Often the only response I get is a blank expression. Time and again, I run across ministries that are doing a lot of good things but have no intentionality, no focus, and no direction. The reason many men's ministries falter is that they are unclear about their ultimate purpose. Without a clear and concise purpose statement, it will be very difficult for your ministry to stay on track. Here are three reasons why you need a purpose statement for your ministry.

1. *A purpose statement keeps you from taking on more than you can handle.*
   Every time I go to a leadership planning meeting, I find myself saying the

same thing: How does this fit into our purpose? Your leaders will come up with some great ideas, but if these ideas don't fit with your purpose for the ministry, you need to set them aside to avoid being lured off track.

2. *A purpose statement helps you make decisions.* When someone has a new idea for a ministry, I always ask two questions: Who is going to lead it? and What is its purpose? Without a purpose statement, deciding for or against a specific activity can be tough. Because everyone has already agreed to our purpose statement, it's the one fair way to determine which ideas work for us and which don't.

3. *A purpose statement keeps you moving in the right direction.* You can do many good things, but what about doing the best thing? Most ministries try to do too much. It's better to start slowly and simply. Reach one group of men and minister to them effectively before you move on to another group. A well-designed purpose statement keeps you on target.

CRAFTING YOUR PURPOSE STATEMENT

It would be easy to swipe someone else's purpose statement, and I've been tempted to do that many times. But the real benefit of working through your own statement of purpose is ownership. In the end, you may end up with a statement similar to what some other group has chosen. That's fine. You'll know that you went through the process and determined what God has put into your own hearts.

You can start the process of writing your purpose statement by having the leadership team read as many passages of Scripture as possible that are relevant to your ministry's mission. Come prepared with some of your own and have the group share theirs as well. Here are a few to get you started: Matthew 28:19–20, John 13:34–35, Acts 1:8, Ephesians 4:11–12, and Colossians 2:6–7. Grounding your purpose statement in Scripture will help you focus on where God is leading your ministry.

Here's the purpose statement for our men's ministry. "By the grace of God, the men's ministry of Elmbrook Church exists to introduce men to Jesus Christ, develop godly character through a deeper relationship with him and other men, and equip them to serve as the Holy Spirit leads."

As your men's ministry grows, it will be important to develop a purpose statement for each new ministry. If you develop small groups, for example, guide those leaders through the process of developing a mission statement of their own that flows from the main men's ministry purpose.

STRUCTURING YOUR MINISTRY

Once your purpose is clearly defined, you need to decide how you will structure your ministry to accomplish your mission. This isn't an easy step for most people. Our natural tendency is to do the same old things we've always done or to grab an idea

Exercise 2: God's Purpose and Your Purpose

1. List verses that speak to the purposes of the church. Some ideas:

   Matthew 28:19–20   Ephesians 1:22–23
   Mark 12:30–31   Ephesians 3:10–11
   John 13:34–35   Ephesians 4:11–12
   Acts 1:8   Colossians 1:28
   Acts 2:42–47   Colossians 2:6–7
   Romans 12:1–2   2 Timothy 2:2

2. From these verses, write down words or phrases that highlight what you believe God desires for your ministry. For example: equip men, evangelize men, mobilize men for service, build disciples, engage the community, reconcile men to . . . , instruct men in . . .

3. Get a copy of your church's purpose statement and ask the following questions.

   What are the major themes in this statement?
   How does that fit with where we are going as a ministry?
   What do we need to incorporate into our men's ministry statement?

4. Now answer the following questions.

   Why does this ministry exist?
   What are we to be as a ministry?
   What are we to do as a ministry?
   How are we to do it?

5. Draft your purpose statement. You might want to start it something like, "Our ministry exists to glorify Jesus by . . ." Remember, what you write will define for everyone the main business of your ministry.

6. Evaluate and revise your purpose statement.

   Is it clear and concise (not longer than two sentences)?
   Does it state our purpose as a ministry?
   Is it easy to communicate to the leaders and the men of our church?
   Does it empower the leadership of our ministry?
   Is it consistent with who we are as a church?

7. Refine your purpose statement. Pray over it and work on its grammar and phrasing. Share it with others and get their input, including your pastor. After a month, come back to it and determine whether it is still what you want.

from a book, a magazine, or a conference. But developing a life-changing ministry requires the programs that will work best for the men in your congregation. For some, it may be a monthly Saturday men's breakfast. For others, it may be a quarterly evening rally. Still others will create a Sunday school class just for men, and maybe only for part of the year. Every situation presents different needs. Every need creates different opportunities. Every opportunity requires a different approach.

As you work through exercise 3, think long-term. Give yourself time. Devise programs that you can put into place over the next five years to accomplish your purpose. Draw on all of the information you have gathered from interviews, surveys, brainstorming sessions, and meetings with your pastor and other church leaders.

ESTABLISHING A TIMELINE

Once you've decided where to start, the next step is to plan exactly how to make it happen. Whether you plot your timeline on a computer program or on paper, you'll want to put things in order, because some things can't happen until other things have taken place. Break jobs down into manageable tasks with reasonable deadlines. Developing an entire men's ministry can be utterly overwhelming, but looking at the small steps along the way feels much more achievable.

Here are three points to remember when establishing your timeline.

1. *Think long-term and take it slowly!* You won't develop your ministry overnight. It takes years to build disciples. Even if you implement one or two straightforward programs, they will need ongoing evaluation and innovation to stay fresh. Everyone wants a big men's ministry right away, but it just doesn't happen that way. A well-rounded, full-blown ministry takes years to build. Think in terms of four to five years to build a healthy ministry to men.
2. *Choose one area to work on.* Whether it's leadership development, small groups, or a men's retreat, it is more important to do one ministry well than to do a bunch poorly. When men sense you are doing things with excellence and purpose, they will be drawn in and pull others in as well. Each year, add one or two more components to the ministry, taking strategic steps in accordance with your five-year plan.
3. *What works in one church may not work in another.* There is no magic formula for ministry. Use exercise 4 to set a timeline for the major ministries you want to see happen over the next five years.

ADVERTISING YOUR MINISTRY

In some congregations, the men's ministry is the best-kept secret in the church. Once you have framed your basic program, advertise it. Make sure your publicity is

Exercise 4: A Timeline for Ministry

1. When do you want to start the various components of your ministry?

   Year One _____

   Year Two _____

   Year Three _____

   Year Four _____

   Year Five _____

2. What must be done in the first year for each of the major ministries you want to start?

   Ministry _____

      Task _____

         When done? _____

      Task _____

         When done? _____

      Task _____

         When done? _____

   Ministry _____

      Task _____

         When done? _____

      Task _____

         When done? _____

      Task _____

         When done? _____

3. Construct your calendar for the upcoming year. Make sure to check the church's calendar to avoid double-booking key activities. Schedule your training meetings, committee meetings, events, seminars, classes, and so on.

4. Evaluate your timeline. Are your goals for each year realistic? Measurable? Open to evaluation? Flexible?

- Is your leadership team functioning properly? Where do you need help?
- Is the pastor being informed to the level he desires?
- Do you have a leadership training program in place?
- Is the ministry balanced between evangelism, establishment, equipping, and extension?

When evaluating your evangelism efforts, ask yourself such questions as, Are our men trained to evangelize? Are they building relationships with unchurched men?

Are our men leading others to Christ? Are we providing evangelistic events? Follow that up with questions about how well you establish new believers in the faith: Are we discipling new believers? How? Are our men trained to follow up with a new believer? Do we have small groups in place for ongoing growth?

When it comes to equipping people, seek honest answers to questions like, Do we have a means for men to discover, develop, and deploy their spiritual gifts? Are men in the church serving based on their giftedness? Do we have a way to train men to be leaders in their homes, their workplaces, the church, and the world? And evaluate your success in extending the kingdom: Are we helping men develop a vision for the harvest? Are we providing opportunities for men to serve across the street and around the world? Have we planned any overseas mission trips for this year? How many entry points do we have in the ministry? (Small groups, large groups, seminars, events, etc.) How accessible are these entry points for newcomers or the unchurched? Do we allow for different levels of commitment? Do we offer a variety of service opportunities? Do we have an intentional and effective way to get men into small groups?

This list is not exhaustive, but it's a start. Develop your own list based on the particulars of your ministry. It is also helpful to evaluate individual activities and events throughout the year. If an event is worth doing, it is worth evaluating.

Evaluations are best when made by both the participants and the men who organized and carried out the program. After an evangelistic outreach luncheon, I sent a letter to ten men who had attended the luncheon and brought a friend. I asked questions like the following.

- Was the setting appropriate for what we were trying to do?
- How was the service at your table?
- Was the food hot when it reached your table?
- Was the message clear?
- Did the program allow for follow-up on the way back to work?
- What should we change the next time we do an event like this one?
- What should we do the same?
- What recommendations do you have for the planning committee?

With these evaluations in hand, the working committee does its own evaluation. We plan an evaluation meeting for a week or so after the event, while everything is still fresh in everyone's mind. We go through each aspect of the event and ask the tough questions.

- Was the flyer or brochure out in time?
- Was the brochure clear?
- Did we use every means possible to get men to the event?
- What could we do differently next time?

This can be a grueling, even painful, process, but it will help your men learn and prepare for the next time, even if it is a completely different program or event. The level of evaluation will depend on the event. Some events need only a quick, ten-minute review, while others will require a full evening of discussion.

BUDGETING FOR YOUR MINISTRY

Another task for your leadership team is to develop a budget for the year and then to ensure that the money is used appropriately. Each church's budgeting process will be different. Find out what the budgeting process is for your church.

I would suggest a zero-based budget. In this type of budgeting, your leadership team looks at the entire year and makes a list of everything they want to do, based on your earlier planning exercises. Decide how much each event and activity will cost. In our church, we have tried to make all of our activities and events self-sufficient. Most of our budget goes for training and promoting the ministry. Here are some categories to think through when developing your budget.

- *Printing.* Ministry brochures, newsletters, posters, letters, and other literature.
- *Postage.* Monthly reminders, bulk mailings, reminder cards.
- *Leadership development.* Training seminars, books, tapes, meetings, appreciation dinner, and leadership retreat.
- *Service or missions.* Brochures, training materials, extra costs for projects.

When budgeting for a specific event, it is best to cover all of your costs with a registration fee. You may even make some money to help offset the cost of the same event next year. We have found that the men in our church are willing to pay for specific activities, which frees up church money for ministries that are unable to pay their own way. When planning a special event, here are some of the things that will need to be included in your budget.

- Food (if you do a breakfast or cookout)
- Publicity (posters, mailers, brochures, radio spots, newspaper ads)
- Honorariums for speakers and musicians
- Sound equipment, props, and other materials
- Facility rental (if needed)
- Transportation and lodging for speaker (if needed)

Effective budgeting requires research and planning. Even though it is a lot of work, a well-planned budget will be a lot more realistic and helpful.

8

PURPOSEFUL PLANNING, EFFECTIVE IMPLEMENTATION

Steve Sonderman

You have spent months planning, praying, and preparing. Now it's time to put your plan into action. If you've been struggling with all the discussion about planning, this chapter is for you—the doers.

Too many ministries around the country are settling for second best. They have become complacent and are happy with just a few events, service projects, and activities each year. But there is more to men's ministry.

SPECIAL EVENTS

Special events are the easiest way to get a men's ministry going. They can be stretched and reshaped to accomplish almost any purpose within your ministry. Special events increase the visibility of your ministry and establish its identity. If you are just starting out, special large group gatherings will provide a forum in which the men of your church can hear about the ministry and its plans.

Special events can be a nonthreatening way for newcomers to become acquainted with your ministry. Most special events can be planned as entry points into your ministry. New men can be encouraged simply to come and listen without feeling compelled to share their opinions or feelings.

Special events can be used to gently encourage men to go deeper in their relationships with one another. Because we know that newcomers will attend our special events, we often include a testimony from someone who has participated in a small group. At the conclusion of the event, we give men a chance to step beyond the more anonymous big event and join a small group.

Special events develop leaders. Many of the key leaders in our ministry are men who started out on special events committees. Such activities pull men into service. Because planning and putting on these events are projects with a defined start and finish, and because men love activity, we usually find that our men are willing to get involved.

Special events are a great way to kick off a new year, because they can give your leadership team a platform to introduce upcoming ministry events and sign men up for the activities. At our fall special events, we set up publicity tables for each aspect of our ministry in order to make them all visible.

Planning a Special Event

Here are some guidelines for planning a special event.

1. *Don't try to do everything yourself.* The most effective way to plan a special event is with a team of men who work together. Involving a wide range of men in the planning process spurs creativity and gives other men a chance to grow in leadership.

2. *Don't start without a coordinator.* Better yet, select cocoordinators. The use of cocoordinators works well to spread responsibility and build accountability. As a men's ministry leader, you can help these cocoordinators recruit the rest of their team members. Before recruiting team members, however, your coordinators should develop brief job descriptions that detail the specific tasks that each man will be doing. Men want to know what they're getting themselves into and how long the job will take. If you pop too many surprises on them, they won't offer to help the next time.

When planning a fall kickoff or other major event, you will want to include the following members on your planning committee: chairman, publicity coordinator, budget manager, registration coordinator, facilities coordinator, hospitality coordinator, program coordinator, food coordinator, worship coordinator, and prayer coordinator. At the beginning of the planning process, have each man develop a job description so that every responsibility is covered without an overlap of duties.

3. *Start early.* A major event can take as much as nine months to plan. Once you have decided what you want to do and when you will do it, put together a timeline to track your progress. List all the things you need to complete and a deadline for each task. Start your timeline as many months before the event as you can and complete it the day of the event.

Keys to Successful Events

Good special events don't just happen. Here's what holds them together.

1. *Purpose.* Early in the planning process, agree on the purpose of the event so that your committee members aren't working at cross-purposes. No event can meet every need among your men. Be specific and stick to your purpose.
2. *Delegate responsibility.* Even if one or two men could stage an event by themselves, it wouldn't be beneficial to them or to the other men of the church. Special events are opportunities to get a lot of men involved and give them a chance to serve.
3. *Timing.* Plan your event with the church calendar in mind. It's easy to be a maverick in the ministry, but you're a part of the church. Don't hinder other ministries by the timing of your events. Case in point: don't plan a men's retreat the weekend after a couples' retreat or a men's event on Valentine's Day or Mother's Day. Believe it or not, it's been done.
4. *Evaluation.* If an event is worth doing, it is worth evaluating. Give the men at the event time to evaluate what they thought of the event and to make suggestions for the future.

Momentum-Generating Events

Effective special events come in lots of shapes and sizes. Plan events that serve your overall purpose and fit the size, scope, and style of your church.

Retreats. A one- or two-night getaway provides an opportunity for your men to set aside the distractions of their lives to fellowship, relax, receive some good teaching, and be exposed to small groups. Many churches plan retreats in the fall to kick off the new calendar year.

Golf outing. This one-day event is a great way to get men outside your church involved. You can have a meal together to share the vision of the ministry before or after you play golf.

Barbecue. Cookouts give men a chance to enjoy an evening of food, fellowship, and fun together. You could roast a pig or barbecue steak or chicken and include music and a short program. Cookouts are a nonthreatening way to draw men in from the fringes and give them a glimpse of your ministry.

Sporting event. Depending on the opportunities in your area, you can gather a group of men to attend a sporting event.

Conferences and seminars. Several nationally known speakers and authors, such as Steve Farrar and Pat Morley, are available for conferences and seminars on men's issues. These events can be citywide, drawing men together from across your community.

MONTHLY OR QUARTERLY MEETINGS

Once interest and involvement have been created by a special event, follow up with monthly or quarterly meetings, strategically planned to keep the momentum going. The timing, focus, and location of these subsequent meetings will depend on the specific vision, needs, and resources of your church and men's ministry. Follow-up meetings are important for several reasons.

- They provide a next step of involvement for men who came to a special event.
- They create opportunities for new men in the church to get involved.
- They build a springboard to get men into small groups.
- They serve as an opportunity to share the vision of the ministry.
- They provide an opportunity for leadership to be developed.

Don't let the planning and implementation of these follow-up gatherings fall on too few shoulders. Spread the opportunity and responsibility as widely as possible to get more men involved and avoid burning out your core leadership team.

1. *Develop a leadership team for each activity.* Designate cocoordinators to call the meetings, develop the team, check that every man on the committee is doing his job, and keep the event in line with the ministry's overall purpose statement.

2. *Delegate responsibilities according to men's interests and gifts.* Some responsibilities include:

Publicity. Place bulletin announcements, develop brochures or newsletters, and send reminders.

Cooking. Prepare the meal or refreshments for each meeting.

Program. Line up speakers, music, testimonies, emcee, multimedia.

Table talk. Recruit discussion leaders and make sure the speaker provides discussion questions that are tied in to his talk.

Greeters. Meet the men when they arrive and give them name tags.

A committee can meet right after the meeting to evaluate and go over any details for the next meeting.

3. *Develop a purpose statement.* I know it sounds redundant, but your team needs a purpose statement to keep your activities on track and in line with the stated purpose of your men's ministry.

4. *Decide on a structure.* There are a lot of ways to do what you want to do. Everything depends on your specific church situation and when your men prefer to meet.

5. *Line up speakers.* There is no magical way to do this. Wherever you find your speakers, schedule them as far in advance as possible. Some churches use outside

speakers exclusively, while others like the consistency of one speaker. You might want to ask your pastor if he would like to speak at these monthly events. If you use outside speakers, make sure to provide an honorarium, lodging, and travel expenses.

6. *Develop a theme for the year.* A well-chosen and unifying theme communicates that you are serious about these meetings and have thought out what you want to accomplish. Everything you do at your meetings should be focused on your theme.

7. *Use your meetings as a bridge to the next step in your men's ministry.* You can announce new small group start-ups, for example, so men can join. Or you can announce service opportunities at church. Continually ask yourselves how you can use each event or gathering to move your men forward in the growth and discipling process.

8. *Follow up with newcomers.* If a man comes to a meeting for the first time, he is there for a reason. Maybe he wants fellowship, encouragement, or guidance. Your leadership team should call these men and ask for feedback on the event. Personal follow-up makes a man feel cared for and counted on. It may open doors to deeper ministry opportunities.

9. *Plan your meetings carefully.* Review your plans with the following questions in mind.

Are the transitions smooth from one part of the meeting to the next?

Does the meeting flow or is it awkward and choppy?

Are there breaks in the meeting so the men can stretch?

Is there an opportunity for the men to talk casually with each other? Don't overstructure your meetings. Allow your men time to meet the simple need for connection.

Do the components of the meeting fit together?

If you have music, are the overheads easy to read? Are there enough songsheets to go around? Newcomers will feel out of place if you sing songs without printed words.

Are the seats comfortable? The heart only hears what the seat can stand.

Is a sound system necessary for the room you are using? Does it work properly?

Is the message practical and relevant? Does it meet the men of your church where they are? Does it have points for the men to apply? Is it biblically based?

PRINCIPLES FOR EFFECTIVE MINISTRY

It's easy to stage a momentum-generating event, but keeping a strong, vibrant, focused ministry together over the long haul is much more difficult. It takes prayer, hard work, and very intentional planning to keep the ball rolling. But no matter what your ministry ends up looking like, no matter what the size or location of your church, certain principles for success apply across the board. Men's ministry is a process, based on biblical principles, to accomplish a purpose. A principle-centered, purpose-driven ministry will avoid weaving to and fro with every fad that hits the church. Evaluate your leadership team and your ministry on a regular basis to make sure that you are sticking close to the following principles.

Principle 1: Ministry Is Relationally Driven

Ministry happens best in the context of friendships. As our ministry has grown, we have had to battle to stay people-centered rather than program-driven. Energy, excitement, and numerical growth will tempt any ministry to spin out another program or string of events. Programs are useful only to the extent that they help build relationships. Authentic ministry happens only when one man gets close to another and develops a friendship. It is impossible to minister to men from a distance.

Jesus is the ultimate model for an up close and personal ministry. Here's how we can emulate Jesus with our men.

1. *Walk with them*. One of the wiser associates on our staff gave me the following sage advice: meet with men on their time schedule, their turf, and their agenda. We build relationships with men by showing up in their world and walking with them.

2. *Listen to them*. When I meet with men, I talk about the news, sports, and weather for a while, then move on to deeper, more personal questions.

How are things between you and your wife?

How are things between you and your kids?

How are things between you and your job?

How are things between you and your Lord?

3. *Love them*. John 13:34 says that we are to love one another just as Christ loved us. Men today are starving for love and encouragement. The adage is true: "People do not care how much you know until they know how much you care."

4. *Pray for them*. End your times together by asking a man how you can pray for him in the coming weeks. Sometimes it's appropriate to pray for him right then. If not, promise to pray for him when you get back to the office.

5. *Scale your ministry to fit your church*. If you're from a small church and you're asking yourself, How can I do all this? don't be discouraged. For you, ministry to men may simply be getting together with a different man from your church each week and asking questions. By building relationships, you are ministering to men. As contacts are made and friendships are established, opportunities for other types of ministry will become evident.

Principle 2: Men's Ministry Is Done by Men

It seems obvious, but the more men you can involve in your ministry, the more effective it will be. Ephesians 4:12 states the principle: We are "to prepare God's people for works of service." The word *prepare* means "to set a broken bone," "to mend a frayed fishing net," "to restore something to its original condition," or "to condition an athlete." The only way a church will come to maturity, Paul says, is if people are deployed into service. You will severely hinder your ministry's development if you try to do everything yourself. The task of the leadership team is to involve other men in the ministry. Always be looking for men who can take on responsibility. Like a coaching staff in sports, the job of your leadership team is to train, develop, and motivate men to serve. It isn't your job to play the game; it's your job to prepare your players to play. Train them, develop their skills, and motivate them to work hard. Your men's ministry will grow only as fast as leadership is developed.

Principle 3: Effective Ministry Is Balanced

In ministry, it's easy to get so caught up in one biblical mandate that you ignore the others. For example, if you pour all your energy, money, and time into evangelism but neglect discipleship, your attendance will be great, but the maturity level of your men will be dismal. It's also possible, however, to spend so much time perfecting your care for one another that you never bother to reach out to those outside the faith. Effective ministry maintains its balance. It isn't easy, but it is possible if you plan carefully and prayerfully.

As you develop your plan, keep the following four biblical mandates in mind: evangelism, establishment, equipping, and extension. You won't be able to address each of these areas the day you start your ministry, but use these points as targets as you move ahead.

1. Evangelism. In Mark 16:15, Jesus tells his disciples to go into the world and preach the Good News. Archbishop William Temple has a great definition of what Jesus meant. He says, "Evangelism is to present Jesus Christ in the power of the Holy Spirit, that men come to put their trust in God through Him, to accept Him as their Savior and to serve Him as their King in the fellowship of His church."

Most of the men in your church are surrounded daily by people who don't know Jesus Christ as their Lord and Savior. It's important to design part of your ministry to reach those in your community who are without God, without Christ, without hope.

2. Establishment. Once men have committed their lives to Christ, they need to be grounded in that relationship. In Colossians 2:6–7 Paul writes, "Therefore as you have received Christ Jesus the Lord, so walk in Him, having been firmly rooted and now being built up in Him and established in your faith, just as you were instructed, and overflowing with gratitude" (NASB).

Even after years of church involvement, most men aren't well grounded in the basics of Christianity. They can say and do the right things, but they have little vitality in their relationship with Jesus Christ. The establishment area of your ministry is a process of grounding men in the spiritual disciplines of prayer, Bible study, Scripture memorization, and solitude. It's here that you give them the skills needed to walk with Jesus the rest of their lives, so they aren't dependent on others for their growth.

3. *Equipping.* You don't want to raise up a bunch of human sponges who attend your meetings solely to take in what they can. The third part of a balanced ministry is getting men out of the stands and into the game. Help your men discover, develop, and deploy their spiritual gifts. Help them highlight areas in the church where they can serve. Help them not only to understand but also to practice good stewardship of time, energy, and money. In short, help them become contributing members of the body of Christ.

4. *Extension.* Mission is the final piece of a balanced ministry. The church exists to take the whole gospel to the whole world. Keep this fundamental truth in front of your men. Around our place, we call it becoming a "world-class Christian." One measure of an effective ministry is how many men you train and send to serve in ministries that reach non-Christians.

Principle 4: Ministry Is Progressive

If faith is a process of growing into Christlikeness, then ministry should likewise be a process of growing Christlike men. Men's ministry is not an isolated event but an intentional series of steps that helps men become fully devoted followers of Jesus. It's easy to fall into the trap of random, unrelated activities. Whenever you plan an event or a new ministry, ask yourself how it fits into your philosophy and purpose. Does it help you reach your goals and objectives or does it just take up time and energy?

How easy have you made it for men to get involved? How many entry points have you created? Different men are attracted to different things. Some want sports. Some like speakers. Some hate to sing. Others love it. Some like large groups. Others prefer small groups. You won't be able to provide all options at once, but as you grow, make sure you create a good mix. As you plan your program, ask whether you are making opportunities for the men to grow in commitment. Make the next step clear—not to exclude anyone but to tap into men's love of challenge.

Principle 5: Start Small and Go Slowly

The biggest mistake many ministries make is that they try to move too fast and start with too many things at once. It is easy to plan a lot of activities and events, but unless there is a strong foundation of leadership and prayer, the ministry will begin to unravel after a couple of years. You would do far better to take the entire first year to develop your leadership for the future. Everything rises and falls with leadership. Once your leadership team is in place and functioning well, start adding one new ministry per year. It is always a temptation to create a wide range of ministries right away to make it appear as though "something is happening." But if you want to develop a lasting and effective ministry for the long term, start small and go slowly!

Principle 6: Be Strategic

Your purpose will lead to your strategy, and your strategy will accomplish your purpose. Pat Morley's Man in the Mirror ministry team has defined three basic aspects to an effective strategy: create momentum, capture momentum, and sustain momentum.

1. Create momentum with low-level, low-commitment events. These may be seminars on finances, parenting, or work, or a men's barbecue with a scheduled speaker. Momentum-generating events have the following characteristics.

They start where your men are and move them to where they need to be.

They provide a safe environment for men to participate and get to know one another.

They give men what they need in the guise of what they want.

They provide a variety of open doors and entry points.

2. Capture momentum by building bridges from one level to the next. Never do an event for the sake of doing an event. Always create a bridge to something deeper. For example, at the end of a golf outing, create an opportunity for the men to join a small group. At the end of every breakfast and special event we do, we encourage our men to join an eight-week study called Men of Change. Over the past two years, we have seen a couple hundred men take this next step.

3. Sustain momentum by getting the men into small groups, developing them as leaders, and deploying them into ministries of service. The key to effectively sustaining momentum is to think through your goals, clearly articulate your purpose, plan your strategies, and follow through with the implementation of each stage of your plan.

9

UPSIDE-DOWN LEADERSHIP

Stacy T. Rinehart

One day, years ago, I told nine different people who worked in our fast-food business, "You're fired!" I was the kind of boss you would never want to work for. I demanded perfection and punished anything less than maximum performance. On that particular day in the late 1960s, nine of the sixty employees who worked for me didn't measure up.

Not long after that, I received a life-changing letter from President Nixon, inviting me for a free physical exam. Of course, I knew what that meant. I passed the exam with flying colors and qualified for an all-expenses-paid trip to Vietnam. But rather than wait to be drafted into the army as a private, I determined to take control of the situation and enlisted in the army's Officer Candidate School.

I was used to giving orders and thought that the best way to exercise control and leadership, and also to stay alive, was to be the commander of other soldiers. Being an officer in the army was my way of being a real leader. I wanted to be as high in the ranks as I could get, so I set my goals for the top.

My leadership model at that time was one in which the real leaders were at the top; they exercised control, kept everyone else in line, and called the shots. Leaders were the ones with real significance, power, authority, and ambition. Nothing in my experience suggested that any other approach was even worth considering.

Less than a week after I finished all my training and became a proud second lieutenant, I was confronted by the greatest leader in history, Jesus Christ. Little did I know how that encounter would change my concept of leadership. Of course, at the time I met him, I didn't know that Jesus is history's most influential leader. I was merely a searching young man, fearful of death in the jungles where I might be sent, seeking answers to life's basic questions.

I prided myself on being a good leader. In fact, for my age, I thought I was a superb leader. But as I grew in my knowledge of Jesus and came to understand his heart and his ways of leading, I changed my thinking. Jesus taught me the life-changing lessons that all of us must learn if we are to serve and lead in his kingdom. As we seek to lead in our men's ministries, we must learn at the feet of the Master how to serve, teach, and inspire other men.

I have made studying Christ's leadership model my focus for the past thirty years. My original approach to leadership, where I could fire nine people in one day, brings me deep shame. I have shared that story, though, so that you could see the distance God has brought me in leadership thinking and practice.

I take some solace in the fact that even the twelve handpicked men who walked with Jesus, watched him, and heard him day in and day out had the same philosophy of leadership that I once had. Two of them, James and John, were brothers. They conspired with their mother to become the top leaders among the Twelve so that when Jesus became king, they would be well-positioned (see Matt. 20:20–24). When the other ten disciples heard about this, they were incensed, because they wanted to be first, too! They often argued among themselves as to who was the greatest. Ambition and thirst for power ran in their veins. In other words, Jesus' disciples represented a cross section of men just like us. That should give us hope.

DESCENDING INTO GREATNESS

Jesus had heard their arguments over the months, but on this occasion, there was outright anger, bitterness, contempt, and hatred toward James and John among the other ten disciples.

Taking the Twelve aside, Jesus acknowledged two kinds of leadership. He said, "You know that those who are recognized as rulers of the Gentiles lord it over them; and their great men exercise authority over them" (Mark 10:42 NASB). "Lording it over" is a model of leadership we all know. It is the boss, commander, or supervisor model. It is the form of leadership that comes naturally to those who think of themselves as real leaders. They are in charge. They exercise authority. They make their mark. They call the shots and have power over raises, firings, layoffs, even lives. They have real significance in the eyes of others. Jesus acknowledged this approach as a normal pattern of leadership. But then he turned leadership upside down with these words, "But it is not so among you."

Following Jesus requires a different approach to leadership, one that contradicts the dominant leadership of our age. I am sure that all twelve disciples were silent and bewildered, thinking, "What's left? What is leadership if it's not being in charge?" In their hearts, James and John no doubt felt rebuked. The other ten must have felt vindicated and convicted at the same time. But surely they all wondered, "What is he talking about?"

Jesus explained, "Whoever wishes to become great among you shall be your servant; and whoever wishes to be first among you shall be slave of all. For even the Son of Man did not come to be served, but to serve, and to give His life a ransom for many" (Mark 10:43–45 NASB).

This was too much! Greatness is what James and John desired. The same was true of the other ten as well. But to become a servant? That's upside down. That's not the way it's done! No one practices this kind of leadership.

It is important that we understand that Jesus did not say it was wrong to want to be a leader or to long for greatness. He simply pointed to a different path to that end. Greatness, according to Jesus, is a descent into servanthood. The issue here is one of identity, not position, title, personality, style, or ambition. Leadership in the body of Christ requires that we take on the identity of a bondservant or slave.

Have you ever observed that the apostle Paul frequently called himself a servant of Jesus? (Rom. 1:1; Phil. 1:1; Titus 1:1). Have you noticed that Peter did the same? (2 Peter 1:1). There is a reason for this. As followers of Jesus, their identity as leaders made a fundamental shift.

In the kingdom of God, real leaders are servants. And as Paul and Peter have shown, servants have real power. They saw themselves not as the men in charge but as slaves who served others out of their relationship with Jesus. For us as men, and as men who minister to men, servant leadership is a radical departure from our normal way of thinking and operating. We are so much like James and John; yet we hear the ring of truth in Jesus' words.

REAL POWER

Because we are steeped in the world's model of leadership—the tactics are part of our nature as men—we must begin by considering how God's design for leadership contradicts what we consider normal. Real power in Jesus' kingdom is not

dominating, overt, loud, or strong

controlling, covert, silent, or passive-aggressive

manipulating through bully tactics or analytical criticisms

imposing the leader's vision or agenda on others

being the boss, supervisor, or senior leader over others

Though our personalities differ and the way we use these tactics may differ, we all recognize the natural drift of our flesh. Jesus says that real power in his kingdom consists of

serving him and his purposes with our actions, thoughts, and words

serving others by helping them see how to follow Jesus

serving others by helping them find their unique place of service in the world, even if it is not in our ministry or small group

Nowhere is the paradoxical nature of servant leadership more evident than when we talk about power. In our culture, having power as an individual or a leader is all about success, strength, and being on top. Power is how we determine when we've made it. There is nothing more upside down about Christ's model of leadership than his refusal to use his power to achieve his ends. Instead, he pointed to a different kind of power: power as an influence rooted in love, power that trickles from the bottom to the top and permeates the whole. From our perspective, this is a strange kind of power. It is not the power of force or control but the power of the Spirit, of humility, of weakness. As Paul learned and teaches us, Jesus' power is perfected in weakness (2 Cor. 12:9–10). Power—real power—as Christ modeled it is the freedom to love and lead without having to throw our weight around to prove we are somebody.

Putting others first and serving their needs is a supernatural act of humility. It requires God's work in us and through us. But servants of Christ are not weak in influence. Paul was a prisoner on a ship for Rome, on his way to stand trial before Caesar. Yet in the storm, when the ship was sinking and all hope was lost, Paul the prisoner influenced even the Roman commander. By heeding Paul, all were saved (Acts 27–28:3). Later, Paul the hero was serving everyone by finding firewood.

Who are the models of servant leadership near you? There's no shortage of those who view themselves as the boss, the greatest, and the one in charge, even in our churches and ministries. But who around you is a real servant?

THE ULTIMATE EXAMPLE

Christ's disciples were full of anticipation. Jesus had entered Jerusalem to a glorious reception of men and women waving branches and shouting, "Hosanna! Blessed is He who comes in the name of the Lord, even the King of Israel." (John 12:13 NASB). What an honor. The Twelve no doubt believed that this would be the time when Jesus would take control of the situation as the Messiah.

They found themselves at a banquet that Jesus put on for them (John 13). They expected him to declare his intentions. They wondered what part they would play in the Messiah's rule. To their complete amazement, their expectations were once again turned upside down. Jesus knew that he was the King of Kings. He knew where he

A Comparison of Power Leaders and Servant Leaders

Power Leaders	Servant Leaders
Feed on the spotlight	Share the spotlight with others
Are the focal point of the ministry	Make Jesus the focal point
Don't develop other leaders	Develop many leaders
Have a high turnover as people leave the ministry	Have a low turnover because people are loyal and stay
Keep the focus on themselves and their agenda	Make Christ the central focus and agenda
Cannot share agendas	Affirm and participate in kingdom agendas
Feed on being in charge and having power	Are committed to being a servant first and foremost
Leave people feeling hurt and abused	Are committed to reconciliation and relationships
Refer to their title frequently	May have a title but seldom refer to it
Are masters of manipulation and abuse those who get in their way	Respect people for their freedom to think, act, and respond
Use power images, offices, and perks to reveal their status	Abhor the thought of using power images
Pull rank to get their way	Never use their position to get their way
Recruit many followers for their work	Develop many followers for the Lord

had come from, what his position was, what his authority was, and where his glorious throne was. He knew. As only the Son of God could know, he knew! Yet because he knew, he rose from supper and put on the garments of a servant, not the garments of royalty. Then he did the unthinkable; he washed the disciples' feet. The most humbling thing he could do to serve them, he did.

The disciples were embarrassed. The Messiah would never do this! Leaders don't do servant things; they do leader things. Why would the King do this? Even Peter protested, revealing his shock that Jesus would do such a thing.

The lesson for us is one of the most powerful examples of what leadership in the kingdom is like. Jesus said, "If I then, the Lord and the Teacher, washed your feet, you also ought to wash one another's feet" (John 13:14 NASB). Some apply this command literally; others take it figuratively. But regardless of our perspective, the message behind the act is that leadership in the kingdom involves being a servant to others.

Several summers ago, we conducted a week-long training seminar in applied ministry. We had a team of Native Americans among our group of Anglo-Americans. During one time of prayer, the sins committed by white settlers against the ancestors and relatives of the Native Americans became central. We could not go on until we had dealt with this issue, until there was reconciliation. The leader of this part of our training felt that he needed to wash the Indians' feet to represent the ultimate humility he felt. Without asking anyone, he went out and got a bucket of water and some towels, came back, and led the whites as they washed the feet of the Native Americans.

A real transformation took place. Stories were shared, and sins were acknowledged with tears and humility. An atmosphere that had been thick with aloofness and polite small talk began to soften. The ensuing prayer was on an entirely new plane. Hearts were joined, and something of consequence was affected in the kingdom—all because a servant leader's actions ignited a transformation.

THE ULTIMATE QUESTION

The heart of spiritual leadership, following the pattern of Jesus, is serving those around you and relating to them as peers before Jesus, serving them not for what you can get but for what they can get by way of intimacy with Jesus and faithfulness to his call on their lives. The question is not, How are they helping me accomplish my vision? but rather, Am I serving them to accomplish the vision that God has given to them or to us as a group? As we evaluate ourselves as leaders, the important question is not, Does the leader have followers? but rather, Does the Lord have followers as a result of the leader's influence?

I am quick to see the flaws of power leadership in others. But when I am honest with myself and look at some of my actions and the desires driving them, I must admit that I have not yet fully embraced servant leadership. I am not the perfect servant, and sometimes I'm not even a poor one. I often lack the patience to allow God to work through the quiet influence of a servant; I want to take things under my control. I say, "Pass me the ball, God, and I'll show you I can run for a touchdown."

When I see this in myself, I cry out for mercy and for the grace to be a servant like Jesus. Though I often fall far short, I still long to become a servant leader. Because

God is the God of patience and kindness, he picks me up and encourages me, much like a father picks up his child when she has fallen while learning to walk.

THE KEY TO SERVANT LEADERSHIP

In the same way that a father serves his children by helping them choose careers that fit their strengths and interests, or as a husband loves his wife and encourages her to maximize her gifts, a servant of others will seek the best for those around him. Our Father does that for us, his children.

The key is to listen to the heart of another. Hear their longings and do all you can to ease their burden and help them accomplish their goals. If you can't serve those around you in a particular area, find someone who can; find someone who will serve them in ways you can't. Even if it means losing a key person in your ministry or study group or losing a close friend who moves away to seek additional opportunities to serve or be developed, you must serve them and love them regardless of the cost.

I have been serving others in this way for many years. Most recently, I have encouraged members of our team to take roles more suited to their gifts. This has cost me dearly in terms of additional responsibilities I've had to take on. But the kingdom has been expanded, and those individuals are far more fulfilled and maximized than they were. I praise God for the opportunity of knowing and being of service to these men and women who have moved away into other roles.

Are you willing to pray that God would raise up people through you, people who will far surpass you in their impact for him?

Servanthood Relationships

Servant leadership is always lived out in relationship to other people. The Bible could rightly be called the Book of Relationships. In our relationships, we

> learn to risk sharing our weaknesses.
>
> say hard words in love to a brother.
>
> let someone really know our temptations and faults.
>
> enter into someone else's pain.
>
> care about the person and not the objective.

Men need other men to serve them in relationship, yet they are afraid to open up and get close enough for someone to see their needs and how they might be served. I am part of a group of men that meets every Thursday at lunch. We are vulnerable to one another, share our difficulties, and receive the ministry that the others offer us. Over the course of eight years, each man has had times when he has needed to be served and other times when he's had the ability to serve others in the group. I don't know how men make it in this culture without a group like this.

This group of men persevered with me through a particularly difficult time I had in a job transition several years ago. I thought I was in the right place and headed in the right direction, but I was in trouble and soon knew it. I brought these guys into the deepest despair I have faced in my ministry. Just their presence gave me hope and kept me going. I faced some difficult career decisions; some I had control over, others I did not. Time has proven that their counsel to me during that time was wise. When I lost objectivity, they kept it and loved and served me through it.

Other guys in our group have faced major health issues, family issues, and financial issues. We never choose when these trials will come, but we are there for each other. Men really need other men to serve them.

Whether you are a leader of men's ministries or simply a man who needs to experience Jesus, I urge you to find some men to meet with regularly. Over time, you will see how to serve each other and, figuratively speaking, how to wash each other's feet.

SERVING THE WORLD

As you move about in your daily life, in your sphere of influence, what ignites your heart? How are you touched by the Spirit of God as you see the needs of a broken world? In every city of this country, every subdivision, school, street, neighborhood, club, and company, there are people who have needs. True servants see the needs of others and meet them. Have you noticed something that really bothers you? Are you sensitive to a need that is not being met? Could it be that the Spirit has allowed you to see that need so you can meet it?

Not every need has my name on it. Jesus, with his divine nature, saw the needs of multitudes, but he didn't meet every need he saw. He served only the needs that the Father asked him to serve.

Chris Mangum, an executive with a paving company in Raleigh, North Carolina, once took a phone call he wouldn't normally take. A Pastor McCoy wanted his church parking lot paved and had called for advice and pricing. Chris is not the person in the company who normally does this kind of estimating, but he picked up the phone nonetheless.

After meeting Pastor McCoy and later doing the work for his church, Chris struck up a friendship with the pastor, and the two men met regularly for lunch to deepen their relationship. This white businessman and African-American pastor had little idea what would happen through their friendship.

At one lunch meeting, Chris lamented, "I have trucks parked today because I can't find drivers." Pastor McCoy shot back, "I have members in my church parked today because they can't find jobs." This dialogue led these two servants to pursue the idea of forming a jobs partnership between churches and businesses in the Raleigh area. Through their efforts, "parked" men and women have become employable through training and mentoring.

It soon became clear that a ministry leader needed to be appointed. The steering committee wanted to choose Chris, but he had already determined that as a white businessman, he shouldn't lead it. Chris suggested that Pastor McCoy was the natural leader. By taking on a servant's role, Chris was looking out for the best interests of the ministry of Jobs Partnership. Likewise, Pastor McCoy took on a servant's role by assuming responsibility for leading the growing ministry, selflessly giving himself to this important work. Both men saw a need and did what they could for the sake of the kingdom. They couldn't meet every need, but the Holy Spirit prompted them to meet this one.

CALLING ALL MEN

It is time to act. The time is ripe for an army of men who will serve those around them. Men who serve are real men; they are powerful men; they are influential men. Not always in ways that the world understands or in ways natural to the masculine soul, but they are powerful in the ways of the kingdom. No man is disqualified from being in this army. No one needs special aptitudes or skills. No one needs special titles, credentials, or training to be a servant. The only need we have is to serve.

There is no competition in this role of servant. The way of the upside-down leader is not the path of upward mobility but rather the way of downward mobility that leads to the cross. On that splintered cross almost two thousand years ago, a servant leader made the ultimate sacrifice in service to his brethren. Now he reigns! May the Spirit give you courage and faith to serve people in your own world.

10

FOUNDATIONS OF CHRISTIAN LEADERSHIP

Chuck Stecker

The greatest need in the church today is for men to become the leaders that God has called them to be. The purpose of men's ministry is to provide the structure and relationships to help men grow into godly leaders and disciple makers. For too long now in our men's ministries, we have focused on getting men involved in activities, rather than focusing our activities on building leadership qualities into our men. Never has the need for godly leadership been more apparent than it is today.

I spoke recently with a woman who is a ministry leader in a local church. With complete candor, she said that she would be willing to cancel every program in the church that did not relate directly to developing men into leaders. "In the long run," she said, "every other phase of ministry would be much stronger if the men in the church would develop into the leaders that God has called them to be."

In his book *Strong Men in Tough Times*, Dr. Edwin Lewis Cole tells the story of his visit to Zimbabwe. While he was there, he was approached by three ladies who told him how the women of the country had banded together to pray earnestly for their men during their fourteen-year struggle to gain independence from Rhodesia. In time, these groups of ladies became known as Esthers. All over the country, Rhodesian women were praying for their nation and praying for their men.

When the fighting abruptly ended and the men returned to their homes, the women perceived them to be passive, complacent, and lethargic. It soon became obvious that the men needed prayer during peacetime as much as they had during the war. The women began praying that the men would resume their responsibilities as leaders of their families and communities. One of the ladies stepped forward and said, "There was a time for Esthers, but today is a time for Daniels." Across the globe, from America to Africa and all points in between, the crying need is for the men of the church to take up the mantle of leadership, not only in the church but within the home and the community.

Men, we need to understand that we are all called to leadership. Because we are created in the image of God, to deny our role as leaders is to deny God himself. We must move beyond a definition of leadership that focuses only on style or personality, and we must come to grips with the foundational principles of leadership from a biblical perspective. But first, let's take a look at what the enemy has done to sap the initiative of men and to destroy our understanding of godly leadership.

THE ENEMY'S ASSAULT ON LEADERSHIP

During my twenty-three years of service in the United States Army, I learned the importance of carefully studying the enemy. We knew that if we understood our enemy's weapons and tactics, we would increase our chances of exploiting his weaknesses and defeating him in battle. The principle is basic. If you know what the enemy is going to do, you will be far better equipped to take advantage of him or stop him. The same is true with our spiritual adversary, the devil. He uses specific tactics to negate or destroy the leadership initiative in men. If we understand these tactics, we can avoid being defeated. The devil uses four basic ploys or maneuvers in his efforts to nullify the leadership of godly men: mystery, confusion, diversion, and condemnation.

Mystery

Satan's first trick is to make men believe that leadership is a deep mystery that can be understood only by a select few. To counteract this ploy, we must understand the difference between a mystery and a secret. Mystery, as it's used in the Bible, is something that even though explained, is incomprehensible in the natural world. We must accept it by faith. Consistently throughout the Bible, the only thing that God describes as a mystery is that Jesus Christ would come and walk this earth as a man, be crucified, die, and be buried, and then be resurrected to sit at the right hand of God. No matter how many times it is explained, the incarnation of the living God in Jesus Christ is incomprehensible, except by faith.

A secret, on the other hand, refers to information that has been withheld or concealed. Once the information has been revealed, explained, and understood, it is no longer a secret. Satan would have us believe that leadership is a mystery, but it's not. It's a secret. As soon as we learn the principles of effective leadership, it is no longer a secret, and we are perfectly capable of understanding and acting upon those principles.

For centuries, men believed there was a mystery to the solar system and the atom. We accepted the order of the universe based on faith. Over the course of time, however, scientists began to reveal the secrets of the created world and to understand the nature of the atom and the solar system. They discovered characteristics that are very clear, orderly, and comprehensible; in other words, no mystery at all.

In the same way that science has unlocked many of the secrets of the universe, we can take the mystery out of leadership. There may be elements of leadership still to be uncovered, but I believe that by studying and seeking God's heart, we can understand and implement his plan for us as leaders.

Confusion

If the devil cannot get us to believe that leadership is a mystery, he may try to convince us that we're simply not gifted to lead. He seeks to confuse us into believing that leadership is based on personality, position, presence, or power. In other words, if you don't have it, you ain't got it. But that's a lie. As the legendary Vince Lombardi once said, "Leaders are made, not born. They are made by hard effort, which is the price all of us must pay to achieve any goal that is worthwhile." The truth is that we are all uniquely and wonderfully made, and as men, we are created to be leaders in one area or another.

You may have heard the story of the man with a severe speech impediment who applied to become a Bible salesman. He presented himself to the manager of the company and said, "I-I-I-I w-w-w-want to s-s-s-sell B-B-B-Bibles." The manager was impressed by the man's boldness but skeptical of his ability to overcome his handicap. Not wanting to offend the would-be salesman, however, the manager proposed a trial. "Take these five Bibles," he said, "and when you've sold them, come back, and I'll give you more." Thinking he had seen the last of the man for a while, the manger returned to his work.

Shortly before noon, the salesman returned to the office, asking for more Bibles. The sales manager was amazed, but he gave the man five more Bibles. At the end of the day, the salesman returned to the office and gave the manager the money for five more Bible sales.

"This is incredible!" the manager said with disbelief. "How did you manage to sell as many Bibles in one day as my best salesman usually sells in two weeks?"

"W-W-W-Well," the salesman explained, "w-w-when I g-g-go to the d-d-door, I s-s-say, 'I-I-I-I am a B-B-B-Bible s-s-s-salesman.' I sh-sh-show them the B-B-Bible and ask, 'W-W-W-Would you l-l-like t-t-t-to b-b-b-buy this B-B-B-Bible or w-w-w-would you l-l-l-like for m-m-m-me t-t-t-to r-r-r-read it t-t-t-to y-y-y-you?'"

This story may appear to be a joke to some, but it illustrates the power of vision, persistence, and boldness in overcoming obstacles and accomplishing the purpose to which God has called us. I have a good friend who has struggled with stuttering his entire life and know the pain he has suffered in his attempts to communicate the love of God to others. But he continues to be used by God to reach people, because it's so apparent to others that his heart is in the right place. All too often, we allow the world's standard of giftedness to tell us that we cannot be the leaders that God has called us to be. We need to adopt the Bible salesman's perspective, quit focusing on our impediments, and instead seek to understand how God has uniquely gifted each one of us. In God's plan for men, leadership is not a matter of "if" but "how." He has gifted us with everything we need to be the leaders he has called us to be.

Diversion

If the enemy cannot get us to believe that leadership is a mystery or that we're not gifted to lead, he may try to divert our frame of reference away from the Bible and will try to lead us into believing that leadership is based on personality, position, presence, or power. To combat this strategy, we must focus on a biblical perspective of leadership.

In addition to reading the Bible, we can turn to several books that have been published in recent years for help in understanding God's perspective on leadership. Some of my favorites are *Moses on Management* by David Baron, *The Leadership Wisdom of Jesus* by Mike Murdock, *Jesus, CEO* by Laurie Beth Jones, *Leading from the Inside Out* by Sam Rima, and *Dynamics of Church Leadership* by Aubrey Malphurs.

To understand leadership, men must have the right frame of reference. The Esthers from Zimbabwe clearly understood this principle when they prayed for their husbands to become leaders according to God's standard.

My aunt Beverly was an incredible cook. She was known in our family for several dishes, but her most legendary culinary creation was her brownies. To this day, if you look in my wife's cookbook, you'll see the recipe for Aunt Beverly's Brownies stuck between the pages. Aunt Beverly's Brownies are the standard by which all brownies in the free world are judged.

When my youngest son was in the second grade, he brought a friend home from school one day. My wife had made brownies, though for some reason not Aunt Beverly's Brownies. Standing in the kitchen, my son and his friend were drinking cold milk and eating freshly baked brownies. During a moment of silence, his young friend spoke up and said, "Mrs. Stecker, these are the best brownies I have ever eaten." Without even lifting his head, my son responded, "Yeah, but he has never tasted Aunt Beverly's Brownies." Even to a second grader, the standard was clear. Once you have tasted Aunt Beverly's Brownies, anything else pales in comparison. Biblical leadership principles are like Aunt Beverly's Brownies. Nothing else compares.

The right frame of reference for leadership is revealed in God's Word. In the lives of Jesus Christ and the saints who came before and after, we learn everything we need to know about the subject of leadership.

Condemnation

If all else fails, the enemy turns to condemnation to try to knock us off the leadership track. He whispers in our ear that we are disqualified for leadership because of our past sins. This single tactic has debilitated more men in the church than any other. If we believe the lies of the enemy, however, we show that we do not understand God's heart or believe his Word. You see, the antidote for the poison of condemnation is truth.

The basis for true leadership is not a lack of sin but a spirit of repentance and honesty before the Lord. We need to understand that our families and the church are not asking us to be perfect as leaders, but they are asking us to be honest, courageous, and transparent. Whatever the devil might try to use in our lives to condemn us and tell us that we are disqualified from leadership, we need to bring out into the open. Once our transgressions have been brought to light, they can no longer be used against us by the enemy.

Men, here's the truth: leadership is not a mystery. By studying God's Word, we can train and equip ourselves and others to be better leaders. Leadership gifts will vary from one man to the next because we are each uniquely made and specifically called by God, but every man is gifted for leadership. If you are a husband or a father or simply a man of God, God has called you into leadership. Don't buy into the devil's lie that you are disqualified for leadership because of your past. Remember, it is his presence, not your past, that sets the standard for leadership.

As we grow into our roles as leaders, we must stay focused on the right standard. That isn't to say that there are not excellent principles in many of the secular books that have been written on leadership. Clearly there are, and I would encourage you to use those as a supplement. Our primary handbook for leadership however, must be the inspired Word of God.

A BIBLICAL FOUNDATION FOR LEADERSHIP

What are the primary characteristics of a godly leader? From the first chapter of the book of Daniel, I have gleaned four foundational traits of leadership from God's perspective: total commitment, submission to authority, accountability, and intentional reproduction.

1. Total commitment. Godly leaders are men who are sold out for Jesus. Total commitment is a decision of the will that we make long before we're confronted with situations that test our leadership. In Daniel 1:8 we're told that "Daniel made up his mind that he would not defile himself" (NASB). Very clearly, Daniel made a decision about where he stood prior to being confronted with circumstances that might have led him to compromise. Total commitment to the cause of Christ requires that we follow Jesus regardless of the circumstances or the consequences and regardless of what everyone else is doing.

Leadership based on circumstances is called situational ethics. Leadership based on consequences is cowardice. And leadership based on what everyone else is doing is people-pleasing. We can not afford to allow these three crippled models of leadership to infiltrate the church. A leader who is totally committed is one who decides to do it God's way, no matter what.

By now you've no doubt heard the story of Cassie Bernall, the Columbine High School student who affirmed her faith in God when she was challenged by the gunman who took her life. In the days that followed the Columbine shooting, there were some who questioned whether Cassie was actually the one who "said yes" or whether it was another student. Regardless of whether she said yes at that precise moment, her redeemed lifestyle in the months leading up to her death had clearly said yes about her commitment to God. Along with several other students who died in the shooting, Cassie had committed her life to Jesus Christ before she was confronted with the consequences.

2. *Submission to authority.* Godly leaders are men under authority. Leadership requires more than just commitment to a cause; it calls us to submit to authority as unto the Lord. Daniel understood this principle and submitted himself to the authority of the Babylonian commander, even though he was not a godly authority. In Daniel 1:8, the young Hebrew nobleman asks the Babylonian official for permission not to defile himself by eating the king's food. All too often as Christians, we act as though standing with God means that we can be arrogant and demanding of what we believe to be God's desire. Daniel shows us remarkable insight into God's heart, because even though God had clearly spoken to him, he made no demands of the guard. Instead, he continued to submit himself to the authority of the guard—even a pagan guard—by asking for permission.

The clarity of God's heart regarding authority is best seen in Romans 13:1–2: "Everyone must submit himself to the governing authorities, for there is no authority except that which God has established. The authorities that exist have been established by God. Consequently, he who rebels against the authority is rebelling against what God has instituted, and those who do so will bring judgment on themselves."

Godly leadership requires that we first submit to authority. Even Jesus submitted to the authority of his Father. Matthew 28:18 says, "Then Jesus came to them and said, 'All authority in heaven and on earth has been given to me.'" Authority did not originate with Jesus but was given to him by the Father in heaven.

We live in a rebellious world with rebellious attitudes. We often disguise our rebellion with phrases like "marching to the beat of a different drummer" or "the entrepreneurial spirit." We must be careful not to confuse the individuality that comes from God with the rebellious spirit that comes from our own deceitfulness. God is calling for men who will submit themselves to authority so that he might place them in positions of authority.

3. *Accountability.* Another facet of godly leadership and submission to authority is the need to submit ourselves to accountable relationships. Accountability is something we give or allow. It is incumbent on us as leaders to give others the right to hold us accountable. Accountability that is imposed only creates resentment and will not result in true accountability.

In the first chapter of Daniel, Shadrach, Meshach, and Abednego, along with Daniel himself, agree to be held accountable for the results of their vegetarian diet. It is reasonable to assume that during the ten-day period of fasting, the enemy tried to attack each one of these young men with doubt and fear. The Bible doesn't say that they met in an accountability group, but I believe that they encouraged each other and held one another accountable.

The consequences of a lack of accountability in the lives of our leaders have devastated our country in recent years. Unfortunately, the lack of accountability has not been limited to political leaders and business leaders but has included religious leaders as well.

An important difference between King Saul and King David might possibly be accountability. In 1 Samuel 13, when Samuel confronts Saul about his disobedience in offering a sacrifice before the Lord, we see a man who has not submitted himself to accountability. When confronted, Saul makes an excuse and tries to shift blame. In contrast, when the prophet Nathan confronts David about his sin with Bathsheba and his complicity in the death of Uriah, David falls to his knees and acknowledges that he has sinned against God. We might reasonably deduce that a lack of accountability might well have been the most significant reason why Saul was told that his kingdom would not endure. David, on the other hand, submitted himself to accountability and was called "a man after God's own heart."

4. *Intentional reproduction.* Godly leaders intentionally pour themselves into the lives of other men. Effective leaders are men who do more than simply manage projects or people; instead, they intentionally reproduce their values in the lives of others. Succession of leadership does not happen by accident. In fact, the mark of a true leader is that he targets others to disciple, mentor, and pour his life into.

Reproduction of leaders can be accomplished in many ways, but it must be done deliberately. In the life of our Lord Jesus Christ and in his relationships with the disciples, we can clearly see the process of selecting men and building them up. To become the leader that God has called you to be, you must seek his direction in identifying other men into whose lives you will intentionally work to reproduce godly character.

Intentional reproduction is the primary difference between a manager and a leader. A manager is focused on control and direction. A leader focuses on deliberate reproduction of godly values in the lives of others.

A true test of the effectiveness of a leader is what happens when he is not around. Think about your own children. It is much more likely that they will do the right things when you are present. But if you have successfully reproduced your values in their lives, they will do the right things even when you're not around. The same is true of leadership at every level. The true test of leadership is the response of those whom you are leading when you are not present to guide them.

We see this principle in the life of Daniel when his friends Shadrach, Meshach, and Abednego refuse to bow down before the golden idol (Dan. 3:16–18). As a result, they were convicted of a crime against the king and were to be thrown into the fiery furnace. A point that is often missed in teaching this passage is that Daniel was not present. If he had been present, there would have been four boys going into the fiery furnace. I believe that the relationship Daniel had with the three other young men was the key to their resolve. His deliberate efforts to reproduce God's heart into Shadrach, Meshach, and Abednego resulted in the strength they needed to stand firm at the moment of trial.

A CALL TO LEADERSHIP

These four foundational characteristics of biblical leadership are easy to say and hard to do. But regardless of what position God has called you to, you are called to be a leader. The decision to accept God's calling must be predicated on an understanding of the basic requirements. The call to responsible, biblical leadership is not something to be taken lightly, nor is it something to be abused.

God is calling the men in your congregation to be committed to him, regardless of the circumstances, the potential consequences, or who else is involved. The time to make that decision is before we are confronted, before our commitment to leadership is tested.

We must decide to be men under authority, not just committed to a cause but submitted to authority. God will not use men in authority until they have proven themselves as men under authority. We must understand accountability and submit ourselves to accountable relationships. Men who refuse accountability increase their potential for moral and ethical failures that will embarrass God and themselves.

We must train our men to intentionally reproduce their lives in the lives of others. Leadership means passing godly values on to others, not just the right things to do but, more important, the right person to be. The greatest need in the world today is for men to be the leaders that God has called them to be, leaders whose lives are based upon the solid Word of God.

Personal Evaluation

1. List three areas in which you struggle to conform to the Word of God and lack the commitment required to lead others. Ask God to help you strengthen your commitment to him.
2. List three areas in which you struggle with authority. Ask God to help you submit.
3. To whom are you truly accountable? With whom do you need to establish an accountable relationship?
4. In whose lives are you working to intentionally reproduce godly values?

11

THE MARK
OF LEADERSHIP

| *Dan Schaffer* |

I n the aftermath of the Columbine High School shooting in 1999, I was struck by the critical need to find men in our culture who can function as restraining, training, and protecting forces. The institutions in our society cannot by themselves help young men become the men they should be. The two youths who perpetrated this heinous crime had obviously lost hope in the normal pattern of life. The hope that sustains can be found only in the spiritual foundation that comes from knowing God. Experience has shown that this spiritual foundation can be laid and modeled only by men who are actively pursuing God and are being conformed to God's image through that pursuit.

As God began to move among us in the 1990s, men with good hearts began launching men's ministries in churches across the country. Churches affirmed leadership committees to administer these programs, and they tended to follow the "events" model that was most evident at men's seminars and conferences. Without realizing it, however, they had stepped onto a treadmill. Early in this process, three problems surfaced.

1. There was no clear understanding of the environment of safety and trust required to allow men to open up and be transformed.

2. To continue attracting men, each event had to be better than the last, with a more well-known speaker and a more entertaining program. Often the men were spectators rather than participants.
3. It was assumed that the goal was to have a men's ministry.

Now that we have stepped into the twenty-first century, it has become evident that focusing on events has not produced the desired results. The hemorrhage of men exiting the church has been slowed, but it has not been stopped. What can we do to alter this spiral and begin to bring men physically and emotionally back into the church?

The key to effectively changing our men's ministries lies with the leadership team. To lead men forward with integrity, our leaders must be the firstfruits of God's work in the hearts of the men in the church. They cannot simply administer a men's ministry program; they must become ministers to men—to each other and to the other men of the church.

We must begin by establishing an environment of safety and trust, but it is even more important to understand and focus on the real goal: pursuing and knowing God. As the core group engages in a passionate pursuit of God, they will establish credibility in the eyes of other men and gain a voice to call them to pursue God. Even though our leaders are not perfect, they must grow enough in their relationships with each other and with God to be transparent with the men of the church. Our leaders must be men who have entered into the battle and who are free to fail but are unwilling to turn back. The challenge is to be men who are committed to pursuing God, despite the barriers.

OBLIGATING OURSELVES TO GOD

In the mid-1990s, I traveled around the country training trainers who were going to train others in the principles of men's ministry. These men were some of the most committed men in the nation. They were there by invitation only. As I listened to them share about their lives, I heard two categories of comments time after time. The first was, "I haven't had my quiet time, so I can't approach God." The second theme was similar but different: "If I don't have my quiet time, I will have a bad day."

In response to these comments, I asked these men about their relationships with God. The majority of their answers confirmed that one of these two statements described their relationship with God, particularly as it pertained to their personal time with him. Let's look more deeply at the implications of these statements.

The first statement, " I haven't had my quiet time, so I can't approach God," illustrates the struggle that the apostle Paul addresses in Galatians 5:1–4. Judaizers had come down from Jerusalem and had begun teaching that belief in Christ as Savior was not enough to make one a Christian. One also had to obey the law and be circumcised.

Paul refutes these claims when he says, "It was for freedom that Christ set us free; therefore keep standing firm and do not be subject again to a yoke of slavery. Behold I, Paul, say to you that if you receive circumcision, Christ will be of no benefit to you. And I testify again to every man who receives circumcision, that he is under obligation to keep the whole Law. You have been severed from Christ, you who are seeking to be justified by law; you have fallen from grace" (NASB).

Some of us seem to feel that by following a prescribed pattern, we can make ourselves more acceptable to God, as though it were our right actions that make us worthy to be loved and accepted by God. Sound familiar? I've fallen into this trap myself. Paul is clearly telling the Galatians, and us, that it is only by grace that we are able to be loved and accepted by God. When we add anything else to that list, we put ourselves back under the law. We *obligate* ourselves to the law. We can do many things to grasp the opportunity to know God, but other than accepting his grace, there is nothing we must do before we can approach him. We don't earn our worthiness; it was given to us through Christ's death.

Throughout the 1970s and 1980s, I was involved in discipling men, and I maintained a regular time with the Lord. Early in the 1990s, I had the opportunity to become involved in the start-up of Promise Keepers. The demands were immense and the hours were long; before I knew it, I was exhausted. I couldn't rise early most days. It just wasn't in me. I was still in the Word and praying, but I began to feel inadequate. I wasn't following the prescribed pattern and I wasn't at all sure that I was acceptable to and loved by God.

After I went through an extended period of struggle, God revealed to me that I had the *opportunity* to know him through our relationship but that there was nothing I could do to make myself more acceptable to him. This revelation set me free, and I began to enter a new dimension of relationship with Jesus as I walked with him throughout the day. Nevertheless, even though I have experienced this new freedom, there are still times when I struggle and feel unable to approach God.

OBLIGATING GOD TO US

The second comment, "If I don't have my quiet time, I will have a bad day," communicates that if we do the right things, we can somehow obligate God to keep us from pain and give us a good day. This trap leads many of us into disappointment, disillusionment, anger, and despair. It is easy to feel that if I "complete the list," whatever that entails, I become more acceptable to God, and he should be obligated to make my life smooth. But what if things don't turn out as I expected? I lose my job? My marriage fails? My child rebels? I get cancer? My wife or child gets cancer? Did I have the wrong list? Do I not know God? Or do I not understand the relationship that God offers me? What should my response be? Have you ever felt as though you've done all the right things and yet God didn't deliver on what you perceived was his part of the bargain? I certainly have. What did that do to your relationship with God?

More than twenty years ago, my wife and I went through the pain of losing our young son. Matthew was born in January of 1977 and seemed to be a happy, bright little boy. When he was about eighteen months old, I got a call one day from my wife, Jan, telling me that Matthew was in the intensive care unit at the local hospital. I immediately rushed over to see him. The doctors thought that he had contracted a virus of the heart and that things would be okay. They weren't okay.

Over the next six months, little Matthew grew weaker and weaker. Even though we prayed diligently, called the elders, anointed him with oil, obtained the best medical resources, and believed that he would be healed, his condition did not improve. Sometime in the fall, I began to realize that things couldn't go on the way they were, but I didn't even want to think about the alternatives. The day before he died, I knew that he was going, even though the doctors were telling Jan that we would have him till summer. I wrestled with God and told him that he could not take my son. After wrestling with God for a number of hours, I realized that he was in control, and I asked him to empty me out so that I could do what was necessary.

When Matthew died, it was not the end of my struggle but the beginning. I contemplated turning away from God. The only reason I did not was because I had told other men for years that Jesus was the answer, and now I had to give him the chance to be the answer for me.

The year following Matthew's death was one of the most difficult in my life. If you had asked me prior to this to describe the relationship between God and his people, I would have given you all the right answers. I would have told you that we are his servants and that we are here to bring him glory. However, even though my theology was orthodox, deep down I had bought into a gospel that said that if you did the right things, had a quiet time, tithed, attended church, and more, God would keep you from suffering. Now here I was. Though I was not perfect, I had done the right things, yet God had not kept me from suffering. Either I did not know God or I didn't understand how my relationship with him was supposed to work.

Over time, God confirmed the nature of our relationship. I had the opportunity to know him and to be part of what he was doing. I could find tremendous significance, but there was no way I could guarantee that I would feel no pain or be more acceptable to God. I was given this opportunity to know him when I became his son, but there was no way that my actions would obligate him to keep me safe or to give me what I wanted.

THE CHOICES WE FACE

The choice we have can be summarized as follows:

Freedom = **Opportunity** = Obedience

or

Slavery = **Obligation** = Legalism

Which equation will you choose? Your choice will determine whether your life is characterized by gratitude and joy or marred by bitterness and disappointment. I challenge you to grasp the opportunity to live in freedom by being obedient to him.

It is clear that Jesus does not need to develop his relationship with me. Instead, I need to know him. The apostle Paul communicates this desire very effectively when he says, "I want to know Christ and the power of his resurrection and the fellowship of sharing in his sufferings, becoming like him in his death" (Phil. 3:10). Paul's consuming passion was to cast aside all of the religious formulas and pursue relationship with Jesus Christ.

I've identified five things that are common to all healthy relationships. These five things are what we might commonly call the godly disciplines: commitment, communication, conflict, covenant, and collaboration.

1. Commitment. All relationships start with commitment. Our relationship with Jesus is no exception. Have you accepted Jesus Christ as your Savior and Lord? If so, then it's time to commit to knowing him. In our ministry to men, we must guide men to commitment to Jesus Christ.

2. Communication. No relationship will last long without effective communication. That's true of marriages, families, businesses, and the church. In our relationship with God, it is the Word, worship, meditation, and prayer that allow us to communicate to and hear from him. Through communication, we grasp the opportunity to walk in his presence. As we minister to men, we must model open communication with our brothers and with God.

3. Conflict. Most men would say that their best friend back in grade school was someone with whom they had conflict. Maybe they even bloodied each other's noses, but then they resolved their conflict and became best of friends. As men, many of us are afraid to wrestle with God. We do not realize that many men of faith have had to wrestle with God—and come out on the other side—before God could really use them. You can see this principle illustrated in Genesis 32:24–28 when Jacob wrestles with God. It was then that God could change his name from "heel catcher" or "supplanter" to Israel, which means "He will rule as God."

In the honesty of conflict, God will change us. How ridiculous it is to think that if we don't tell the all-knowing God of the universe how we feel, he won't know. We must grasp the opportunity to wrestle with God so that we can experience his friendship. Are you able to wrestle with God the way Jacob did? What needs to happen so that you can? What can we do to help the men in our churches learn to grapple honestly with God?

4. Covenant. After we have committed ourselves to God, learned to communicate with him, and are able to work through conflict with him, it is time to begin to covenant with God as we serve him. A covenant is an executed agreement determining how two or more parties will relate to one another. Grasping the opportunity to pursue God involves understanding the commitment God has made to us as his children. For us to grow in our relationship with him, we must grasp the opportunity to offer ourselves in service to him. We are not instituting a new list of commandments but rather verbalizing and executing our commitments to him.

What commitments have you made to God? What additional commitments do you need to make? In our ministry to men, we must model godly covenants by making our commitments a matter of public record. Will you grasp the opportunity to covenant with God today? Will you show other men how to grasp this opportunity, as well?

5. *Collaboration*. Every healthy relationship produces something. In a marriage, it may be children and a lasting impact on the community. In a business, it may be a product or a service and income for those who work there. Healthy relationships produce positive products for everyone in the relationship. When we relate to God, the product of our relationship is collaboration. Collaboration, or colaboring, is the opportunity we have to be a part of what God is doing in our world. When God formed us physically and again when he redeemed us spiritually, he gave us certain gifts. We have the opportunity to offer those gifts back to him and to use them to establish his kingdom wherever we are. In our ministry to men, we must seek ways to collaborate with each other and with God to accomplish the Lord's purposes here on earth. May we not fail to take the opportunity to discover and utilize the gifts that God has for us.

Five Questions Every Man Should Ask

1. *Commitment*. How would you describe your commitment to Christ?
2. *Communication*. How do you communicate with Christ?
3. *Conflict*. What conflicts do you have with the Lord?
4. *Covenant*. What covenants do you have with Christ?
5. *Collaboration*. In what areas are you collaborating with Christ?

PART THREE

LAYING
THE FOUNDATION

12

GETTING MEN TO JESUS

Gordon England

M en are notorious for not asking directions. They might grab an old map from the glove box and try to figure out where they're going, but they're just as likely to try to feel their way by intuition. But even if a guy condescends to using a map, it isn't going to show all the roadblocks, barricades, construction zones, detours, bridges out, and other obstacles on the road to his destination. Apply these same principles to a spiritual journey, as we seek to get men to Jesus through evangelism, and the road to glory can be even more complicated.

Make no mistake, there's only one "highway to heaven," and that's through the atoning blood of Jesus Christ, but depending on where a man is when he starts, it might take some careful steering to get him over to the main road. When we present the gospel to our non-Christian friends, it is imperative that we give clear and comprehensive directions for getting to the truth. If our friends don't understand the message, they're bound to take a wrong turn and end up somewhere they don't want to be.

STARTING WITH A GOOD MAP

If we want to lead other men to Christ and teach the men in our congregation how to do the same, we must begin with a good map. Of course, there is no better guidebook than the Bible for leading a man to Jesus Christ.

In our ministry to men, we must equip them with the skills and knowledge to use the Bible to discover God's truth and to present it in a way that relates to men. Useful tools, such as the Roman Road or the Four Spiritual Laws, that use a sequence of Bible quotations to guide a man from recognizing his need to accepting God's provision of salvation can be helpful. These and many other resources are excellent representations of the biblical message of salvation through Jesus Christ, but they may not relate to a man and bring about the desired commitment.

AVOIDING ROADBLOCKS, DETOURS, AND OBSTACLES

Handing someone a map, and even tracing the route with our finger, doesn't guarantee that he'll reach the desired destination, because there may be obstacles on the road to redemption. A major roadblock to understanding the Bible and its message of hope and forgiveness is figurative language. Even if we use a modern translation of the Bible, spiritual language can sound otherworldly and mysterious.

Spiritual concepts are often described in symbolic terms that can be confusing to an unchurched reader. Take, for example, the phrase "open your heart to Jesus." What does an expression like this mean to a man who is a stranger to God? He may sense the deep sincerity and passion in these words, but the mental picture he composes may be confusing. Are we talking about a physical heart—the blood pump that keeps us alive—or a figurative heart-shaped box of chocolates that symbolizes romantic love? Neither image seems to fit. Your friend may have said to his wife when he proposed marriage, "I love you with all my heart," but even then, he probably hoped she wouldn't ask him exactly what he meant. It might be more comfortable for a woman to express her love for Jesus using intimate language, but most guys would experience cognitive dissonance. In their minds, romantic words don't fit with the spiritual context.

How about this line from an 1879 hymn by Joseph Parry: "Jesus, Lover of my Soul, let me to Thy bosom fly." I can just hear some guys I know saying, "I don't think so. I'd better play golf next Sunday. I feel a little embarrassed even thinking about the word bosom while sitting in church." You get the point. Old poetic images with secondary meanings don't translate well into a contemporary culture in which biblical allusions are not well known, much less understood. In our ministry to men, we must present the truth of the gospel in language that men can understand.

How can we explain the spiritual concept of knowing or relating to God? Here are four images that most men can readily identify with.

1. *God as Father*. Every man wants to have or to be a great dad. Even if a man's relationship with his own father was less than ideal, we can explain how God is the ultimate and intended Father of us all—the one who sets the standard for what an earthly father should be.

Telling Your Story

Every Christian man should be able to tell another man how he came to know Christ. You can do this in several ways.

1. *Let your words reveal your faith.* You don't have to explain the four spiritual laws in every conversation. However, your words should be filled with an honest appreciation for what the Lord has done, even when you're talking to a non-Christian!

2. *Share faith stories.* No doubt you've seen God do remarkable things in your life. Tell people about the answered prayers, the changes in your life, and the times the Lord has brought you through something difficult.

3. *Prepare a testimony.* Take the time to write a simple, two-minute testimony that describes what your life was like before you met Christ, how you became a Christian, and what a difference it has made in your life.

2. *Jesus Christ as the older brother.* Most guys look up to and admire their older brothers. In the same way, we can look up to Jesus as our example. What guy wouldn't say, "I want to be like him," when looking at Jesus?

3. *Christians as colaborers together with Christ.* Our society admires team players, and everyone wants to be teamed with the superstar. Jesus sets the example and shows us how to live. When we team up with him, we know that we're not alone in this quest. As mature believers, we can encourage our younger brothers to "follow me as I follow Christ."

4. *Called to a noble, sacrificial task.* Deep in the heart of every man is a longing for significance. Christ's call to "take up your cross and follow me" reaches deep into a man's character and summons him to commit to a calling of substance and sacrifice.

The Detour of Self-Justification

Men are masters of self-justification. We're wired that way. Our simplistic sense of fairness suggests that God, whom we fancy in our minds according to our own image, will balance the deeds of our lives on the scales of justice. Most guys live their unredeemed lives as though the preponderance of their good deeds and intentions will outweigh anything bad they have done. When engaged in a spiritual discussion, many men quickly retreat to the passive position of "letting God decide." They say, "I do the best I can, I try to be fair and not hurt anyone, and when God weighs the good against the bad, I think I'll come out okay."

What causes the same man whose response borders on road rage if anyone passes or cuts him off on the highway to adopt such a passive posture when confronted with

How to Write a Testimony

1. Speak to God and ask him to speak through you.
2. Follow a simple outline: your life before Christ, how you met Christ, and your life after receiving Christ.
3. Start with an interesting sentence and offer a good conclusion.
4. Include relevant, thought-provoking personal experiences. Give enough detail to arouse interest.
5. Use some Scripture verses to help you explain the gospel clearly.
6. Avoid negative statements about others and Christian jargon like "sanctified" and "redeemed."
7. Build your testimony around a theme—something characteristic of your life.
8. Lift up Christ as the only means of eternal life.

spiritual issues? Most guys prefer to take the detour that allows them to say, "I don't want to deal with it today. My attention is taken with concrete, tangible, real things of business, family, and entertainment. All this stuff about morality, mortality, and ethics puts me on a road where I don't feel comfortable, so I'll just stay over here on the detour as long as I can." He may look over to the main highway every now and then to see if the traffic is moving, but often it takes a catastrophic event like a funeral or a tragedy in his life to wake him up to the realization that the detour isn't getting him where he wants to go.

If we have been careful to establish meaningful, committed relationships with our unsaved friends, the best challenge to the detour may be an "in your face" statement, such as, "You really don't want to wait for justice. You need to plead for mercy now, like the rest of us!"

The Barricade of Self-Reliance

Self-reliance is as masculine as the Y chromosome. The notion that "I can fix it myself" can block a man's understanding and acceptance of God's truth. The barricade of self-reliance is built with the following blocks.

- As men, we don't want to owe God anything.
- We equate control with independence, and we don't want to have to depend on anyone.
- We assume that behavior rather than character is the issue with God, and we act no worse than the next guy.

- Most men process in a linear sequence. We can live according to a set of rules, but freedom in Christ is another matter.
- An intimate relationship with God is unpredictable, and therefore, intimidating.

In confronting the barricade of self-reliance, we have several factors in our favor. First of all, the "I can fix it myself" mentality implies that the man understands that something needs to be fixed, that he is not meeting the expected standard, whatever that might be. Most men who have had at least some exposure to church recognize that there is a God to whom they are accountable. Finally, it implies that at least as a matter of discussion, he is willing to do something about his situation.

It is axiomatic that a man doesn't own anything he doesn't buy. I had an experience with a friend named Jack that illustrates this reality. I had been talking to him about the Lord for several months, and one day I invited him to lunch. He happily accepted. After we had enjoyed some good food, conversation, and humor, it was time to return to work. When the check came, I picked it up, because I had invited Jack to have lunch with me. He quickly suggested that we split the tab. I thanked him but said I wanted to pay, because I wanted it to be my gift to him. He looked nervous but didn't protest.

As we started to stand up, he said, "Let me get the tip." Again I thanked him but said I had already put it on the credit card and I didn't want him to do anything other than enjoy the time we had spent together. He looked frustrated, but again he didn't argue.

As we walked out the door of the restaurant, he said, "I'll buy next time." It was time to let the other shoe drop, so I said, "No thanks, Jack. I invited you here today because I appreciate you and want to honor you. I don't want to reduce that to merely trading lunches. This lunch was a gift, no half-payment due, no shared tip, and no future obligation."

When he looked confused, I added, "On a small scale, this lunch illustrates how you are approaching God, Jack. He's offering you the gift of salvation and you don't want to receive it. Your only obligation in receiving a gift is your acceptance of it. Its price may be as simple as a thank you, but by your acceptance, you acknowledge that we share a bond of friendship. Accepting a gift from God works the same way, yet you're resisting it. You want a half-and-half deal—your part and God's part; or you want to throw in the tip—God did most of it, but I'll add a little to it! What God wants is for you to freely receive what he has freely given. The challenge is that our resistance keeps us from getting what we can't earn. In the New Testament, the apostle Paul tells us that 'the wages [what we earned] of sin is death, but the free gift [what we received but didn't earn] of God is eternal life through Jesus Christ our Lord'" (Rom. 6:23 LB).

Jack accepted Christ that day.

The Pothole of Control

Control is our greatest prize and often our worst enemy. Sometimes our efforts are downright funny; other times, they're simply pathetic. When men overuse control, power, and direction with their wives, it is sad and often hurtful. In a relationship with God, a man who insists on being in control will eventually end up in isolation, estranged from God.

God designed us to function interdependently. This is true in our marriages, in work, in team relationships, and especially in the body of Christ. All of God's gifts are for the common good. Men can relax and be real with God and other people when they realize that they are accepted and valued and that they don't have to wrestle with life on their own. It is only insecurity that says, "If you know me, you may not like me." Insecure men continue to grasp for control while trying to hold God at arm's length. What a sad predicament.

The Missing Bridge between Sin and Behavior

There is a vast difference between character and image or reputation. In our superficial society, it is easy to think that "keeping up appearances" is the highest virtue. But when we become more concerned about who others think we are rather than who we are in the eyes of God, we can easily twist the cause-and-effect relationship between our behavior and sin. Before long, the bridge washes out altogether, and we're left with a strictly performance-based standard of righteousness. Consider the typical sermon about sin. It is easy to fall into the trap of believing that you are a sinner

because you drink

because you cheat on your wife

because you gamble

because you steal if you can get away with it

In this scenario, we think that all we have to do is clean up our behavior and we'll be acceptable to God. But God looks at matters from an entirely different perspective. He looks at the heart of a man and says, Because you are a sinner

you drink

you cheat on your wife

you gamble

you steal if you can get away with it

A man may do none of these things, and yet he's a sinner; his sinful behavior is the result of his nature. When a man finally realizes that he sins because he is a sinner (not the other way around), then we need to ask him the question, Can a sinner

Leading Men to Christ

If you're going to lead men to Jesus, you must know the words to use to get them there. A sample script would probably include the following essentials.

- *God loves you and has a plan for your life.* No matter what you've done, there is a God who made you and loves you.
- *Man is sinful and separated from God.* Each of us has sinned, and that sin has created a barrier between us and God. (Use Rom. 3:23.)
- *Our sin will lead to eternal separation from God.* Since God is perfect, he won't allow our sin to go unpunished. The punishment for sin is to spend eternity apart from him. (Use Rom. 6:23.)
- *God sent his Son, Jesus Christ, to make peace.* Jesus died on the cross to pay the penalty for our sins. Believing in him is the only way we can be freed from our sins and gain acceptance into God's family. (Use Rom. 5:8.)
- *Every man must decide for himself.* Each person is given a choice: either to accept Jesus Christ and his gift of life or to reject it and try to make it to heaven on our own. (Use Rom. 10:9–10.)

go to heaven? Isn't that the bottom line? If behavior is the result rather than the cause, the cause must be addressed.

Why are men afraid of a relationship with God? Why do they insist on trying to fix their own behavior instead of choosing a relationship with the living God through Jesus Christ? When you consider that the power of God and the blood of Jesus Christ cleanse us from the inside out and that the influence of the Holy Spirit brings lasting, positive change in our lives—and eternal life as the ultimate bonus—why would any guy in his right mind not jump at the opportunity? The problem is that the obstacles and roadblocks we've discussed make it hard for men to see where they're going. Men want a clear road map they can follow, and it is our responsibility as Christian men and pastors to untangle the mystery and point them in the right direction.

Wrong Turns and Dead-End Streets

Even when a man sincerely sets out to pursue God, he's susceptible to wrong turns and dead-end streets. The goal of men's ministry is to come alongside our brothers and walk with them in genuine friendship as we all make our way toward God's purpose for our lives.

Some men take the path of denial. They think they can escape responsibility to God by claiming he doesn't exist. The Bible states the truth in simple language, "The fool has said in his heart, 'There is no God'" (Ps. 14:1 NASB). If you have a friend who has taken the wrong turn of denial, tell him to put it in reverse and get back to the road of reality.

The New Age Movement, the counterfeit religion of our day, is another wrong turn and dead-end street. Whether it's secular humanism, revived Hinduism, pluralism, animism, relativism, or simply "different strokes for different folks," New Age thinking leads a man down the dead-end street of thinking he can control his own destiny. Any philosophical system will have some moral value and order, but in the final analysis, they can all be summed up by the words of Proverbs 14:12: "There is a way which seems right to a man, but its end is the way of death" (NASB). The bridge is out. Only Jesus Christ can span the gap from mortality to immortality.

THE UNFINISHED ROAD

God is calling men to himself. He wants to draw us into a relationship—not simply to an event. The gospel, if received, involves giving up all that I know of myself to receive all that I know of God. The road is not the prize. The journey is not the prize. Relationship with God through Jesus Christ is the prize of our salvation. The unfinished road stretches toward the horizon because we haven't yet arrived. If we had arrived, we'd say, "That's mine, I'll go on to other things." But because we walk by faith not by sight, the road unfolds before us as we walk. And as we journey with Jesus, we learn how to depend on God and become interdependent with our fellow pilgrims along the way. The good news is that we walk in the light together, rather than in the darkness of isolation, when we surrender our control to the higher calling of the good and acceptable and perfect will of God.

13

TEACHING MEN TO PRAY

Dale Schlafer

V

ince Lombardi, the legendary coach of the Green Bay Packers, began training camp the same way each year. He would gather the players around him and, taking a football in his hand, would yell, "Gentlemen, this is a football!" Now, you might ask, didn't his players know a football when they saw one? Of course they did. But this was Lombardi's way of getting back to basics. Every year, he approached camp as if no one had ever heard of a football or had ever run any of the team's offensive or defensive plays. And almost every year, the Packers were contenders for the NFL championship. In a sense, my purpose is the same in this chapter. I am not trying to suggest that your prayer life is less than championship caliber, but I do want to establish the primacy of prayer in the building of a championship-caliber men's ministry.

PRAYER MUST BE LEARNED

The most obvious point to make about prayer is that we must learn how to pray.[1] In Luke 11:1, one of Jesus' disciples says to him, "Lord, teach us to pray just as John also taught his disciples" (NASB). In other words, prayer is not natural for most people. Prayer needs to be taught. Most people would say that they talk to God. In fact, a

---

[1]The following outline was used by Pastor Wesley Campbell in a sermon on December 2, 1999.

recent survey showed that 90 percent of Americans pray. But in that same poll, most of the respondents said that prayer is boring and that they don't enjoy it.

Too often, we tell the men in our congregations to pray, but we give them no help or models. We somehow expect them to be able to pray the minute they come to Christ. If prayer is a relationship, and it is, then we must teach men how to develop an effective prayer relationship with God.

If you have worked with men for very long, you know that building close relationships is not a man's strong suit. Give a man a task, and he is right at home. But ask that same man to establish a relationship with someone, and he's a lot less comfortable. Now consider what it is like when we say to a man, "You need to have a quiet time and pray to God. Have a relationship with the King of the Universe!" We are almost guaranteeing his failure. But give that same man some directions and suggestions on how to build a relationship with God or, better yet, model how to pray so he can see it in action, and he will be much more willing and able to take that next step.

Men operate best with procedures. Once a man becomes comfortable with the model, he begins to try some new ways on his own. But unless we supply the initial help, we can almost guarantee that our men will be weak in prayer or prayerless. If you were coaching football, you would never allow a player to step onto the field unprepared.

PRAYER IS WORK

We must also recognize that prayer is work. Hebrews 5:7 says that during his days on earth, Jesus "offered up both prayers and supplications with loud crying and tears" (NASB). In other words, Jesus didn't just read through his prayer list in some unemotional way until it was completed. No, Jesus was involved in his prayers "with loud crying and tears." It was hard, emotional work. It costs to be a man of prayer. It costs in time. It costs in energy. It costs in sleep!

As you may know, there is an on-site intercessory prayer team that prays during every Promise Keepers men's conference. Because my wife was involved with these teams, I would often go to the prayer room to pick her up after the meeting was over. As I looked at those dear people who had gathered to pray throughout the conference, I saw folks who were incredibly tired and spent. They had fought spiritual battles, and they were exhausted. Sometimes I believe we give men the wrong idea concerning prayer, that it doesn't require effort. It may be easy to say prayers, but it is incredibly difficult to really pray.

PRAYER IS LISTENING TO GOD

Prayer is not a monologue in which we do all the talking. Think about our earthly relationships. What kind of a conversation would it be if we did all the talking with our spouse or a friend? It took me a while to learn the importance of listening to God, because the tradition I grew up in did not emphasize this part of prayer. It crystallized for me, however, in 1989, when I was a delegate at the Lausanne II conference in Manila. Delegates came from more countries than were represented by the United Nations at that time. This focused time of worship, prayer, and evangelistic strategizing became a life-changing experience for me.

The highlight occurred one afternoon when we were introduced to an old Chinese pastor. We were told that he had been in prison for almost twenty years. Most of that time had been served in solitary confinement. The Communists hated him and gave him the worst job they could, working in the cesspool of the prison. It was such a filthy job that his guards would not stay there.

As best I can remember, this is what the pastor said: "This cesspool became my garden. For since no one was there, I could talk out loud to my Master, which I was not permitted to do in my cell. I could sing quietly to my Master, and I could hear from him." Then he shared how God had ministered to him in his "garden." Near the end of his remarks, he began to sing in Mandarin a song that every delegate in the room knew because of the tune. He sang: "I come to the garden alone, while the dew is still on the roses. And the voice I hear falling on my ear, the Son of God discloses. And he walks with me and he talks with me, and he tells me I am his own. And the joy we share as we tarry there, none other has ever known."

More than a decade later, this song still reverberates through my being. Prior to the Lausanne II conference, I had rarely taken advantage of listening to God in my prayers. Spurred on by the challenge offered by that elderly Chinese pastor, I began to study in the Bible and from church history about listening to God. Any reading of history makes it clear that listening to God has always been part of prayer. Jesus himself says that the Spirit of God "will not *speak* on His own initiative, but whatever He hears, He will *speak*; and He will *[tell you]* what is to come" (John 16:13 NASB, emphasis mine). Oh, the change that has come to my life and ministry as I have learned to listen for the voice of God! Listen to what God is saying to you, in your prayer, from God's Word, and by his Spirit.

PRAYER MUST BE REGULAR

We must set aside regular times for prayer. Throughout the Bible, you'll find men and women who set regular times for prayer. Daniel "continued kneeling on his knees three times a day, praying and giving thanks before his God, as he had been doing previously" (Dan. 6:10 NASB). "They were continually devoting themselves to the apostles' teaching and to fellowship, to the breaking of bread and to prayer" (Acts 2:42 NASB). As Stanley Jones was fond of saying, "You cannot expect God to come into the occasional, if you refuse him in the continuous." There needs to be a fixed time each day when we go into our prayer closet.

Throughout church history, prayer is always referred to as a discipline. Discipline is always required to accomplish any worthwhile goal. If you want to be the best free-throw shooter on the basketball team, it takes hours of practice. If you want to sell the most insurance policies in your company, it takes discipline to achieve your goal. Every important achievement takes discipline. And along with the discipline comes its companion: drudgery. Let's face it, discipline day after day gets hard. But if you stick to the discipline long enough, it finally leads to delight. That's exactly what happens in prayer. Through the centuries, men have acknowledged the difficulty of the discipline of prayer and the drudgery that accompanies it. But great delight occurs when we break through to a wonderful intimacy with God.

REGULAR PRAYER HAS A REGULAR PLACE

We all know that we can talk to God wherever we go, but a disciplined prayer life will have its own space as well. There is something special about having a place where we know we are going to meet God.

I have a number of friends who have built special prayer closets in their homes for this purpose. I know others who have curtained off the space under the basement steps to use as a place of quiet. In the homes where I have lived, I have always had a special chair and a place that has been my quiet time location. It is important for us to pray daily in a special location.

PRAYER IS PERSONAL

God loves you and delights in spending time with you. How do those words strike you? If you're like most men, your immediate inclination is to take the concept of God's love and make it theological. "Yes," we say, "'or God so loved the world, that He gave His only begotten Son, that whoever believes in Him should not perish, but have eternal life.' God loves the world, and because I've received him as my Savior and Lord, he loves me." In a way, we keep God at arm's length by theologizing the passages that talk about his love for us. But God's love for us is very personal and intimate.

Recently, I was convicted by the Holy Spirit that I needed to deepen my experiential knowledge of God. I had a good, theological grasp of God's love in my mind, but my feelings were in need of further engagement. I began to spend a great deal of time in the Song of Solomon, the wonderful love story of a bride and groom. Numerous interpretations of this lyrical book have been offered, but most would agree that it speaks of the bride of Christ, the church. In this context, God is the lover, and we are the bride. As men, we might have difficulty adopting the feminine perspective, but listen to what God says to you: "You have ravished my heart, my sister, my spouse" (Song 4:9 NKJV).

Do you believe that? God's heart is ravished by you! In the NASB, this passage says that we make God's heart "beat faster." He loves you. And there is not one thing you can do to earn it. Nor does your sin affect his love for you.

Elsewhere, the king says to his bride, "Arise, my darling, my beautiful one, and come with me.... Show me your face, let me hear your voice; for your voice is sweet, and your face is lovely" (Song 2:10, 14). I can hear some guy saying, "This is mushy! This isn't manly." Brother, don't you get it? God loves you, and he's not hesitant to tell you so. Meeting with you somehow fulfills a longing in God's heart. Yes, you and I have a great need to be with God, but have you ever realized that he wants to see your face and hear your voice?

> **Arise, my darling, my beautiful one, and come with me.... Show me your face, let me hear your voice; for your voice is sweet, and your face is lovely.**
>
> Song of Songs 2:10, 14

Not only that, but "the Lord your God is with you, he is mighty to save. He will take great delight in you, he will quiet you with his love, he will rejoice over you with singing" (Zeph. 3:17). God loves you so much that he's in heaven right now singing over you.

To become effective in prayer and to teach other men to pray effectively, we absolutely must absorb these truths deep into our emotions and feelings. Why? Because we don't go into our prayer closet out of Christian duty. We don't go simply to get something. Instead, we go to bask in the love of the one who loved us and gave himself for us. God loves us; that's why we take time to pray. Being in love changes everything!

PRAYER IS PASSIONATE

Prayer also gives us a chance to tell God how much we love him. We're to have an intimate and passionate relationship with Jesus. That is, in our prayer time, we have the opportunity to tell the Savior of our love for him. As men, it is sometimes difficult for us to express our love to God. In fact, I read recently that Christian leaders are being encouraged not to talk to men about loving God because it is too difficult a concept for men in the twenty-first century to grasp. Bunk! We know what it is to love and be loved. After all, that's what separates Christianity from every other religion in the world. God wants us to be in a love relationship with him. God loves us, and we can tell him of our deep love and affection. "We love [or have the ability to love], because He first loved us" (1 John 4:19 NASB). While ministering in Iowa recently, I contracted a bacteria that caused bleeding in my stomach. As a result, I spent two nights in the hospital. Though my situation was serious, I have had no further problems, but God used my sickness as a wake-up call in my family. On my second day in the hospital, when I was free to call my kids, my twenty-eight-year-old son said to me, "Dad, I thought you were immortal." Of course, he knew that someday I would die, but he'd never thought about it. So when I went to the hospital, it dawned on him that someday I *would* die.

When I got home from Iowa, my son came to visit. We had a great time together, laughing, talking, and reviewing my hospital experience. As he was leaving, he gave me a kiss and a big hug, as he always does, then got into his car. He sat there for a moment, then got out, walked around the car to where I was standing, and gave me another big kiss and hug. Then he got back in his car. This time, he started the engine, but then he got out once again. He came back over to me and said, "I love you, Dad," and gave me a third kiss and hug. How do you think I felt? "That's my boy! He loves me!" Even now, months later, I am basking in those three kisses and hugs! How do you think God feels when we tell him that we love him? "That's my boy; he loves me!" Men, we take time to pray so that we can renew our love relationship with our heavenly Father. You always spend time with the one you love!

PRAYER IS SURRENDER

Yet another reason to pray is to surrender. That is, we have the opportunity to surrender our purposes, our plans, and our wills into the hands of God, acknowledging his superiority as our Creator. As Stanley Jones puts it in *How to Pray*, "Prayer, then, is the surrender of the wire to the dynamo, of the flower to the sun, of the student to the processes of education. The Gulf Stream will flow through a straw provided the straw is aligned to the Gulf Stream, and not at cross purposes with it. You as an individual, surrender to God and then—shall I say it?—God surrenders to you—His power is at your disposal. You are working with an almighty purpose and an almighty purpose is working with you."

Prayer is never trying to get God to do our will. It is not trying to bend the Almighty to accomplish our purposes, but rather it is to cooperate with his design for our lives.

A PATTERN FOR PRAYER

Over the years, I have discipled many new converts to Christ. Almost invariably, they will ask, "What do I say when I pray?" This question must be taken seriously, because we know that men have a difficult time communicating in intimate relationships. For most men, prayer is difficult. I usually answer this question by telling men to "pray the Bible." That is, to take the prayers of the Bible and pray them back to the Lord.

The Psalms are a great place to start in learning how to pray the Scriptures. Let me demonstrate, using Psalm 19. I would start like this: "Father, I come into your presence now through the work of Jesus Christ, my Savior. I worship you Father, Son, and

Holy Spirit. With the psalmist of old, I say [begin reading Psalm 19]: 'The heavens declare the glory of God; the skies proclaim the work of his hands. Day after day they pour forth speech; night after night they display knowledge' [vv. 1–2]. Lord, as I look at the sunrise this morning, I realize again what a great creator you are. The colors today are just awesome. How do you bring all the colors together? My God, day after day and night after night, you display yourself for all to see. 'There is no speech or language where their voice is not heard. Their voice goes out into all the earth, their words to the ends of the world' [vv. 3–4]. Thank you, Lord, that everywhere on this earth your glory is displayed. 'In the heavens [you have] pitched a tent for the sun, which is like a bridegroom coming forth from his pavilion, like a champion rejoicing to run his course. It rises at one end of the heavens and makes its circuit to the other; nothing is hidden from its heat' [vv. 4–6]. Thank you, Father, that every day you bring the sunlight, and it brings warmth and light to the earth. Father, your creation is awesome, and it is all about you. It is to bring glory to you. I praise you, my God. 'May the words of my mouth and the meditation of my heart be pleasing in your sight, O LORD, my Rock and my Redeemer' [v. 14]. Lord, may everything that comes out of my mouth today and everything that I think about be pleasing to you. You know that I have that meeting with Joe today, and we really disagree. Help me to please you by the way I speak. In Jesus' name, I pray, Amen."

This simple approach of praying the Scriptures has been used to help numerous men learn how to pray. By the way, I always encourage men to pray out loud while walking around, no matter what kind of prayer they are engaged in. Why? So they will know when they have stopped praying. Wes Campbell, speaking to the World Congress of Intercessors and Prayer Leaders, once said, "Praying out loud, or prayer mumbling out loud, will take our minds and hearts kicking and screaming into the presence of God and help us to focus. It's hard to think about anything else when you are talking."

Once a level of comfort has been reached in praying the Scriptures, you can help men to understand the various parts of the prayers they have already been praying. Examples of adoration, confession, thanksgiving, supplication, and intercession are laced throughout the prayers they have been reading from the Bible. Praying through the Bible creates an easy transition to a man's own extemporaneous prayers.

PRAYER HAS A CORPORATE EXPRESSION

In addition to instructing us to make time for private prayer, the Bible is clear about the necessity of joining with other believers for corporate prayer. The book of Acts describes many such prayer meetings. To encourage corporate prayer, we must design opportunities for men to pray in small groups, in local church prayer meetings, and with groups of men and women from their city. Widespread corporate prayer has long been missing from the church of North America. But this is beginning to change as more small groups are created that bring men together for support and prayer. In a growing number of cities, pastors are coming together, across denominational and racial lines, for prayer. And large numbers of Christians have gathered together for extended services of worship and prayer. As a revivalist, I am excited about these developments, because historically, revival has always been preceded by seasons of prayer.

January 1999 marked a very significant event in the history of the United States. After an absence of almost one hundred years, a National Prayer Accord was once again presented to the church, signed by denominations and associations representing more than 200,000 churches.

The Call

We humbly, yet strongly, request all churches and all Christians to join together, at a minimum, in the following five rhythms of prayer:

- by *daily* spending time with the Lord in prayer and in the reading of His Word, so as to yield ourselves fully to the control and empowerment of the Holy Spirit.
- by *weekly* humbling ourselves before God by designating a day or part of a day (Friday, if possible) for united prayer with fasting, as the Lord leads.
- by *monthly* designating in individual churches one service for concerted prayer, emphasizing this call, with special focus on its neighborhood applications.
- by *quarterly* assembling in multi-church prayer events, emphasizing this call, with special focus on its citywide application.
- by *annually* participating in nationwide prayer events, emphasizing this call, with special focus on its national and global applications.

—National Prayer Accord

In January 2000, more than 35,000 Christians gathered at the Bank One Ballpark in Phoenix, Arizona, for a worship and prayer service. "Pray Lubbock" was the designation given to a movement of corporate prayer in Lubbock, Texas. I could write an entire book about what God is doing across America through cross-denominational, cross-racial corporate prayer. David Bryant puts it so well in his book *The Hope at Hand*: "If we know historically that this groundswell of prayer is a gift of God; if it is biblically accurate to teach that God has not only ordained the end but also the means (the end being world revival, the means being the prayers of his people); if this massive chorus of prayer is increasingly focused on nothing less than national and world revival; and if when God stirs us up to this type of praying he does so because he is actually ready to answer us—how can we believe otherwise that world revival is bearing down on top of us?"

My dear brother, nothing is more important for your life or ministry than prayer. Become a man of prayer and teach other men to do likewise!

Two resources I have found particularly helpful in praying the Bible are:

Kenneth Boa, *Handbook to Prayer* (Trinity House).

Wesley Campbell, *Praying the Bible*, a series of CDs covering most of the prayers in the Bible (Revival Now Resources, 1-888-738-4832 or www.revivalnow.com).

14

LEARNING TO WORSHIP

Rick Kingham

Texas Stadium. The home of the Dallas Cowboys of the National Football League. A classic stadium that has witnessed its share of exciting games and championship-caliber football teams. A roof covers most of the stands, but there's a hole over the playing field, which the local fans will tell you is designed to allow God to watch his favorite team play. Every Sunday that the Cowboys play at home, thousands of screaming fans jam the stadium to cheer on their hometown heroes. But on one particular day so vivid in my memory, football wasn't on the schedule, though God definitely came to visit Texas Stadium. More than 60,000 men from Texas and across the Southwest packed every available seat in the stadium for a Promise Keepers rally. Some men came merely out of curiosity. Others came at the invitation of a friend. Some were there because their wives had given them a Father's Day gift that they dared not refuse.

When the gates opened at 4 P.M., I stood to watch as God answered a prayer I had prayed many times. I had long desired to see the day when men would rush to get a good seat in anticipation of an opportunity to worship together. Promise Keepers began with a dream of thousands of men filling a football stadium singing "Amazing Grace." I remember Coach Bill McCartney's words in those early days: "Something happens when God's men get together; it's off the charts." Now here they were, as in many other cities around the nation. They'd come to celebrate; they'd come to see and hear; they'd come to fellowship. Boys and men joyfully gathered as one to sing loudly—and with attitude.

For some, this event was like attending their first professional sports game. Others experienced the thrill of looking around at thousands of other men who were ready to declare their commitment to Jesus Christ. Seeing so many Christians in one place was a joyous revelation for some who had thought they were standing alone.

As a board member and vice president of Promise Keepers, I had already participated in nearly forty of these stadium events, but from the opening note of the first explosive song, I knew that this would not be just another night. As the worship continued with great, swelling enthusiasm, the men I watched were connecting with God—many for the first time. This was a sovereign moment in time. I sensed that God was pleased with his sons. I knew that we were standing on holy ground.

The men began to sing the great hymn "Holy, Holy, Holy" with hands uplifted, hearts engaged, and tears streaming. Overcome with joy, I cried out as loudly as I could (although only God could hear me above the praise), "God, this is what it's all about! You've brought your sons, as in the Old Testament, to appear before you and worship you as King and Lord." The men responded to the worship with thunderous applause, as though releasing their joy and adoration for the Lord with a shout was the only appropriate action. That scene is indelibly etched in my heart.

If you have experienced the thrill I've described or have enjoyed the heartfelt worship of a retreat campfire where God's presence was hotter than the heat of the flame, you know that God is up to something in the lives of men in our generation, calling them to worship him. Throughout our land, churches are experiencing revival and renewal. Dr. Jack Hayford, no stranger to the importance and reality of worship says, "We are due for another reformation—a reformation of worship. We need a reformation to sweep through Christian worship today, providing spiritual food for a relationally disintegrating and spiritually thirsty society."

I believe that worship holds the key for the renewal of the church. Worship and praise encourage a heightened activity of the Holy Spirit as men give greater glory to God the Father and the Lord Jesus Christ. Sincere worship creates an awareness of the presence of God that is desperately needed by today's confused generation.

EXPLODING THE MYTHS ABOUT MEN

What we have witnessed over the past few years has blown away a major myth in the church: that today's men can't be encouraged to worship. Promise Keepers, Man in the Mirror, the National Center for Fathering, Point Man Ministries, and a host of other men's ministries involved in the National Coalition of Men's Ministries are proving that men will worship God with great passion and intensity when given an atmosphere of freedom to express who they are. The struggle we have is providing them with that environment of openness and encouraging them to praise God as only men can. But a new sound is being heard across the land. By the millions, men are taking up the command given in Revelation 19:5: "Give praise to our God, all you His bond-servants, you who fear Him, the small and the great" (NASB).

For the most part, worship doesn't exist in every church or men's fellowship like it does in a stadium full of men intent on forgetting everything else and focusing on God. The awesome experience of the huge gatherings is not the experience of most men on a regular basis. While serving with Promise Keepers, I received many letters asking how we could help churches to experience the level of worship found at the stadium events. Some of that excitement comes naturally from the size of the event, but don't believe that you cannot enjoy the same passion in a smaller, local gathering. The size of the crowd might be considerably smaller, but the passion doesn't have to be less. There are things we can do to enhance our worship and to create a culture and environment of openness in our churches that will allow men—and women—to express their love and passion for God to its fullest measure. Worship cannot be forced, but it most certainly can be encouraged.

SINGING SHEPHERDS

The first thing we must do is to establish the truth that men don't sacrifice their masculinity by lifting praise to God. That's a childish notion left over from junior high school, when most guys gravitated toward wood shop, drafting, and athletics, while few applied their talents to band, choir, and drama. We must affirm in our churches that praising God with reckless abandon is a very manly pursuit. Look at King David, the "Sweet Psalmist of Israel." He was no wimp. As a young shepherd, he killed a lion, a bear, and a giant. He also grew up playing his harp and singing beautiful melodies to the Lord.

As leaders, we must understand our importance as role models. I've watched men in their church groups at a stadium event look to see if their pastor was participating before they felt that it was okay to clap, shout, or raise their hands in honor to God. Don't underestimate the value of giving permission, even though it may not be verbally communicated. Those of us who lead men must encourage them to sing with all their hearts and ability. This may not seem all that important, but over the years, I've heard from enough men to make me believe that it is. Unfortunately, the pattern in many churches on Sunday morning is that the worship leader stands up front endeavoring to get everyone to join in, while the pastor stands off to the side failing to participate.

Not everyone can sing with equal ability, but together we can passionately praise our God. Early in the development of Promise Keepers worship philosophy, a choice was made to value passion over perfection. Though we were joined by some of the best musicians and singers around the nation through Maranatha! Music, we didn't strive for perfection over passion. When an atmosphere is created that allows men to make a joyful noise together, they really get noisy. Pastors and music directors, who for the most part are trained in music, can hinder the worship of men by over-emphasizing perfection. Set your men free to passionately praise God, even if it doesn't sound like Take 6 or the Brooklyn Tabernacle Choir.

PASSIONATE APPEARANCES

Passion doesn't always look very dignified. But God is looking for a generation of men who are not so self-absorbed that they worry what everyone around them thinks. The guys at the stadium events feel free to express themselves because they know that they have an audience of one. Many of them clap, shout, laugh, cry, dance, and raise their hands. Some of them do these things in spite of their traditions or comfort zones.

If your church becomes a place of worship where men can be less self-conscious, it will only take a little encouragement to get them to express it. Again, King David is an excellent example. First Chronicles 15:25–29 tells the story of when he brought the ark of the covenant back to the city of Jerusalem after its long absence. Great shouts and rejoicing accompanied this symbol of the presence of God as it was restored to the people.

As the glory of the Lord returned, David removed his ephod and danced and cel-ebrated. His lack of concern for what anyone thought is remarkable. He gleefully twirled, shouted, and rejoiced. His explosive joy could not be contained. His passion for God spilled over like a young boy who shakes a soda-pop bottle and lets it spray freely. At that moment, David was modeling the joy that God expresses over his people.

"The LORD your God is in your midst, a victorious warrior. He will exult over you with joy, He will be quiet in His love, He will rejoice over you with shouts of joy" (Zeph. 3:17 NASB).

God rejoices over us with singing. With intense emotion coming from his entire being, he pours out his love, affection, grace, and joy. David could do nothing less than imitate God's explosive, passionate joy. Neither can we.

First Chronicles 15:29 also tells us that when we celebrate, not everyone will like it. David's wife Michal surely didn't. She despised him for his extravagance. Perhaps she had learned from her father, Saul—who was always concerned about what other people might think—to value dignity over worship and appearance over praise. When men begin to radically worship God in our churches, there will inevitably be those who will criticize and admonish us to contain our joyful celebra-tion. Don't pour water on the fire of God's Spirit out of concern for how things look. Let's be more concerned with what God desires than with what other people think.

RIGHT RELATIONSHIPS RELEASE WORSHIP

Right relationships are the key to releasing men to worship joyfully, passionately, and radically. Jesus himself highlighted this truth in Matthew 5:23–24: "Therefore if you are presenting your offering at the altar, and there remember that your brother has something against you, leave your offering there before the altar and go; first be reconciled to your brother, and then come and present your offering" (NASB).

It is clear that if we want our worship to excel, we cannot detach it from the way we relate to others. A lack of freedom and joy that inhibits our worship may be caused by our poor relationships with God and others. Clearing the way for God to manifest his presence in our churches may entail reconciling relationships with our brothers. I've heard countless stories about the freedom and joy that is released when hearts are open, pure, and united.

"Behold how good and how pleasant it is for brothers to dwell together in unity! It is like the precious oil upon the head, coming down upon the beard, even Aaron's beard, coming down upon the edge of his robes. It is like the dew of Hermon coming down upon the mountains of Zion; for there the LORD commanded the blessing—life forever" (Ps. 133:1–3 NASB).

God is clearly moving mightily among the men of our day. He is calling us to come and worship him. Under the proper leadership, all men will sing and praise God—loudly. And when the Lord looks down and sees his sons singing with passion and bringing him pleasure, he'll favor us and our churches with joy.

THE PASSIONATE PURSUIT OF GOD

True worship of God involves more than our emotional response or physical movement. It springs from our hunger for intimacy with God. The church must encourage meaningful encounters with God, or we've missed our calling. Enjoying God through our worship is neither excessive nor abusive. In fact, it should be the normal experience for all believers.

The way worship is modeled in the church can hinder rather than encourage men to worship. Our leaders must be men who enjoy intimacy with God and exhibit a freedom in Christ that will draw men into active participation. Sadly, most leaders do not possess a personal theology of worship or model a lifestyle that reflects a hunger for God.

One of the essential dynamics of the stadium events I've attended is a flexible environment that allows for freedom of expression. Because of the diversity of men who attend these events, from a broad range of the body of Christ, one style, tempo, or liturgy is not given preference over another. Likewise, our churches should not abandon one style for another just because they want a more contemporary approach. The men's gatherings of the last ten years have shown us that we can experience the historical substance of hymns and the freedom of praise choruses together in balance. The leaders of men's ministries in the local church would do well to learn that lesson.

> *O Breath of Life, come sweeping through us*
> *Revive Thy Church with life and power*
> *O Breath of Life come cleanse, renew us*
> *And fit Thy church to meet this hour.*

BUILDING AN ATMOSPHERE OF WORSHIP IN THE LOCAL CHURCH

When men believe that they can encounter the risen Lord in the midst of their local congregations, they will be encouraged to worship with all their hearts. The following practical steps will help you encourage men to worship.

1. *Pray for the men of your church.* Pray that the Spirit of God will draw their hearts into worship. God honors prayer that is in accordance with his will, and he clearly desires for us to worship. Don't keep your desire for greater worship to yourself. Express your heart to God.

2. *Make worship a topic of discussion and study.* Your men's small groups, Bible studies, and prayer breakfasts are good opportunities to discuss and study worship. Most men have very little knowledge and experience when it comes to a Biblical explanation of worship. Because they lack a personal theology of worship, they have no basis upon which to build. A great place to start is with a study of the forms of worship found in the Psalms.

3. *Teach men to worship as a way of life.* Too many men have accepted less than God's best for them in experiencing him. Worship has been isolated to the time when we gather together on Sunday morning instead of describing the fullness of what we do in honor of God before his throne. Bring men to a place where they can live a lifestyle of worship. Help them to understand the value of prayer, solitude, disciplined study, confession, and singing to the Lord.

4. *Create opportunities for men to worship in a safe environment.* Men need space. If you walk into a room of men, you'll see them spread out all over, because men function best when given room. Space is more than a physical principle. Provide a safe environment, time to adjust, and an opportunity to grow before asking too much of them. Too many leaders have failed or become discouraged because they forgot that not everyone is as comfortable as they are with singing loudly and participating expressively.

5. *Use music designed for men.* Don't expect your men to sing songs that are written for someone with a high range. Men love to hear themselves sing in big, bravado tones. Get the music down in a range where they can get to it.

6. *Identify men in your church who have musical talent and give them opportunities to use their gifts.* Nothing is more encouraging than hearing another man use his voice

to the glory of God. Singing is not the only form of public worship, of course. Those who read Scripture, take the offering, preach, and pray are also participating in worship. The goal is for every person in church to participate in some way, even if they are sitting in a pew. Learn to use the men of your church to assist in the worship service, and therefore enhance their participation in the worship of our God.

7. *Challenge the men who have caught the vision for worship to encourage other men to participate.* Something happens when men worship together. Men like to know that others are involved. It is good if they are asked to participate by someone other than the leader.

8. *Make worship tapes and resources available to your men.* Let the men of your church catch the vision for worship by experiencing it in their car, home, or office. Organizations that minister to men have learned how valuable music is to the family. Many times, the same songs the men like have become the favorite music in the home. Consider picking up some of the Promise Keepers music on CD or finding some music that lifts your spirit and playing it in your home, your office, and your car.

9. *Don't get discouraged.* Men don't change quickly. You won't develop a dynamic atmosphere overnight, but it *will* happen as you establish a consistent, inspiring, open environment in which God can be glorified.

15

ENCOURAGING VITAL RELATIONSHIPS

Geoff Gorsuch

I f you want to see a vibrant men's ministry flourish in your church, you cannot afford to overlook the most essential ingredient of success: vital relationships. You can follow every step in this book, but if you neglect vital relationship building among your men, you'll never see an effective men's ministry grow in your church.

Successful small groups begin with leaders who model genuine Christlike relationships. Are you willing to spend enough time together in your core group to develop vital relationships? Are you willing to share your hearts with one another, including both struggles and victories? Are you willing to rely on each other for personal prayer, encouragement, and exhortation in your relationship with Christ and others? Are you willing to serve your families and the men in your church in order to demonstrate godly leadership?

The process of building vital relationships among men can be likened to a baseball diamond (fig. 4). Each base represents a stage of development. The process begins when we step up to the plate and declare our desire and determination to become more like Christ. Whether we get on base and how well we progress around the bases depends on our willingness to open ourselves up to other men.

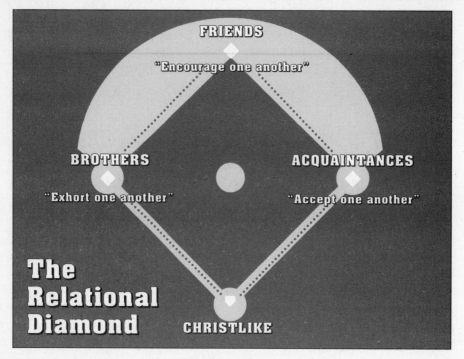

FIGURE 4

FIRST BASE

Acquaintances

The key to reaching first base in our relationships with other men is acceptance. "Accept one another, just as Christ also accepted us to the glory of God" (Rom. 15:7 NASB). As we become acquainted with other men in the context of a small group, we should focus on the following objectives.

- Develop trust-building activities
- Accept one another as we are
- Establish parameters for ongoing relationship (who, what, when, where, why, and how we're going to get together)
- Define our purpose as a group
- Agree on confidentiality

Effective men's small groups include three key elements: (1) sharing and relationship building, (2) prayer for one another's personal needs, and (3) applying God's Word. In building a strong foundation in relationships, there's no substitute for spending time together. The more opportunities the men in your group have to get together in a variety of activities, the quicker everyone will bond and trust will be established.

Though activities alone do not guarantee solid relationships, men need the interaction to get to know one another better. Men will enter more easily into the task of trust building when it is accomplished in the context of shared experiences. Activities may range from sporting events to social gatherings, depending upon the tastes of the men involved, but the goal is always the same: to help men accept one another in Christ.

Conversations at the acquaintance stage will be lighthearted and casual, but the important thing is that men learn how to listen to one another. As the relationships progress, your men will begin to explore options and will arrive at forms of activity and styles of communication that meet their needs. Although a fully developed purpose statement may not be determined until the group has been meeting for a while, the essential elements—what the group wants to do and why—should be settled as soon as possible. In most cases, the group's purpose will be well established by the time it approaches second base.

Getting to First Base

Key questions:

1. What are some enjoyable activities that your church can sponsor to help your men get better acquainted?
2. What common interests, hobbies, or topics do your men have that would draw them to small groups?
3. How can your core group help the men in your church to become involved in men's small groups?
4. How will you encourage your men's small group leaders to share their hearts, pray for their men's personal needs, and help the men in their group apply God's Word to their lives?

SECOND BASE

Friendship

At second base, the relationships progress to the level of friendship. The focus here is on encouraging one another, developing good discussion skills, and learning how to resolve conflict. "Therefore encourage one another and build up one another, just as you also are doing" (1 Thess. 5:11 NASB).

The word *encourage* comes from the same word as one of the names of the Holy Spirit. This word means "called alongside to help." To encourage one another, then, is to be vitally involved in what the Spirit is doing in the lives of our brothers in Christ. Either verbally or through our actions, we can affirm God's view of our brothers. In doing so, we move from accepting them to helping them. Encouragement is taking an active role in a brother's life.

Sliding into second implies friction. When men commit to a small group gathering, their expectations for the group may need to be adjusted in an honest and respectful way. Conversations will pass from the superficial level to the level of ideas and opinions. It is important for the leader to model effective communication and conflict resolution as the group grows closer. Your small group leaders should be prepared to ask open-ended questions that encourage discussion and to use differences of opinion in their small groups to help their men develop mutual respect.

When men are encouraged to fully express themselves on men's issues, they develop a bond of trust with each other. This trust produces a camaraderie based on mutual respect. Without this, the group will inevitably dissolve. Time and care must be taken to work through relational differences and to allow the men in the group to unite around common interests and commitments. Don't try to steal second by rushing the process. It takes time for men to feel comfortable with each other.

Men need to know that after they've shared their lives, they will not be "benched" through betrayal of trust or a lack of commitment. Our small groups must be havens of safety, where "perfect love casts out fear" (1 John 4:18 NASB). As each man gives his best to God and each other, he will move out of isolation and into vital relationships. The team will learn what it means to live as brothers. They will grow toward Christlikeness.

Sliding into Second

Key questions:

1. How can you tell if the men in your small groups are sensing the freedom to share how they really feel?
2. What open-ended questions are your small group leaders asking to help their men to express their beliefs and ideas?
3. How will you help your small group leaders communicate to their men that it's okay to disagree and that a goal for the group is to understand where each man is coming from, not winning arguments?

THIRD BASE

Brotherhood

As communication and commitment to one another deepens, we round third base by teaching and exhorting one another. "Let the word of Christ richly dwell within you, with all wisdom teaching and admonishing one another with psalms and hymns and spiritual songs, singing with thankfulness in your hearts to God" (Col. 3:16 NASB). Thus we become the brothers that Christ intends for us to be.

The apostle Paul says that speaking the truth in love, we are to grow in Christ (Eph. 4:15). How do we grow spiritually? How do we become the men that God wants

Dynamics to Avoid in Your Small Group Ministry

1. *Domination*. Don't allow one or two men in your small group to dominate the conversation or group discussion. Hogging the stage causes others to withdraw or not interact with the group, and these men will soon become disinterested spectators. The way of group domination is not the avenue for growth.

2. *Intimidation*. Avoid intimidation at all costs. Some men in your group will be insecure. Others will have been intimidated most of their lives due to physical size, wealth, appearance, family, job, or how long they have been a Christian. Until you know where everyone in the group stands, be careful about going too deep or assuming that all members know all the Christian terms and their meanings.

3. *Humiliation*. Some men belittle others in order to appear funny or secure. This habit of sarcasm or cutting remarks will undermine trust and intimacy in a group. If one person is picked on in jest by another and other people laugh, he might sense that everyone is ganging up on him.

4. *Interrogation*. Most men will not open up when faced with a battery of questions that appear confrontational or "in your face." Though shooting straight is the best way to approach a small group, grace is still a vital characteristic of a Christlike attitude.

5. *Fabrication*. To gain the most from a small group, all members must be honest with one another. The truthfulness of answers will depend greatly on the group's commitment to confidentiality.

6. *Agitation*. Not everyone has a great day every day. Coming to a small group and being confronted with personal shortcomings may not be pleasant. Treat one another with patience, grace, and gentleness.

7. *Procrastination*. Follow up on action points within the group, to make sure that everyone is making time to grow in their commitments. If a brother stumbles, the others should pick him up and carry him, if necessary.

8. *Hesitation*. When a man in your group has a definite need, don't just say you will pray. Do it on the spot! If he has a physical need, pitch in and help him out.

9. *Capitulation*. Never give up on the members of your small group. "Let us not lose heart in doing good, for in due time we will reap if we do not grow weary" (Gal. 6:9 NASB).

us to be? Growth comes from truth shared through meaningful relationships. Through "teaching," we learn how God wants us to live. Admonishing involves helping each other apply those truths, even when it is difficult. We all fall short, but we must keep trying! An effective small group can become God's means of loving correction to help us apply the truth to our lives. This is exhortation as God intended it to be—brothers lovingly prodding one another to do their best.

Brothers are the sons of a common father. If you are a child of God and I am a child of God, it is undeniable that we are brothers. The same royal blood has been shed for us. We are heirs of a common spiritual inheritance, so as brothers we should be available for one another. Brothers stand in defense of one another. Brothers fight for each other, and at times may even die for each other. In a manly way, they learn to love one another.

At third base, after much coaching and time spent together, we should feel free to exhort one another as we face life's challenges together. At this point, as brothers, we are vitally interested in helping each other reach home plate: growth in Christlikeness. Our focus at this stage is on team building, learning to worship together, establishing and honoring covenants, and allowing accountability.

Too many groups approach third base and then turn right! In other words, they never get around to exhortation. They never establish covenants or accountability. They never enter the struggle for moral excellence together. They never really worship. Part of the problem may be that they have cut across the diamond from first to third without establishing the necessary friendship dynamics at second base. Once men have genuinely accepted and encouraged each other, they should be ready to admonish one another and offer accountability. Having studied and discussed God's Word together, they should have discovered where they really are in Christ and where they need to be. Cooperation based on mutually shared needs and respect for each other's strengths should now replace old, self-protective patterns.

Rounding Third

Key questions:

1. What are your small groups doing that demonstrate their interdependence as brothers?
2. How can your core group encourage the men in small groups to enter into covenants and commitments with God and one another?
3. From among the men in your core group, who can you ask to regularly check that you are following through on the commitments you've made to God and each other?

Good Habits for Small Groups

1. *Concentration.* The key to establishing effective communication in a small group is good listening. Without good listening skills, there is no small group. Look at the man who is speaking, don't interrupt, and don't be distracted by thinking about what you are going to say next—listen and learn.
2. *Facilitation.* Keep the conversation uplifting and progressive in growth. Make sure the discussion questions are open-ended and require more than a yes, no, or maybe response. Be sure that you leave enough time for everyone to be involved.
3. *Punctuality.* Set a time for your small group meetings and be on time. Tardiness or consistently running over the allotted time will kill a group before long. Make your group a priority and stay within the time parameters.
4. *Imitation of Jesus.* Demonstrate the grace, acceptance, understanding, compassion, and unconditional love of Christ to the members of your group.
5. *Participation.* If the group is to succeed, everyone must be involved. This involvement includes opening one's life honestly before others.

HOME PLATE

Christlikeness

Your investment in the lives of the men in your small groups pays off as they become servant leaders to their families, friends, communities, and church. As each man is helped around the bases by his brothers, momentum builds toward Christlikeness. This may be a lifelong commitment and process, but complementary skills will fall into place as men reap the benefits of teamwork and begin serving the body of Christ. As insight about life is shared, God's truth will be applied in a framework of mutual accountability, encouragement, and prayer.

With the support of his brothers, the dream that each man had as he stepped up to the plate will be within his reach. Together we can become men of genuine integrity. We can become more like Christ! "I in them and You in Me, that they may be perfected in unity, so that the world may know that You sent Me, and loved them, even as You have loved Me" (John 17:23 NASB).

The focus during this stage is on teamwork, serving one another, defining and developing each man's unique contribution to the body of Christ, and reaching the world for Jesus Christ.

Heading for Home

Key questions:

1. How can you tell if the men in your church are becoming servant leaders?
2. What are some ways that your core group can help your men to identify God's calling in their lives and to discern what gifts and talents they have to fulfill that call?
3. If your small groups ended today, would your men have impacted anyone's life for Jesus Christ outside of the groups? Why or why not?

NOT EVERY SWING IS A HIT

Being a mature man has never been easy, but the Bible teaches us that there are spiritual resources available to help us face the challenge. God has given us his Spirit, his Word, and one another so we don't have to do the job alone. In that light, we must decide: Will we still insist on going it alone, or will we become part of a group of men and assume our role as a brother in Christ?

Each phase serves its purpose to keep us in the game, but each stage also has its limitations. Not every acquaintance we make will become a friend, and not every friend will be as close as a brother. Our emotional capacity and ability to draw close to others is too limited. However, if we keep stepping up to the plate and taking a few swings—pursuing vital, meaningful relationships—we can become the brothers of a few. And that's what the game is all about. "Let's play ball!"

16

OVERCOMING PREJUDICE

Robert Sena

Prejudice: an opinion formed without taking the time and care to judge fairly. A biased opinion, attitude, or tendency formed unfairly or unjustly.

Prejudice is a demon that is not exclusive to the secular world. It has penetrated the lives of Christian individuals, families, churches and all levels of Christian organizations. We read our Bibles and worship in church; we build small group studies around books such as *Experiencing God*, *The Mind of Christ*, and *Spiritual Awakening*; and we declare that we are Spirit-filled believers in Almighty God; yet we continue to tolerate strongholds of prejudice, racism, hatred, and bigotry in our lives.

NORTH AMERICAN SAMARITAN

I first encountered prejudice at a very young age. In New Mexico, where I grew up, the Hispanic pride my parents untiringly taught me was not the prevailing attitude of the predominantly Anglo culture. Hispanics were considered second-class citizens or trash—the Samaritans of the Southwest.

When I went to school, I spoke Spanish and ate traditional foods during the lunch period. I can still hear the offensive laughter of the white kids as they talked about the "garbage" I ate for lunch. Yet now those very same people pay high prices for the same food in restaurants. I still remember the embarrassment and anger that welled within me as I stood in the hall outside the classroom, banished for having spoken in my native tongue. The words "You are in America now; speak English" still cause me to react, because I am a fourth-generation American Hispanic, born right here in the United States.

When I received my call to ministry, I went to my high school counselor to request that she send my grades to the colleges in the area, because I wanted to prepare myself for the ministry. She responded, "No college will accept a dumb Mexican to be a part of their student body." Her rude answer was painful, but what really crushed me was that I knew she was a member of one of our churches in town.

Many pastors of the sponsoring churches where I served would describe me as their "Mezcan pastor" and rub my hair as they introduced me to other pastors. Many times, these same leaders would say to me, "Bob, you are different. You aren't like the rest of the Mezcans."

I was not allowed to go into the same barber shops or eat in the same places as others. My new bride and I were told as we sat at a Five and Ten soda fountain that they didn't serve Mexicans.

The accumulation of these acts of prejudice tore away at my self-worth. I remember standing in front of the mirror and scrubbing my face raw with a wash cloth, trying to lighten the color of my skin, with tears running down my cheeks because I wanted to be a part of the predominant culture.

The years of experiencing prejudice gave birth to and fostered a deep hatred in my heart toward white people. I became cynical, suspicious, and distrusting. Despite all the blessings the Father had given me, I wasn't happy. I was doing exactly what the Lord had called me to do—evangelism and church planting—but I wasn't happy and fulfilled as a Christian. I had a beautiful, dedicated, and supportive wife and four children, yet something was blocking my relationship with the Father, my wife, and my family.

TRANSFORMATION THROUGH SILENCE

An Anglo football coach in Roswell, New Mexico, who was also a Southern Baptist deacon at the First Baptist Church, was one of the many instruments that God used to restore my self-image and change my perspective of non-Hispanics. Coach Laird helped me to realize that not all white people are racist or prejudiced, that Christians are different, and that it is all right to be Mexican.

During my Doctor of Ministries spiritual formation class, I became acquainted with the discipline of a silent retreat. In 1995, prior to a missions conference in Glorieta, New Mexico, I decided it was time to stop and listen to God. A six-hour period of prayer and fasting turned into a time of spiritual reflection, confession of lingering sins, and surrender of my life to the lordship of Christ. God spoke to me about my broken relationship with one of my brothers who is walking a different spiritual path; he convicted me of the need to give my wife and family priority time; and he revealed the negative feelings that I was harboring in my heart as a result of the racist environment, the paternalistic attitudes, and the hatred I had endured. I had never sincerely dealt with these issues that haunted my spirit and emotions. But when I did, God set me free from the anger and hatred I held in my heart.

As a result of Coach Laird's impact on my life's pilgrimage and through prayer and the healing of the Holy Spirit, I no longer harbor bitterness, hatred, and anger in the closets, crevices, and deep, dark hiding places in my soul. That doesn't mean I no longer feel righteous indignation and the need to speak out when I see injustice, racism, prejudice, and bigotry. I do, but my motives, attitude, and approach are different. I've ceased practicing reverse prejudice.

What about you? Are you guilty of practicing the sin of prejudice? Do you form negative opinions about people who don't look like you, talk like you, or eat like you? Do you form opinions about others without attempting to know or understand them?

MAKING CHANGES

What can you do to combat the sin of prejudice in your life? Here are some guiding principles, for individuals as well as men's ministry groups and churches.

1. *Stop demanding that everyone be just like you.* The first church conference, described in Acts 15, shows the Jerusalem church dealing with the problems of prejudice and conformity. There were some in the group who were willing to welcome others into God's kingdom, as long as they conformed to Jewish customs. But Peter stood up and addressed the assembled church leaders, saying, "Brethren, you know that in the early days God made a choice among you, that by my mouth the Gentiles would hear the word of the gospel and believe. And God, who knows the heart, testified to them giving them the Holy Spirit, just as He also did to us; and He made no distinction between us and them, cleansing their hearts by faith. Now therefore why do you put God to the test by placing upon the neck of the disciples a yoke which neither our fathers nor we have been able to bear? But we believe that we are saved through the grace of the Lord Jesus, in the same way as they also are" (Acts 15:7–11 NASB). The result of Peter's exhortation and the elders' subsequent action was that the new believers "rejoiced because of . . . encouragement" (v. 31 NASB). Be an encourager, not a judge.

2. *Stop insisting that everything be done your way.* One of the most significant barriers to intimacy with God and with others is our attitude that says, "Everything must be done my way." Adam and Eve first walked this path when they disobeyed God in the Garden of Eden. When we insist on having our own way, we miss out on all the ways that God wants to surprise us with his grace and mercy and love.

3. *Repent of your prejudice toward other races and ethnic cultures.* In relating to people of other cultures and races, everyone has said and done things they should not have. Even with our best intentions, we make mistakes. We must repent of our negative attitudes and renounce our negative actions. Though we may live with the consequences of our mistakes—and the mistakes of others—we must determine not to perpetuate prejudice in our generation.

Once we have repented and have sought forgiveness where necessary, it's time to move on. Rehashing old news in your mind or in a group will not help anyone. Ask God to help you to be open and caring with others. Remember the apostle Paul's example in Philippians 3:13–14: "But one thing I do: forgetting what lies behind and reaching forward to what lies ahead, I press on toward the goal for the prize of the upward call of God in Christ Jesus" (NASB).

4. *Seek opportunities to make friends across racial and cultural lines.* We must look for ways to connect with others at a friendship level. Among friends is where the best barrier breaking takes place. Once you have made a friend, he can introduce you to many of his other friends.

5. *Learn to celebrate your own culture.* Every culture has unique characteristics that we can appreciate and celebrate. The principle that you cannot love others until you love yourself applies to culture as well. Celebrate your culture without idolizing it. Most people are interested in cross-cultural experiences. The more you know and appreciate your own culture, the richer your interactions with other cultures will be.

6. *Learn to celebrate other cultures.* Look for the good in every culture. Be as conciliatory as you can when you find things that you do not appreciate. But remember, not everything has to be done your way.

7. *Understand the difference between a process orientation and a task orientation.* Many minority cultures are process oriented. They place a higher value on the process of getting somewhere, rather than the act of getting there. They tend to get bogged down in the details of a project. Process-oriented individuals ask a lot of questions about consequences and how the given options will affect others.

The prevailing culture in the United States is task oriented. Anglo-Americans tend to place a higher value on getting somewhere, rather than on the process. They tend to be very focused on the goal or task at hand, and consequently they accomplish a lot. Task-oriented individuals ask a lot of questions about how to get the job done better and more quickly. Understanding the differences between process and task orientation can smooth over relations between individuals from differing cultures.

8. *Be willing to allow minority persons to fail.* Sometimes we remember failures for too long. And sometimes we let failures keep us from trusting others. Always expect the best of others, but don't expect perfection.

9. *Differentiate between race and culture*. Race refers to the distinct physical attributes that identify a particular people group. In our society, we seek to eliminate the structures that mistreat people because of their race.

Culture describes the sum of the customs, habits, and practices of a given group of people. In the process of Americanization, we seek to leave intact the patterns of relating (customs) of a given ethnic group, but we do not force it upon people.

10. *Help to remove the barriers of racism and prejudice*. Prejudice and racism are learned behaviors that often result from ignorance. We cannot deny that racial and cultural differences exist, nor should we try. Racial and cultural questions and concerns can be addressed openly in a warm and friendly manner. Develop a philosophy of "different but equal."

11. *Help to remove the barriers of racial and ethnic myths and stereotypes*. Every cultural group has a set of given traits that unites them. Make an effort to approach each minority person as an individual. Avoid the myth that all minorities are uneducated and poor. Do not assume that an ethnic person was born outside of the United States and does not speak English. Remember that preserving native languages is an important part of keeping a culture alive.

12. *Help to remove the barrier of fear*. We must set aside our fear that others will take advantage of us and deal with one another in an atmosphere of mutual trust and respect. We must overcome our fear that we will lose power and control. Remember, God is the one who is in control.

PART FOUR

BUILDING
THE FRAMEWORK

17

TRANSFORMING YOUR MEN'S MINISTRY

| *Rod Cooper* |

I was the team chaplain for the Houston Oilers back when Earl Campbell was in his heyday. The players often talked about their desire to have a "no cut" contract. Then if they ever got hurt, they could not be cut from the team and would continue to be paid. A buddy of mine, named Mike, played linebacker for the team. He was six feet three inches tall and weighed 235 pounds, all muscle, tall, dark, and handsome. To put it bluntly, he was a stud. On the field, he was good, but not quite good enough. At the end of training camp one year, he got cut from the team. When he told me the news, he asked me a question that floored me.

"Rod," he said with all sincerity, "now that I'm no longer playing with the Oilers, will we still be friends?"

I was shocked. "Of course we will, Mike," I replied. "I like you, not because you play ball but because you're who you are." Man, was he ever relieved. You see, he was caught up in an environment that said, "If you do not perform, you are out—both professionally and relationally."

I find that many men in the world would like a no-cut contract. They would like to know that even when they are not performing their best or are hurt, they are still on the team and do not need to fear competition. But that is not how the world operates, and sad to say, it's often not how the church operates either. Consequently, many men continue to play hurt and stay isolated from one another. They stay in hiding because they think that it's not okay to admit they don't have it all together, especially spiritually.

After my friend Mike had been out of football for a while, I asked him what he missed most about playing. I was surprised by his answer. He said that the best times were in the huddle on the field, because in the huddle you felt safe. It was a place of encouragement, direction, support, and correction. It was also a place where you could regroup for the next phase of the battle, knowing that you had ten other guys on your side, committed to the same purpose. Mike said that it was especially nice to draw into the huddle when they were playing away games in hostile stadiums where it seemed they not only had to battle the other team but also the negative environment. On the road, the huddle was a sanctuary, a place you could retreat to for encouragement to keep going.

CARRIED TO THE FEET OF JESUS

Like Mike and his former teammates, every man needs a huddle, a safe place where he can go to be refreshed in order to persevere through the battles in his life. If a man is going to win—not just survive—the battle of life, he must have a huddle of good men around him to cheer him on and bandage his wounds. He needs to know that other men will celebrate with him in the good times and bring help and healing in the bad times. He needs the kind of friends that the paralyzed man had in Mark 2:1–5.

Let me set the scene. Jesus had entered the small village of Capernaum, which was his base of operations in the northern part of Galilee. He went to a small house, possibly the house of Peter and Andrew (see Mark 1:29). His presence in the village was soon discovered, and the house began to fill with people, to the point that they were overflowing onto the porch and out onto the street. Some people came in the hope that Jesus might heal them from their diseases and ailments. At least that's what four men carrying their friend on a stretcher hoped.

"And they came, bringing to Him a paralytic, carried by four men. Being unable to get to Him because of the crowd, they removed the roof above Him; and when they had dug an opening, they let down the pallet on which the paralytic was lying. And Jesus seeing their faith said to the paralytic, 'Son, your sins are forgiven'" (Mark 2:3–5 NASB).

To understand the commitment of these men to their friend, we must understand what they were willing to do to help him. The typical peasant's house in Palestine was usually a small, one-room structure with a flat roof accessible by means of an outside stairway. The roof was usually made of wooden beams covered with thatch and compacted earth to shed the rain. Tiles were sometimes laid between the beams and the thatch. When the four men brought their friend to Jesus, they saw the size of the crowd and realized it was impossible to enter the house through the door. Not to be deterred, they carried their friend on his stretcher up the outside stairway to the roof and began ripping up the compacted thatch and earth with their bare hands. When a large enough hole had been formed, they lowered the man through the newly exposed beams to the floor below.

Can you imagine the look of shock on Jesus' face when all of a sudden he heard the roof being ripped off over his head, the debris started falling down around him, and he saw this man being lowered down right in front of him? What a scene. Jesus was so impressed that he healed the man not only physically but also internally (Mark 2:5, 11).

Why? Because of their faith. Please don't miss this important principle. The paralyzed man was healed because he had faithful friends who stood by him and carried him to the feet of Jesus. This man had a huddle.

Three Keys to Effective Friendships in Men's Ministry
From Mark 2:1–13

1. *The men went and got their friend.* Isn't that what we need and want from our friends? These men were so committed to their friend that they pursued him and looked out for his well being. They were there for him. Every man needs that kind of commitment from his friends.
2. *The men did whatever it took to meet their friend's need.* Notice that they worked as a team to carry him to the house and tear through the roof to get him help. Every man needs a team that will help remove the obstacles in his life so that he can be healed. We have all been paralyzed in some area and have needed the help of our huddle to remove obstacles and bring healing.
3. *The men brought their friend to Jesus.* These men knew that Jesus had the ability to bring healing to their friend. They had *faith.* Every man needs friends who have faith in him and in Jesus. Men need other men who will bring them to Jesus when they can't get there themselves, so that true healing can take place in their lives.

What does it take to create a successful huddle? What kind of relational environment is needed to sustain a man when he faces the problems and perplexities of life? Two types of relational climates prevail in most men's groups: conformity and transformation. One will sink a man spiritually, and the other will sustain him. Let's look at the characteristics of each.

THE CONFORMITY ENVIRONMENT

The conformity environment is based on measuring up to a strict set of standards, often based on appearance and performance. A man in this climate may feel that he has to be good or perfect to be loved or accepted. Expressing emotions—especially anger—is generally discouraged. In this atmosphere of repressed emotions, however, men may have difficulty trusting each other.

Sadness, anxiety, and emptiness frequently characterize the mood in a conformity environment. Men may feel frustrated, angry, and dissatisfied, and these feelings may persist despite their best efforts at prayer and Bible study. Men may feel more afraid of God than loved by him and may experience a pervasive sense of guilt, even about small, unimportant matters.

There can be a prevailing sense that it is somehow "unspiritual" to enjoy life, and freedom in Christ can be replaced by a checklist mentality, in which men try to follow a list of rules in order to be spiritual.

Sadly, these characteristics describe a good number of men in today's men's ministries, especially in so-called accountability groups. Wellington Boone, a national speaker for Promise Keepers, put it well when he said, "Accountability groups are not merely for 'sin management' but should help a man grow into the image of Jesus Christ." Your men's groups should not be places where a man is bound by a set of rules and hammered if he breaks them. An effective huddle is a place where a man can admit his weaknesses and have teammates who will help him grow through these weaknesses and into Christlikeness.

THE TRANSFORMATIONAL ENVIRONMENT

What kind of environment did Jesus create for his men's group? If ever there was a group that was constantly not measuring up, it was the disciples. But instead of expecting his men to conform to some high, unattainable standard, Jesus created a transformational environment that brought out the best in his men and helped them to grow spiritually. A transformational climate is characterized by the following four traits.

1. Acceptance and security
2. Openness
3. Teamwork
4. Loving accountability and growth

Let's compare each of the characteristics of a transformational environment with its counterpart in the conformity environment.

Acceptance and Security

The Pharisees were a religious group in the New Testament that loved to keep the rules. They operated according to the conformity environment model. Rigid rules. Severe consequences. One clash between Jesus and the Pharisees occurred when Jesus and his disciples were walking through some grain fields on the Sabbath (Matt. 12:1–8). Because they were hungry, the disciples began picking heads of grain. Seeing this, the Pharisees accused the disciples of breaking the law. According to the rules of the Pharisees, picking the heads of grain was harvesting, which was work forbidden on the Sabbath. By rubbing the kernels between their hands before eating them, they were threshing, which was also forbidden.

But look at Jesus' response. He reminds the Pharisees of the Scripture that says, "I desire compassion, and not a sacrifice." Jesus knew that the rules were made for man, not man for the rules. In a transformational environment, a man is accepted where he is, and then his friends help him get to where he needs to be. The focus is always on the needs of the man (compassion) and not on keeping a list of rules (sacrifice).

A transformational climate also offers a sense of security, especially when a man screws up. Have you ever played Nintendo? That's a conformity environment if there ever was one. There are certain rules, and you had better follow them. If you don't, you're immediately punished. You may lose points; you may lose a "life." Lose enough lives, and you're done—game over. The Pharisees would have loved it!

The Pharisees once brought to Jesus a woman who had been caught in the act of adultery. What these men were doing there is another story, but suffice it to say that the woman had been found out. The Pharisees brought her to Jesus and wanted him to condemn her. After all, she'd been caught in a sin deserving of death. Game over. But Jesus turned the tables. He asked the Pharisees to examine their own hearts before condemning the woman.

As the accusers began to slink away, Jesus told the woman that he didn't condemn her, and he commanded her to go and sin no more. He offered a redemptive solution. Notice that Jesus did not overlook her sin, but he first made it clear that there is no such thing as spiritual superiority. When he said, "He who is without sin among you, let him be the first to throw a stone at her" (John 8:7 NASB), he leveled the playing field. A transformational environment is built on the attitude of "there but for the grace of God go I." A man can feel secure in knowing that he can share his guts and the team will not pick up stones to throw at him but will be there to help him "sin no more" in that area.

Jesus always focused on transformation, not conformity. By contrast, Luke 11:39–43 tells us what was important to the Pharisees. They cleaned the outside of the cup and didn't care what was inside. They tithed down to the smallest seed from their gardens—and made sure that everyone knew it—yet they neglected God's larger law of justice and love. In the Sermon on the Mount, Jesus said that when the Pharisees prayed, they prayed loud and long so that everyone would hear. But Jesus said that what was important was what was inside a man. It was the substance of his prayers that mattered, not the volume.

Openness

Emotional Openness

I have a picture of a laughing Jesus that one of my clients gave to me. Jesus is depicted in the middle of a big belly laugh, with a huge grin on his face. Children

CLIMATE OF ACCEPTANCE AND SECURITY

Conformity	*Transformation*
1. Conformity to rigid rules	1. Rules empower righteousness
2. Punishes wrongdoing	2. Focuses on redemptive solutions
3. Appearances are important	3. Substance is more important than appearance

loved being with Jesus. He was even accused of partying too much. Why? Because he made people feel safe. And because they felt safe, they could be open with him.

The emotional climate of the Pharisees was tense and rigid. There were so many rules, so many laws. Break any one of them, and you were unclean. The question the disciples asked about the man that was born blind (John 9:1–3) reflects how the culture of that day viewed disabilities. Was it his sin or his parent's sin? It was a blaming, judgmental time. Jesus' response put matters into perspective. It was no one's fault that the man was blind, "but it was so that the works of God might be displayed in him" (John 9:3 NASB). Jesus reached out to the man and gave him safety, acceptance, and care.

Jesus ate with sinners and tax collectors. He let prostitutes minister to him. He touched lepers. All who came into contact with Jesus were allowed to be themselves. No pretense, no faking. Every man needs that kind of acceptance and emotional openness, friends around whom he can just be himself. A safe environment where he can voice his frustrations, fears, and failures and know that they will not be used against him. If you want to keep a man stuck, don't allow him to share his emotions. But our churches and our men's groups should be safe havens where a man can let it all out and then process it.

Intellectual Openness

Have you ever noticed that with Jesus, there were no dumb questions? In fact, he invited questions and open discussion. Even when James and John asked for the seats on his right and his left in glory, Jesus did not rebuke them for asking. Peter asked, "What do we get for following you?" To us it sounds like a selfish, rude question. But not to Jesus.

Now, don't get me wrong. Jesus did hold his disciples accountable. For instance, when Peter chastised Jesus for talking about his death, Jesus told Peter in no uncertain terms to quit buying into Satan's agenda. There was accountability, but it was couched in love.

In a conformity system, values are rigidly held and contrary views are unacceptable. There were no untouchable areas with Jesus. In the Sermon on the Mount, he talked about sex, money, adultery, and divorce. He talked politics, and many times he talked about his own death. This same openness permeated his entire life. He started a conversation with the Samaritan woman at the well and offered her living water. He ate with sinners because he knew they needed a physician.

A transformational men's ministry will allow men to bring up tough issues—even opinions that might not be popular—so that the men can work through them. Healing comes when men are allowed to get the secrets out of their lives. If your group does not allow for emotional and intellectual openness, your men will never progress along the path to healing and Christlikeness.

EMOTIONAL AND INTELLECTUAL CLIMATE

Conformity	Transformation
1. Tense, tight, defensive	1. Comfortable, safe, trusting
2. Blaming and judgmental	2. Spontaneous, accepting, caring
3. Contrary views unacceptable	3. No untouchable areas, free and wide-ranging discussions

Teamwork

Just like on the football field, the huddle is a place for coordinating teamwork. All for one, and one for all. Two stories in the Bible represent Jesus' approach to teamwork. In Luke 10, Jesus sends out seventy disciples to minister in the surrounding communities. He gives them instructions and turns them loose. When their mission is successful, does Jesus feel threatened by their success? Does he fear that they are stealing the limelight? No. The Bible says that he rejoiced greatly.

After Jesus rose from the dead, he sent his disciples out again. Matthew notes that some of the disciples were doubtful about Christ's presence. So he comforted them, giving them authority to accomplish the task that lay ahead. How many of you have been in a position of having responsibility without authority? It's not a good way to accomplish something. But Jesus gives his followers the authority, and he shares the responsibility. And he promises his presence throughout the process.

Every man wants to know that he has the support of his friends. A man doesn't mind being confronted with the truth when he knows that those who confront him will be with him when he has to face reality and make painful changes. Confrontation without commitment leads to destruction.

I once heard a story of a man who had committed adultery and needed to tell his wife. He was scared and knew that there would be incredible pain and disruption in his family. He told the men in his huddle, and to a man, they began to weep with him, recognizing their own vulnerability. They agreed that he needed to tell his wife. When it was time for the husband to break this painful news to his wife, the men went as a group and shared in the responsibility of helping him as their teammate and the husband and wife as a couple to begin the process of healing. The wife was devastated by the news, but knowing that these men were going to be there during the restoration process helped to salvage that marriage and restore that brother to fellowship.

THE TEAMWORK ENVIRONMENT

Conformity	Transformation
1. "Just do it" mind-set	1. Team oriented—*we* can do it

Loving Accountability and Growth

I've been in both conformity-based and transformational huddles. In a conformity environment, love is conditional, based on behavior. You could be "in" one week and "out" the next. In a transformational environment, love is unconditional. The chart below shows some of the defining characteristics of each group:

THE ACCOUNTABILITY ENVIRONMENT

Conformity	Transformation
1. Controlling. Lists of shoulds and should nots. Focus on behavior.	1. Relational. Developed spiritual disciplines. Encouraged to question, think, express, and work with feelings to become aware and responsible. Focus on process.
2. Punished by others for wrongdoing. Interaction remains superficial and task-driven.	2. Teammates guide, confront, and encourage. Relationships are warm, relaxed, trusting, and based on mutual respect.
3. Gotcha!	3. Believe the best for each brother.

Guess which group I left feeling beat up, never quite measuring up, and often feeling alone in the process? The other group I left encouraged, convicted, and hopeful that I could do what was needed to change, because these men were squarely behind me, urging me on toward Christlikeness.

I currently have a huddle that I meet with on Wednesday mornings. These men are my lifeline. I will never forget the time I shared my frustration concerning my communication with my wife, Nancy. My brothers began to lovingly probe me with questions and pinpointed the fact that I was traveling more than 50 percent of the time. They also pointed out that communication was tough because when I was at home, I would veg out and not take the time to communicate. I defended myself, but they put the ball squarely back in my court. They said, "Rod, you didn't make a vow 'till death do us part' to Promise Keepers, but you did to Nancy. Don't you think it's time to change?" They were right. They not only have helped me to take more time for Nancy but have helped me to see how to cut back on my schedule to be at home more—to be a promise keeper. They did not let up on me, but at the same time, they helped me in the process. These men held me accountable by locking arms with me, not by shaking their fingers at me.

TRANSFORMED BY JESUS CHRIST

If you want to see the results of a transformational environment, look at the disciples of Jesus after his resurrection. They went from being fearful followers with little faith to being leaders and the foundation of the church. Peter went from cowering in an upper room to preaching fearlessly before crowds, getting arrested in the process. Did this change result from conformity to a set of rules? No, Peter had been transformed by Jesus Christ.

Does transformation mean that you and I will never fail? No, but failing doesn't mean that you're out of the game. Jesus gave his men the freedom to fail. Look at John 21. Peter had denied Christ three times. Now he's out fishing, because it's the one thing he knows how to do. The men in the boat have been hard at it, with no success. Then a stranger on the shore calls out, "Cast the net on the right-hand side of the boat, and you will find a catch." When they do, they catch so many fish that the nets begin to break.

All of a sudden, John realizes who the stranger on the shore must be, and he says to Peter, "It is the Lord." When Peter hears that it's Jesus, he does the only rational thing he could do; he covers himself, jumps into the water, and heads for shore.

The next part of the story is special and illustrates my point. How does Jesus confront Peter? Does he shame Peter for his denial, shake a finger at him in rage, belittle him, or let him know that he just doesn't measure up? No. First, Jesus makes breakfast for Peter. Eating a meal together demonstrates fellowship. Then Jesus asks the most penetrating question, "Do you love me?" You know the story. Three times

Jesus asks Peter, "Do you love me?" Then he *restores* Peter to a strategic position in front of his peers. Jesus lets Peter know that just because he failed, it doesn't mean that he's a failure. He could start fresh. Jesus transformed Peter by his love. As disciples of Christ, we're to go and do likewise.

THE TRANSFORMATIONAL MAN

Here's what a man from a transformational environment looks like.

1. In relationships, he establishes clear lines of communication with his family and encourages their growth. He sets appropriate limits. He expresses his emotions appropriately, especially anger. He is trusting and trustworthy. He recognizes that he is secure in his relationship with Christ.
2. His moods are characterized by a general state of fulfillment and contentment.
3. In his spiritual life, he trusts in the character of God—whether he's emotionally up or down. He deeply loves God and feels loved by him. He feels shame when appropriate and seeks repentance and reconciliation. He enjoys life and lives by biblical principles.

Jesus said, "Come to Me, all who are weary and heavy-laden, and I will give you rest" (Matt. 11:28 NASB). We might paraphrase this verse to say, "Come to me, all who are tired of the game, all who have fumbled, all who are bruised and broken, and I will give you a place to huddle." If our ministry to men is to be transformational, if we're going to help men go deep with Christ and keep their commitments, they must know that the huddle is a place of rest and safety.

18

BECOMING A SPIRITUAL PARENT

Phil Downer

Many of the New Testament writers describe their ministries in terms of parenting. Paul calls the Galatians "my dear children"; he tells the believers at Thessalonica that he cares for them "like a mother caring for her children"; and he calls Timothy his "son." John repeatedly addresses those to whom he writes as "my children." Peter encourages his readers to long for the milk of the Word of God so they will grow. Even the writer to the Hebrews talks about spiritual infancy and the importance of moving toward maturity in Christ. We're all called to become mature and to make disciples of others (Matt. 28:19).

If you are going to disciple a fellow believer, you need to take the approach of a parent. Even if the person is your peer, you need to decide in your mind that you are offering spiritual guidance the way a father tries to guide and assist his son. With a baby Christian, you'll need to be attentive, giving a lot of individual attention, explaining things, and protecting the new believer from harm. Babies don't know much; more important, they don't know that they don't know. So the greatest thing you can do for a new Christian is to create a strong personal bond so that he knows he can rely on you. The church has a tendency to create discipleship programs as a substitute for personal care, putting people through a particular curriculum in hopes of helping them mature. That's a recipe for failure, because a new believer doesn't need information as much as he needs a meaningful relationship with a spiritual parent. Within the context of a trusting relationship, he can receive information.

A Christian needs to understand the Scriptures in order to grow, but without a relational context, it is easy to get the mistaken notion that spiritual maturity is simply a matter of having all the right answers. Genuine spiritual growth, however, occurs in relationship with a family of fellow believers, in which the new Christian has a model to follow, a guide to lead him, and the strong support of mature believers to help him through the hard times.

My spiritual parents taught me responsibility, helped me discover how to pray and study God's Word, and encouraged me to develop a love for people. The love, support, and accountability they offered were invaluable. I also saw their willingness to stick by me, even when I failed.

It takes patience and love to be a spiritual parent, but if you try it, you'll experience the joy of seeing new believers move down the path of maturity. Some things will change quickly; others will change slowly. God knows the needs of each person and is working in each life to help establish growth. We want instant maturity in our culture, but the spiritual life is a marathon, not a sprint. It takes time to learn how to live as Jesus would. Nobody just shows up to run a marathon; they train and prepare themselves for the race. The Christian life is all about preparation. What we do flows out of who we are, and God is in the business of changing who we are. A spiritual parent can be a mighty tool in the Lord's hand to shape the life of a new believer in training.

CHANGING FROM THE INSIDE OUT

We don't send babies to school to teach them how to grow, do we? So why do we send spiritual babies to discipleship classes? New Christians need education, but more than that, they need close, nurturing relationships. The personal attention that a spiritual parent can offer is much greater than what the new Christian could get from a classroom.

It used to be that people growing up in this country were shaped not only by parents but also by aunts and uncles and grandparents. We've lost much of that because of the mobility of our modern age, but the good news is that the church still offers an extended family experience. As brothers and sisters in Christ, we can disciple others as part of a team. No one individual has everything it takes to bring another to maturity, but collectively, every healthy Christian community does. Together we can teach the skills of spiritual survival and can nurture the character of those new to the family.

The Spirit of God is at work in our lives, helping us to become like Christ. We'd all like to see continual upward growth, but in reality, most of us experience a "three steps forward, two steps back" pattern. Some people seem to get stuck in perpetual babyhood, which can be disastrous. A church made up of immature believers soon begins mistaking immaturity for maturity. They substitute carnality for holiness, los-he's living to please God. If you insist on some particular behavior, he'll quickly sense that your love and commitment are conditional, and he will look for a better relationship elsewhere.

We need to allow space for God to work in our disciples, understanding that he is ultimately in control. Our role is to listen to a problem, encourage a right response, and then have the freedom to forgive when a Timothy decides to take a wrong turn and suffers the consequences.

A second common pitfall is the problem of overcontrol. My tendency early in my Christian walk was to try to protect my Timothys, to shelter them from other influences beyond myself and a handful of other like-minded men. My narrow-mindedness ignored the workings of the body of Christ and God's desire that he be in charge of the growth of his children. After all, these were his disciples, not mine.

In one of my early discipling relationships with a man, I had covered all the bases pretty well except for financial stewardship. My wife and I had always been big givers; the problem was, we were also big spenders. We looked at our finances as being 10 percent God's and 90 percent our own. Because of my own immaturity, I never offered my friend help in the financial area, and he suffered from my narrowness and unwillingness to share input from others. I learned something from that relationship: I am not an expert in many areas, so I'd better learn to listen to those who are. Remembering my own shortcomings has saved me from being overly controlling with different men on various occasions.

A third pitfall is assuming that everyone is just like us. We need to allow room for different backgrounds, personalities, and positions. For example, if your Timothy is a cofounder or owner of a business, he may feel free to be a vocal supporter of Christ in the workplace; but if he is the youngest member on a team of lawyers, his position may dictate that he keep his mouth shut and pursue a ministry of prayer until God gives him an obvious opportunity to speak.

Your Timothys will be different from you. Don't expect that just because you like classical music, the men you disciple will share your taste. We need to help others grow in accordance with their own bents. If you're discipling someone who is a technician and you're a generalist, you may need to seek the assistance of someone else who can relate to the man in his own context. You can still have a strong relationship, but you'll find yourself more effectively reaching and understanding men if you learn to speak their language.

Overprotection is another pitfall that spiritual parents fall into. Typically, we want our children to be perfect or competent before taking on new challenges. Just as it is important for our natural children to stretch and take on areas in their lives in which they may fail, it's important to let your Timothys do the same. For example, new Christians in dead churches are often asked to serve on the board. Your disciple's nat-

ing their ability to impact the world for God's purposes. But a man who has been properly discipled grows up into maturity. That's why the writer of Hebrews says that "solid food is for the mature, who *because of practice* have their senses trained to discern good and evil" (Heb. 5:14 NASB, emphasis mine).

It seems that the more I know about God, the less comfortable I am with myself. I keep wanting to improve the old me, but that can't happen. God isn't interested in the old me; he wants to remake me into a brand-new me. He wants to transform me completely. I fear being co-opted by our culture, becoming more comfortable with the things of this world than the things of God. But if God is at the center of how I view the world, my life is bound to change. I'll begin to see things his way. I'll find myself surrendering some things I thought I couldn't live without. His values will eventually become my values. When this happens, my behavior will start to change. What I do will begin to line up with who I am.

Christians often think that changing our behavior reveals our maturity, but God wants to change us from the inside out. He's not satisfied with simply watching us try to change ourselves. Instead, the Spirit changes us as we walk close to him, as we spend time in the Word and in prayer, and as we learn to imitate Christ. If he can help us see the world from his perspective, our worldview and values will change, having a significant effect on our behavior.

The role of the spiritual parent is to keep new Christians close to the Spirit. Let them see how God has changed your life. Reveal your God-given perspective and values to them, so they can begin to think in a whole new way. Remember, our goal is not to change all of the world at once, but to help change one life at a time. As God works through us as spiritual parents, we'll see him change other people from the inside out.

The discipleship process mirrors the growth process. We have to understand that new believers will progress from child to adolescent to adult, so we must adjust the focus of our relationships accordingly. As a spiritual child, the new believer requires daily feedings, attention, and some diaper changes. The diaper changes come not always when the baby asks for it but rather when he needs it. If he has made a mess of his life, as a spiritual parent you are there to help clean it up. You'll sometimes have to ask the hard questions and hold him accountable for his actions.

As the spiritual child becomes an adolescent, a more two-way and consensual relationship develops, rather than strictly father to son. Adolescent believers will have doubts and ask questions about the faith, and it's your role to try to answer them.

Often, growing believers need to try things on their own and make their own mistakes. It is advisable at this stage to get them involved in evangelism and discipleship, so they can share the excitement of bringing someone else to maturity. Their early attempts to share their faith or disciple someone may be marked by a few disasters, but along the way, they'll discover that God wants to use them in the lives of other people.

What's important is that you don't want the men you are discipling to think they will always be spiritual babies dependent upon your instruction. Move them into some activity in which they can stretch their spiritual muscles by getting involved in the lives of others.

Two-way communication is essential for the adolescent stage of discipleship. Rather than always considering yourself the leader, foster mutual respect and approval. If you never listen to the man you are discipling yet expect him to take your advice, you will end up with rebellion. I once discipled a brand-new Christian, a man sixteen years my junior, who wanted help with the challenges of his family, his job, and his walk with the Lord. Along the way, he asked how he could pray for me, and I briefly mentioned a problem I was having with an associate named Del. My young friend started asking questions, and I found myself becoming irritated, because in my prideful heart, I didn't believe that this spiritual baby could possibly have much wisdom about my situation. After about ten questions, he asked me, "Phil, if you were to do it over again, would you hire Del?" After I told him no, he said, "Well, then you need to admit your mistake and let him go."

I was struck by his abrupt conclusion and began to explain that it would be unfair to simply cut Del loose. After listening to my rationalization, this brand-new believer went on to point out the biblical principles that God has a wonderful plan for our lives (I could hear myself saying those same words several weeks before), that Del was God's child, and by my keeping him in the wrong position, I was perhaps depriving Del of God's best in his life. At that point, I had to admit my blind spot. I took the advice, and it was absolutely the perfect result for both Del and the team.

Had I ignored my young friend, not only would I have lost the benefit of his wisdom, I probably would have lost his respect. No one wants to be ignored. No one likes to feel unappreciated. This man was a successful businessman, and my treating him like a child would have killed any mutual respect we had established. Respect and communication are two of the most important elements of the discipling relationship. They reveal trust, appreciation, honesty, and your belief that the other person is growing in the Lord.

LEADING BY EXAMPLE

While serving with the U.S. Marine Corps in Vietnam, I found myself in charge of a team of new marines patrolling a territory infested with booby traps. These little devices were nearly impossible to see on the jungle trails, but if they were stepped on, they could turn a man into a mass of raw flesh. They were one of the hidden enemies that haunted our every step in Vietnam.

While we were on patrol, two of my men tripped a detonator, and we had to medevac them out before taking up positions for our night ambush. With the scent of the explosion still in our nostrils and our comrades' screams of pain still ringing in

our ears, we moved down the trail several hundred meters with great caution. Our team was to establish a position on a small knoll that looked like a perfect vantage point but was also likely to be booby-trapped. My temptation was to send one of the new marines to scout the area and set the machine-gun position, but I knew it was my responsibility to look out for these men's lives. Because I had greater experience in dealing with booby traps, I knew that I should be the one to clear the area.

On my hands and knees, I crawled along the trail to the clearing, searching every inch as I went. As I squirmed along the ground, I could picture what would happen to my head if I tripped a detonator. The men behind me, who had been with me for only a few hours, knew nothing about my leadership or my concern for them, but after I took the risk to sight out the trail and clear the area for the machine-gun position, they gave me loyalty and respect beyond belief. We forged an alliance that carried us through fierce battles.

Sometimes you'll have to risk your neck for someone you're discipling. Discipleship often means sacrificing ourselves for another man. But God calls us to protect the men he entrusts to us. Our disciples' growth and protection comes ahead of our personal interests.

One of the most exciting things about discipleship is when your spiritual sons become not just brothers in the faith but mature spiritual warriors on whom you can depend. Sometimes they'll even grow into spiritual big brothers. Many of the men I've discipled have gone on to master aspects of the faith far beyond my own expertise. At times it can be humbling, but it is also wonderful to realize that you had a hand in helping a man grow to spiritual maturity. It's fulfilling to see how a man's obedience to Scripture can lead to tremendous growth in both spiritual things and professional pursuits.

THE PITFALLS OF PARENTING

We must be careful to approach our spiritual children in love, particularly those of us who have had terrible parental role models in our lives. A spiritual parent should never become an autocratic or authoritarian figure. If we treat our Timothys in such a way, they will exit the relationship quickly. If a spiritual parent is demanding or impossible to please, he will never develop the long-term relationship necessary to the discipleship process. But if we sacrificially and unconditionally love the individuals God has entrusted to our care, discipleship will become the most fulfilling ministry imaginable.

One of the most common pitfalls of parenting is performance-based relationship. We often make the same mistake in parenting our disciples that we make in our families: making our children, both spiritual and natural, feel that our love and acceptance depends on their performance. Performance-based discipleship can lead to legalism and is always destructive. Remember, the disciple isn't living to please you;

ural inclination may be to try to change the church. Although you may want to counsel your Timothy as to the difficulties and challenges inherent in that process, once he
has it in his mind that he wants to do it, you must be careful not to break the relationship just because he hasn't followed your advice. Support him in his endeavor, offer
your wisdom and encouragement, and let him learn the hard lessons if he needs to.

Parents also want to protect their children from sin, but if you give your child a
list of do's and don'ts, you'll often just drive his behavior underground. Set up some
sort of regular accountability session with your Timothy in which both of you are
checking on each other and learn to openly share both your joys and your struggles.
You can't protect your Timothys from temptation, nor can you take responsibility
when they fail, but you can arrange for open communication so that there is someone they can talk to about what they are facing.

Some of the best friends I have on earth are the men I have been involved with
in discipleship. We've been through some severe challenges over the past twenty
years, and it's often been not just our spiritual parents but our spiritual children as
well who've come to our aid, support, and counsel at crucial moments in our lives.
We've grown as brothers in Christ and have developed the love and commitment
that brothers have toward one another.

If you will invest in the lives of men and choose to make a significant difference
in their lives rather than settling for worldly success, you can be part of God's plan to
change the world. If you ask the Lord for the name of one man you can disciple and
form an alliance with—spending time with him, holding him accountable, and developing a relationship that will thrive as you both mature through the spiritual life
cycle—you'll find that you have a friend who is closer than family. You'll find fulfillment that can never come from making money or acquiring material possessions.
Instead, you'll have the satisfaction of knowing you are one of the links in the chain
that stretches back to the Lord Jesus Christ. And at the end of time, God will weigh
the eternal impact of your life by your spiritual children and grandchildren. You have
a chance to be part of the greatest ministry ever. It all starts when you make the decision to come alongside a friend and help him to grow.

For more information on discipleship, contact us at PhilDowner@DNA
ministries.org.

19

WORKING WITH MEN WHO FAIL

Steve Farrar

Reed Joseph was adopted as an infant into one of the wealthiest families in America. He went to a very exclusive prep school in upstate New York, then headed west after graduation to play football at Stanford. Upon graduation from Stanford, Joseph immediately enlisted in the military. He spent the majority of World War II making bombing runs over Germany and returned a highly decorated military hero. He then picked up an M.B.A. at Harvard and a Ph.D. at Yale. Reed Joseph was a success. He was the last guy you'd expect to be wanted for manslaughter. But that's exactly the charge that would change his life and end his career.

In his early thirties, Joseph decided to make a run at politics. Going for broke, he ran for the United States Senate and won. His string of successes continued. But it all changed one evening when he got on the subway.

After enjoying the premiere of a new play on Broadway, he and his wife decided to do something they hadn't done in years. Just for fun, they would take the subway back to their hotel.

As they were running to catch the waiting train, Reed and his wife heard a man screaming. Reed turned and saw an elderly Hasidic Jew, wearing the traditional black suit and hat you see so often in New York City, being beaten by a guy who had to be at least six feet six and three hundred pounds. The old man's face was gushing blood from the relentless blows. In a flash, the senator bolted toward the assailant and brought him down with the form that had made him an all-American linebacker twenty years ago.

Quickly the assailant was on his feet, now charging Reed with a piece of pipe in his hand. Sheer instinct, combined with Reed's military training, resulted in a survival-training blow to the attacker's throat. The man collapsed on the platform, gasping for air that wouldn't come. Within seconds, he was dead, and so was the senator's career. He was forty years old, and he was finished.

THE TRUE STORY

This really happened. Except the man's real name was not Reed Joseph. And he wasn't an American. He didn't go to Stanford, didn't fly bombers over Germany, he wasn't a senator, and he never took the subway. But other than that, it's a true story.

His first name wasn't Reed, but his adoptive family could have called him Reed, because they found him among some reeds along a riverbank. Instead, they called him Moses.

His last name wasn't Joseph, but it could have been, for he was a descendant of Joseph, the great Israeli prime minister of Egypt. That's why his Jewish family was in Egypt. Moses was brought up in the palace and was treated as the grandson of Pharaoh. He was probably educated in the college that had grown up around the Temple of the Sun, a place biblical scholar F. B. Meyer notes has been called "the Oxford of Ancient Egypt."

But Moses wasn't just a student; he was a statesman and a soldier, "a man of power in words and deeds" (Acts 7:22 NASB). At age thirty-nine, Moses had it all: power, prestige, education, wealth, and a career with unbelievable potential. By anyone's standards, Moses was successful. By virtue of his military leadership and his membership in the house of Pharaoh, he was a logical choice to rule the entire country one day.

Something about the story of Moses has a contemporary feel to it. Many people today are devoting their lives to reaching the top of the pyramid. Moses was in line to *own* the pyramids—until he made a very costly mistake. One day, he saw one of his Hebrew brothers being beaten by an Egyptian taskmaster. Moses went to the man's aid and killed the guard. With one impulsive act, Moses fell off the pyramid and became a fugitive.

HOW COULD YOU BE SO STUPID?

Why did Moses take it upon himself to defend a Hebrew slave? Stephen, the early Christian martyr, gives us particular insight into what was going on in Moses' mind when he moved to defend his Jewish brother. Apparently, he had a broader purpose than just defending a helpless slave. In Acts 7:24–25, Stephen says of him, "And when he saw one of them being treated unjustly, he defended him and took vengeance for the oppressed by striking down the Egyptian. And he supposed that his brethren understood that God was granting them deliverance through him, but they did not understand" (NASB).

Acts 7:25 makes it clear that Moses knew he had been chosen by God to be the deliverer of Israel. He was right about the task but dead wrong about the means and the timing. As a result of his miscalculation, note what happened: "On the following day he appeared to them as they were fighting together, and he tried to reconcile them in peace, saying, 'Men, you are brethren, why do you injure one another?' But the one who was injuring his neighbor pushed him away, saying, 'Who made you a ruler and judge over us? You do not mean to kill me as you killed the Egyptian yesterday, do you?' At this remark, Moses fled and became an alien in the land of Midian" (Acts 7:26–29 NASB).

Moses instituted his own plan to bring about the Exodus, and it didn't work. But these events give us some clues about the kind of man Moses was. Stop for a minute and think about what he was trying to accomplish. His goal was to take two million slave laborers, plus women and children, out of Egypt and back to the land of their fathers. These people were the economic backbone of Egypt. Yet Moses believed they would follow his leadership, revolt against Egypt, and find their freedom. It takes a special kind of man to attempt that kind of rebellion. He must have had great self-esteem. He must have had great self-confidence. He must have had great courage.

Moses believed in himself. He knew he was gifted and well connected. And he knew he had what it would take to pull off the Exodus. He knew it because he had succeeded in everything he had undertaken up to that point in his life. That's why he fully expected to be successful in this venture as well. Moses was a mover and shaker, a leader with a capital L. But this time he hit a brick wall.

THE FATAL FLAW

The account in the book of Exodus of these same events gives us another key detail about Moses: "Now it came about in those days, when Moses had grown up, that he went out to his brethren and looked on their hard labors; and he saw an Egyptian beating a Hebrew, one of his brethren. So he looked this way and that, and when he saw there was no one around, he struck down the Egyptian and hid him in the sand" (Ex. 2:11–12 NASB).

Notice the fatal flaw in this account. As Moses contemplated going to the aid of his Hebrew brother, the Bible says "he looked this way and that." In other words, he looked to his left and then to his right. But he never looked up.

There is a type of self-confidence and self-esteem that is healthy and good. But there is an excessive self-confidence that is harmful to one's spiritual health. A harmful self-confidence is usually characterized by prayerlessness. We're so busy instituting our plans and following our instincts and so confident it will all work out as we have planned, that we never bother to look up to the Lord in prayer. It's not that we are going against God; it's just that we don't have a sense that we really need to depend on him. We think we can handle things without bothering the Lord.

In John 15:5, Jesus says, "I am the vine, you are the branches; he who abides in Me and I in him, he bears much fruit, for apart from Me you can do nothing" (NASB). The person with excessive self-confidence doesn't really believe that last phrase. He may accept it intellectually, but he doesn't believe it experientially. That's exactly the same mistake Moses made, which no doubt made his failure particularly bitter. He knew that God had placed him in a position of power and authority to secure the release of the children of Israel. There were no other Hebrews in positions of power or influence like his. He was it. Or rather, he used to be it. His golden opportunity and his people's shot at freedom were over.

Moses experienced the original midlife crisis. At age forty, he went

from palace to pasture

from success to failure

from wealth to poverty

from significance to insignificance

from privilege to persecution

from freedom to flight

from a purposeful life to no purpose whatsoever

from a great future to a grim future

May I remind you that all these events happened overnight? You've heard of overnight successes. Moses was an overnight failure. He lost it all in just twenty-four hours. That's what you call major league midlife crisis.

MIDLIFE CRISES

Many men experience some type of transition around the age of forty. Midlife is when men are forced to come to grips with the changes that have occurred in their lives. Consider the changes that Moses faced at the age of forty.

Moses had a change of address. He went from the palace of Pharaoh to the pastures of Midian. That's like going from the White House to running a gas station in the middle of the Mojave Desert. There was no Hilton Hotel in Midian. It seemed godforsaken territory.

Moses had a change of vocation. Once a leader of men, now he was the leader of sheep. Imagine the psychological and emotional trauma that Moses experienced with such a dramatic shift in his life. This guy could lead a nation. He wasn't cut out to lead sheep. But there he was in the middle of the desert, playing den mother to a flock of woollies.

Most men derive their sense of self-worth from what they do. All of a sudden, Moses wasn't doing anything, except trying to find enough grass and water to keep those sheep alive. I think he must have experienced a tremendous personal identity crisis during those years, don't you?

Moses had a change of status. We generally gauge cultural success by an elevation in privilege, power, and wealth. Moses had it all and lost it, which makes me think that he must have struggled with depression. Generally speaking, depression stems from some type of loss (unless, of course, it results from a chemical imbalance). Whether a man loses his wife, his job, his sense of identity or self-worth—whatever the loss is—it can bring depression. Even the most talented man is still very human.

Emotional rejection can strike men at any time in life. Moses could understand his rejection by Pharaoh. At least that made some sense. But what didn't make sense was the rejection by his own people! It always hurts when rejection comes from inside our own camp. It might be from a friend, a loyal coworker, a spouse, or some other trusted person. That's why the wounds are so deep. We thought they were on our team, and they rejected us.

After leading Britain to victory over Germany in World War II, Winston Churchill had earned his place in history. By the power of his will and personality, Churchill had "transformed cowards into brave men," in the words of one historian, and the British had defeated the Nazi war machine. Then, on July 25, 1945, not quite three months after Germany's defeat, the British people showed their thanks to this great man by voting him out of office. Churchill was rejected by the very people he had helped to save! He had pulled them together as a nation, and then with victory in hand, they turned on him. When his wife told him that defeat may in fact be a blessing in disguise, Churchill responded, "If it is, then it is very effectively disguised."

That's how Moses felt. He could see no blessing in his circumstances. He could see nothing positive about his new position in life. And from a human perspective, he was right. Moses was wounded; Churchill was wounded; and perhaps there are wounded men in your local congregation. As ministers to men, we must draw close to men in crisis and assure them that the God who oversees and controls the events of history is overseeing their lives as well. And he knows exactly what he is doing. A man may have lost control of his circumstances, but God has not. If we help our wounded men to remain teachable, God will make sure that they finish strong.

A MASTER'S DEGREE IN CHARACTER ACQUISITION

God was far from finished with Moses. Although Moses felt that God had removed his hand from him, nothing was further from the truth. Instead, God was enrolling Moses for a master's degree in character development.

Unemployment 101

Moses was a scholar, a statesman, and a soldier. The kind of guy who isn't looking in the classifieds for a job. With such credentials, jobs usually come looking for you. When you have that kind of track record, it seems that every other call is from a headhunter, looking to see if you would be interested in a more lucrative position.

Moses had always been a success. Now he was out of a job. It's hard for a guy like that to be unemployed. But that's exactly what he was. It probably took a week or two for the reality to set in, but eventually it did. This was no lateral move; it was a permanent setback.

It's easy for us to read this stuff in the Bible and kind of blow right by it. But we can't afford to do that if we want to minister to men who have failed. Guys who lose their jobs are stunned, hurt, wounded, embarrassed, and humiliated. Unemployment 101 is a tough course to take. It inevitably attacks a man's sense of self-worth. I certainly struggled with those feelings when I found myself unexpectedly enrolled in this course.

For nearly a year, between my first and second pastorates, I was out of ministry. During that time, I interviewed with seven different churches, and every one turned me down. I couldn't believe it! Most churches, it seems, don't want to hire a "former pastor." They want to hire a current pastor.

I felt like a failure. I was really hurting. That's what happens to most guys who take Unemployment 101, though not everyone is honest enough to admit it. For me, it was a time of suffering. If you have men in your congregation who are enrolled in Unemployment 101, they may be suffering as well.

Here's the good news about Unemployment 101. The suffering caused by this challenging course qualifies men for ministry. Every man who knows Jesus Christ is in the ministry. And it is suffering that equips us for the unique task God has set aside specifically for us. He has not shelved us. He is simply retooling. And we are the tools.

Remedial Waiting

Moses was in a tremendous hurry to accomplish his timetable. After all, he was nearly forty! If he was going to achieve his appointed purpose, then he needed to get with the program. Peter Marshall once observed that "we are in such a hurry that we hate to miss one panel of a revolving door." I've got some bad news for you. You may be in a hurry, but God is not. He rarely uses FedEx to build character into our lives. He doesn't e-mail or fax it to us. Godly character takes time to build. Lots of time.

Can you believe that God took forty years to build character into Moses? Most men want character in forty minutes, and even that is pushing it. That's why Remedial Waiting is such a difficult course. But it is absolutely necessary for the character remodeling that God is undertaking in our lives. Are the men in your congregation at a place in their lives where they are tired of waiting? They may be waiting for a promotion, waiting to conceive a child, waiting for their business to turn around, waiting for employment, waiting for their house to sell, waiting for their child to finish cancer treatments, waiting for that blanket of depression to finally lift.

If we're going to minister effectively to men, we must make the commitment to stay the course with our men while God is working on their character. We cannot afford to become impatient and say, "That guy's been out of work forever! I wonder if he even wants to find a job?" or, "That guy's never going to change. He's always so negative!"

Instead, we must persist with words of encouragement and actions that communicate support. Men need to know that they are right on schedule. Maybe not on their own schedules, but on God's schedule. He knows precisely what he is doing in our lives. Every trial has a beginning, middle, and end. We cannot determine where we are in our trials, but we can covenant with one another to persevere together.

Intermediate Loneliness

Sometimes, God calls us to take a course in Intermediate Loneliness. Loneliness is never a pleasant experience, but isolation is often an opportunity to get to know God better. God had to get Moses off by himself so that he could have his undivided attention.

Loneliness is tough. It's tougher on us than most of us realize. Research has demonstrated that prolonged loneliness can even effect us physically. At Ohio State University College of Medicine, scientists found that patients who scored above average in loneliness had significantly poorer functioning of their immune system. In Sweden, a ten-year study of 150 middle-aged men found that social isolation was one of the best predictors of mortality. A report published in the journal *Science* determined that social isolation is as significant to mortality rates as smoking, high blood pressure, high cholesterol, obesity, and lack of physical exercise. In fact, when age is adjusted for, social isolation is as great or greater a mortality risk than smoking.

In our society, loneliness usually results from social isolation, which can be highly destructive for men. In our men's ministries, we must create opportunities for men to connect in genuine friendship, support, and encouragement. As leaders, we must draw men into interaction with one another and build a network of supporting relationships. When the bottom falls out of a man's life, he will know where he can turn for support.

THE BOTTOM LINE

Moses must have felt like an absolute failure. He had lost his career, his status, his reputation, his family, his friends, and his future. If that had happened to you, wouldn't you feel like a failure? Of course you would. Any human being would feel that way.

That's why many men in your church are struggling with failure right now. If they have experienced a setback in their lives, they struggle with failure nearly every waking moment. It could be a career setback, a relational setback, or some other major loss in life. They are in the desert just as Moses was in the desert. They may not be wandering around on sand dunes looking for an iced tea, but they're in a spiritual desert. They feel like failures, but they're not. God has simply pulled them aside to draw them closer to himself and build their character.

I like Miles Stanford's insight here: "Many believers are simply frantic over the fact of failure in their lives, and they will go to all lengths in trying to hide it, ignore it, or rationalize about it. And all the time they are resisting the main instrument in the Father's hand for conforming us to the image of His Son!"

Henry Ward Beecher wrote, "It is defeat that turns bone to flint, and gristle to muscle, and makes people invincible, and forms those heroic natures that are now in ascendancy in the world. Do not, then, be afraid of defeat. You are never so near to victory as when defeated in a good cause."

Everyone fails. But the true failure is the one who doesn't learn from his setbacks. That's why a teachable spirit is so important. When men are in the midst of a desert, the fastest way out of that desert is to ask God to let them learn everything he has for them in that experience. Encourage men who are undergoing testing to stay open and teachable. God isn't trying to ruin us; he is rebuilding us so that we can be used strategically. And the people God loves to use most are those who have learned to depend completely on him. For many of us self-sufficient, confident types, that doesn't come easily.

Humility means that someone has a proper self-confidence, a proper self-esteem, and a proper kind of godly courage. That kind of character only comes from being in the furnace of affliction and hardship. No wonder it was said that "Moses was very humble, more than any man who was on the face of the earth" (Num. 12:3 NASB).

If you're working with men who feel like failures, then you are in good company. As John Gardner pointed out, "There are not very many undefeated people around." Our society is intoxicated with the idea of success. That's why we are so afraid of failure. But as Erwin Lutzer describes it, if you know Jesus Christ, you should know that failure can be the back door of success. God uses our failure to equip us for future success.

When you look behind the scenes at some of the most successful people in all of history, you will find that they were not unacquainted with failure. And it was failure that became the bedrock that enabled them to handle the triumphs that came later. God is big enough and grand enough to take even our defeats and turn them to our ultimate advantage. You see, some defeats are more triumphant than victories. But that's something only God can accomplish.

20

MEN OF ALL COLORS
Unity in Diversity
Haman Cross and Thomas Fritz

My (Haman Cross) family experienced biblical unity on the most horrifying night of my life, when my oldest son was involved in a car accident and had to be flown by helicopter to Grady Hospital in Atlanta. On the way to the hospital, my heart ached as I pondered my son's possible fate. All I could do was pray. Then the Lord impressed upon me to call some prayer warriors to intercede on my son's behalf. My list included friends from various backgrounds, and they came from all over to the hospital. Black, white, and brown. Rich and poor. Old and young. Before the night was over, so many prayer warriors had gathered that they had to move us to a bigger room. The hospital workers weren't used to seeing so many white people in this regional hospital located near the 'hood. They asked questions because they saw something different: a diverse group of Christians praying for the healing of a black teenager. They saw Jesus that night in a picture of unity within the body of Christ. And as the pray-ers were kneeling, God was healing.

Unfortunately, the body of Christ doesn't always reflect Jesus so clearly. In fact, my first significant racial conflict was in the church. Now, I had seen a "for whites only" sign in front of a restaurant north of Hattiesburg, Mississippi, when I was en route for army jungle training there. And I had been subjected to some "selective assignments," digging dirty waste holes while the other soldiers were given more desirable tasks. And I'd been almost run down near the army base, by a car full of white guys calling me a derogatory name for Negro. But until I had my eyes opened at a church in Clarksville, Tennessee, I did not believe that Christians who claimed to be saved, sanctified, and filled with the Holy Spirit would be racists. Yes, I was quite naive.

After months of visiting this church (I was the only black person in the congregation), I was convicted by the Lord that I had not yet been baptized. I had been a Christian since age six but had never joined a church. When I shared with the pastor my commitment and desire to be baptized, he somehow managed to delay dealing with the subject. Week after week, he would postpone giving me a date for baptism.

Finally, after many weeks, a young man who led our discipleship team confronted the pastor in my presence. I listened with tears streaming down my face as he shared the reasons for his hesitation. He had no problems personally with my baptism, he said, but he was concerned about the reaction of the board of deacons and the congregation. I was shocked and speechless.

Please understand that this was the best church I have ever attended. The pastor was top notch when it came to vision and Bible teaching. In fact, it was under his preaching that I committed my life in full surrender to Jesus Christ.

Convicted by the Spirit of God, the pastor heard his own words and finally agreed to my request. As it happened, the shock that shook my foundation was the shock that shaped my destiny. I just prayed and gave it to the Lord. I learned how to forgive. I learned to trust God. I had faith in God, but I still practiced holding my breath, just in case they accidentally held me under the water too long. When I came up out of the water, I heard loud harmonies of "amen."

THE CHURCH IN DENIAL

Some Christians want to ignore or downplay matters related to race or ethnic relationships. They wish that the issue would simply go away. When racial reconciliation is mentioned, you can see the frowns, nervousness, and gradual glazing over of their eyes. You hear various remarks and excuses, such as: "Why can't blacks get along with us?" "They seem to be happy doing things among themselves." "God looks at our hearts, not the color of our skin." "I don't see color, I'm color blind." They either don't see the problem or don't want to see it. But all these comments and attitudes, in essence, are attempts to obscure the fact that we have a problem among Christians when it comes to racial reconciliation.

Other Christians will admit that there is a problem, but they have given up trying to solve it. I've heard some white friends of mine complain that they have to start all over again every time they meet new African Americans. "Why do I have to explain and convince them that I love them or that I am not like other, ignorant white people?" they lament. "Why do I have to confess and repent over and over until I'm red in the face? It's not fair, and I'm tired of it." Do you feel that you have to prove yourself to African Americans time and time again? If so, press on! If you give up, you'll miss an opportunity to overcome the greatest barrier to the fulfillment of the Great Commission.

THE BIG SQUEEZE

I have attended five major Promise Keepers events, where I have heard various speakers give emotional, passionate, and inspiring messages on the topic of racial reconciliation. After each appeal for reconciliation, the predominantly white audience is challenged to meet and hug an ethnic man in the stadium. Picture for a moment a ballpark filled with 50,000 white men and 5,000 African Americans, Hispanics, and Native Americans. Instantly, the majority of men in the stadium start looking for a person of color to give a big, strong, manly hug. I didn't mind a few hugs, but fifty is too many. Can you imagine trying to explain to your wife that a bunch of white Christians squeezed you to death after the reconciliation message? I quickly learned my lesson. I now move toward the back during these messages to get a head start in running away from these reconciliation huggers. Seriously, the messages are inspiring, but the follow-up is tiring. And what happens after the rally ends? Expectations are high, but the actual experience of change falls woefully short.

I recall hearing a speaker some years ago give an illustration of how hard he and his staff had worked to put on an event in an auditorium. Everything was ready: the lighting, the sound, the seating, and the multimedia presentation. The speakers were prepared, and the music was ready to fill the air. But something was missing. It seems that a small detail had been overlooked. In all their preparations, they had forgotten to advertise the seminar. When the curtain went up, the auditorium was empty. The very ones they wanted to reach were absent. Why? They had failed to make contact.

Racial reconciliation takes more than good intentions and a few dozen hugs. It demands our undivided attention to make contact with each other. When we do this, we will see beyond the superficial and begin to experience the supernatural. Otherwise, this notion of men coming together in one accord is incomplete.

We need to understand why our past ways of dealing with racial unity haven't done the job. To begin with, we are only skin deep in our views. This is evident when we use terms like "color blind." When I hear someone say, "I don't see color, only another Christian," I want to reply, "If you don't see color, why are you talking about it?"

I am black by design. God knew what he was doing when he created me. Most seminaries, pastors, and teachers don't deal with this subject, but God made us all the way we are. If you don't see color, you don't see me. How can you claim to be color blind yet continue to make decisions out of partiality? Let's face it, we're all guilty, and that's a sin.

COLOR OR CULTURE?

Historically, Christian leaders have shirked their responsibility for dealing with the problems of racism, partiality, and diversity. Reaching the goal of unity has been measured by how successful we are in integration. The tendency among white evangelical Christians is to encourage ethnic minorities either to melt into the majority—the place of superiority—or return to their own communities and churches—the place of inferiority.

We can easily have the false idea that all we need to do is to get some multicolor faces in our men's group or congregation. But the issue is deeper than faces. We have to understand culture and history. Yes, we should be color blind when it comes to justice, but to develop good relationships, we need to become culturally sensitive.

We need to have a better understanding of the term "racial reconciliation." Do you know that a good number of black Christians struggle with this popular "Christian" politically correct term? The idea seems to be to foster harmonious relationships between ethnic men and white men. But to what end? I prefer the term racial partnership.

As Clarence Shuler says in his book *Winning the Race to Unity*, "The strength of the term racial partnership is that, first of all, it implies that equal parties are involved. Secondly, partnership implies a working together for a desired goal or result. Successful partners know the desired goal is worth some personal sacrifices. It is working through differences that build strong, close relationships. None of us, even as Christians, has it all together, but together in Christ, we have it all." Let's do together what we cannot do without one another. Together we must confront racism and injustice with the intensity that we deal with abortion or other favorite evangelical issues.

MELTING POT OR SAVORY STEW?

Next, we need to understand the concept of the melting pot. Most nonethnic Christians in this country want African Americans to become like them. The expectation is that Blacks, Hispanics, and Asians will accept and assimilate the values and norms of the majority culture. African Americans don't want to be less black and more white. They don't want to be forced to accept the majority culture in order to be accepted.

In a melting pot, all of the added ingredients blend into the rest of the pot. Excuse the expression, but we are going to pot with this misconception. A stew pot, or perhaps a tossed salad, would be a better picture of ethnic diversity.

"Part of the thrust of American education has been to forget one's past, and become part of the new America," we read in *A World of Difference*. "There continues to be a great pressure or heat to melt us into a uniform culture in America.... Those in power have purposefully attempted to keep the country from fragmenting

The Changing Face of America

The presumption that the "typical" U.S. citizen is someone who traces his or her descent in a direct line to Europe will [soon] be a part of the past.

By 2020, a date no further into the future than John F. Kennedy's election is in the past, the number of U.S. residents who are Hispanic or non-white will have more than doubled, to nearly 115 million, while the white population will not be increasing at all. By 2056, when someone born [in 1990] will be sixty-six years old, the "average" U.S. resident, as defined by Census statistics, will trace his or her descent to Africa, Asia, the Hispanic world, the Pacific Islands, Arabia—almost anywhere but white Europe.

—*Time*, April 9, 1990

into its many component parts. They say if the country is to survive it has to have some basis for unity. Therefore, the approach from the last millennium has been to do this by being a melting pot. . . . The melting pot is real . . . [but] it is not an even mixture of all people and ideas. It is unbalanced and biased. Those who want to melt have to accept a culture that is dominated by certain [subcultures]. The further down the scale you are, the harder it is and the longer it will take you to melt."

If you add an ingredient that measures 5 percent into a pot of 95 percent, when the new component melts, it will become what's in the pot. When you add a distinct ethnic culture into a dominant culture, the smaller group risks losing its identity and being swallowed up by the dominant culture. How do you think it feels to be part of a meltdown?

In a stew pot, on the other hand, each component—however small—contributes to the flavor of the stew while maintaining its unique distinction. Not everyone is a carrot or an onion, but you can taste both and it's good. If everything were pureed together, the pot would be bland and tasteless. Jesus did not intend for the dominant culture to win. That is not what he had in mind when he spoke of being "perfected in unity" in John 17:23 (NASB).

The church in North America has always been dominated by European culture. But is the European tradition the only true way? The preaching, music, and worship in my church may not sound like yours, but it is biblical. You might ask why black choirs sing the same phrase over a thousand times: "What a mighty God we serve." After two or three repetitions, maybe you're ready to say, "Okay, we got that, but what we really need are more great hymns of the faith, eight stanzas of sound, orderly, doctrinal truths."

Is there not room for both in the contemporary church?

Some Christians would say, "It's fine for you the way you worship and preach." But don't just pass judgment and move on down the road. Can you appreciate and celebrate who I am and where I come from? Do you understand that I have something to bring to the table? Diverse ethnic cultures bring spice to the dominant culture. Contemporary gospel music, for example, often considers the emotions and feelings. The Christian life is not all brains and thinking. There is a time for thinking and a time for expressing our emotions. May we do both in such a way that they may know we are one.

At the same time, let us celebrate our differences. We are all fearfully and wonderfully made. We all tend to react to that which is different. We all have a tendency to work out our own sense of favoritism and partiality.

> We affirm and strive toward the biblical mandate of unity. Unity requires an intentional engagement in reconciling the body of Christ. The development of ministry does not necessitate integration, as it is commonly understood, for without effective ministry strategies to the ethnic populations of this nation, there will be no reconciliation. It is impossible to reconcile with someone who is not present.

UNITY IN DIVERSITY

Diversity is good. The church is a heterogeneous body, a pluralistic body made of varying races and ethnic groups, as millions are added to the body seeking the abundant life promised. Already, one in every four Americans is a person of color. Clearly, with such increased diversity, faith-based institutions need to enlarge their focus from being exclusive to being inclusive of the larger sociocultural context. If the body of Christ is to grow, it must take into account its varied cultural and kinship networks; its socialization experiences and communication styles; its culturally defined attitudes and behaviors, typical male-female interactive patterns, and the role of the family.

It's not so bad that ethnic groups meet in different churches where they are in an environment to receive the Word of God. The issue is not that we must include other races and cultures in the ministry of the church. The issue is the church's outreach across ethnic and social lines. And we can add to that our ability to have ongoing relationships with different ethnic and socially diverse congregations.

Unity arises out of polarity. Bearing the image of God includes the color of our skin as well as the content of our hearts. Race is a nice thing to have. The consummate nature of the Godhead is the expression of fullness of being. We can celebrate our diversity and share it with others without compromising our uniqueness in the body of Christ. There is unity in diversity as long as there is no partiality. The world has yet to see the way unity among believers can work.

BUSTING DOWN THE WALLS

Several years ago, my (Thomas Fritz) collaborator on this chapter, pastor Haman Cross, started a church in Detroit with the goal that it would be a black, middle-class congregation with a vision to reach the poor and the lost. The mission statement was "the up and outers reaching the down and outers." When the church was five years old, some white families began to visit. They came of their own accord, without any particular invitation or strategy by the church. One morning, a white family joined this black, middle-class church. Then another family joined. Pastor Cross was blown away as more whites continued to join, week after week. Through this process, God forced him to tear down his prejudice and the partiality in his heart. Then, gradually, God began to re-create and clarify his vision for the church. He saw it as an opportunity to visualize what a church committed to reconciliation could look like.

The picture of completeness is found in John 17:20–24: "My prayer is not for them alone. I pray also for those who will believe in me through their message, that all of them may be one, Father, just as you are in me and I am in you. May they also be in us so that the world may believe that you have sent me. I have given them the glory that you gave me, that they may be one as we are one: I in them and you in me. May they be brought to complete unity to let the world know that you sent me and have loved them even as you have loved me. Father, I want those you have given me to be with me where I am, and to see my glory, the glory you have given me because you loved me before the creation of the world."

I recently had some plumbing problems at my house when a section of water pipe broke. To fix the pipes, the plumber had to reach them. The only problem was, the pipes were behind the walls. And the walls had to be broken in order to repair the damage. In like manner, God wants us to surrender with humility so he can break down our inner walls of pride and stubbornness.

Haman Cross teaches the concept of busting down walls or barriers that divide the collective body of Christ. The walls are built with bricks made of hate; partiality; attitude of superiority; fear; play-it-safe, middle-of-the-road complacency; ignorance; social pressure; political maneuvering; isolation; indifference; apathy; and the list goes on and on.

In his book *Cross Colors*, Haman says that we must tear down the wall of self-rejection. Whether you were born white or black, it is no mistake. It is God's design. God always knows exactly what he is doing. The diversity he introduced into the human race was an intentional and loving act. It was mankind who turned race into an issue rife with division and contention. Anytime we tease, jest, or ridicule a person about an unchangeable feature, we are guilty of mocking the Creator. We must find security in who God has created us to be. Accept God's design. The unchangeable characteristics of an individual include parentage, racial background, national heritage, time in history, gender, birth order, brothers and sisters, physical features, mental abilities, age, and death. God designed them all.

We must bust down the walls of thinking that integration and assimilation (the melting pot) is the avenue to cross-cultural and racial partnerships. Charles Gilmer, director of Impact in Campus Crusade for Christ says, "Integration and assimilation actually has the effect of selectively targeting ethnics who are more fully engaged in the mainstream of American culture. Our mandate is to take the gospel to those ethnic Americans who are not currently being reached, discipled, and mobilized. Therefore, we must take the ministry into their context, not ask them to leave that context in order to be developed in ministry."

Once the walls are down, we must become bridge builders to help our brothers cross over into unfamiliar territories to meet new brothers. Bridges are a means by which we move into different cultural, ethnic, and social environments. Building a bridge requires strength and commitment, because bridges are made to be walked on. And not everyone who crosses your bridge will have an attitude of understanding. Some will make you feel that you must prove yourself each time you meet a person of a different ethnic group. Are you willing to be hurt? Are you willing to be misunderstood? What about having to think differently? Don't wait to cross that bridge when you come to it, start now.

I am so thankful that Jesus bridged the separation of sin with his death on the cross. Bridges are expensive. Jesus paid the price with his life, and he calls us to present our lives to God as living sacrifices.

"Therefore I urge you, brethren, by the mercies of God, to present your bodies a living and holy sacrifice, acceptable to God, which is your spiritual service of worship. And do not be conformed to this world, but be transformed by the renewing of your mind, that you may prove what the will of God is, that which is good and acceptable and perfect" (Rom. 12:1–2 NASB).

A GREAT MULTITUDE FROM EVERY NATION

As Christian men, we have the opportunity to make a difference with a commitment for unity. Not just for cosmetic purposes or decoration, but trusting God to bring together diverse colors to make a declaration of the gospel to the lost world. We can help bring credibility to the gospel. Consider taking these steps.

- Share the issues in this chapter with your men's group.
- Pray for true unity.
- Seek to make some connections with men from other cultures.
- Develop relationships with men who are different from yourself.
- Seek reconciliation among believers.
- Since true reconciliation begins with confession and repentance, encourage your men to consider their attitudes and perspectives toward others.

Let's remember that unity in diversity will be with us in heaven, so let's start now to bring it to pass on earth.

"After these things I looked, and behold, a great multitude which no one could count, from every nation and all tribes and peoples and tongues, standing before the throne and before the Lamb, clothed in white robes, and palm branches were in their hands; and they cry out with a loud voice, saying, 'Salvation to our God who sits on the throne, and to the Lamb'"(Rev. 7:9–10 NASB).

21

FROM SUCCESS TO SIGNIFICANCE

Phil Downer with Chip MacGregor

What is the most important thing that has ever happened in your life? Was it completing your education? Deciding on a career? The birth of your first child? For me, it was realizing that God was recruiting me to play a part in his eternal plan. He has called me to impact the world, even after I'm no longer here. He wants me to help him fill up his eternal kingdom.

It's true—God has taken a risk and called me to work with him. He wants me to take people who are far away from him and bring them near. He wants me to take people who are near and help bring them to maturity in Christ. The Lord has called me to mentor and disciple men so they will reproduce themselves in the lives of others. God is calling me to join ranks with men like the apostle Paul, by faithfully helping other people grow up in Jesus Christ. Rather than merely achieve success at some career while I'm on this earth, the Lord wants me to take a significant role in shaping the lives of others. That's the job to which he has called all Christians—including you.

Paul understood this responsibility. When writing to his young protégé, Timothy, he said, "You therefore, my son, be strong in the grace that is in Christ Jesus. The things which you have heard from me in the presence of many witnesses, entrust these to faithful men who will be able to teach others also" (2 Tim. 2:1–2 NASB). In other words, Paul understood that his role was to pass on God's message to trustworthy people, who in turn would pass it along to others. Paul became a spiritual father to Timothy, and as Timothy passed on the message, Paul became a spiritual grandfather and great-grandfather. Four generations are represented in that verse: Paul, who trained Timothy, who trained faithful men, who in turn trained others.

Through the centuries, God passed on his message of salvation through ordinary people, and one day someone told you. Most of us didn't come to know God by reading a tract but through a relationship with a friend or family member who loved us enough to tell us the truth. They became our spiritual parents, part of a chain that leads back two thousand years, to Jesus Christ and his twelve disciples. If we are faithful, that chain will lead into the future, adding more new links than we can even imagine.

The people who have made up that chain have been ordinary men and women, but they've been given a supernatural power that has allowed them to conquer kingdoms, influence lives, and alter the course of history. And they have done it all one by one, spreading the love of God and taking his message and the new life it promises to every part of the world. Each person who loves Jesus Christ brings a new dynamic to the cause and a new circle of people who can be changed by his love. Every relationship is unique and carries special opportunities, which is why friendships are so crucial to God's agenda.

Early in my career, I was a lawyer, focused on my own success and living to please myself. Then I met the Lord. A woman named Liane Day took the initial steps that would eventually lead this reprobate lawyer to a saving knowledge of Jesus Christ. Liane was a new Christian, still reeling from the blow of her husband's leaving and an unwanted divorce, which had catapulted her into the work force without a college education in order to provide for her two children. However, Liane had a friend who loved her through the turmoil, led her to Jesus, and began discipling her. One day, Liane found herself at a baby shower, sitting on a couch next to my wife, Susy. She didn't know that Susy was a successful lawyer, or that she was about to divorce me. She simply sensed that this woman next to her was struggling in some way, so Liane reached out and shared her faith in Christ with my wife.

Those two women began working through a popular one-on-one discipleship series called Operation Timothy, a Bible study and sharing time produced by the Christian Business Men's Committee (CBMC). It was Liane's great sense of God's power and unmatched peace that caused Susy to be attracted to her the first time they met. Through that study and their growing friendship, my wife realized that a relationship with Jesus Christ was possible and that it was probably the missing ingredient in facing her biggest problem—living with a tyrannical husband. It was Liane who suggested to Susy that they figure out a way for me to attend a CBMC outreach luncheon. There, a builder from Birmingham, Michigan, named Paul Johnson shared the gospel with me. That led to my coming to Christ and getting acquainted with Dr. Jim Lyon.

My life was never the same after meeting Jim. He went over God's assurance of my salvation, answered my questions, and helped me cement the decision to give my heart to Jesus Christ. But our relationship didn't end there; it was just the beginning. For the next three years, Jim met with me each week. I became his Timothy as he shared his life with me and helped me mature in my faith. He didn't merely offer information or assume that going through a workbook would provide me with adequate training. He opened up his life, sharing his joys and struggles, so I could observe how a godly man lived. Mine was supposed to be a new life in Christ, and Dr. Jim made sure that I got a chance to see how that new life was active in another man's life.

Jim wasn't perfect, of course. But without his example, I would have had no idea how the Christian life was different from my pagan lifestyle. Jim wasn't just having a Bible study with me; he was passing on his faith and his life. He was giving me spiritual training so I could become a soldier in the army of God, fully equipped for spiritual battle. And the whole process started because one divorced young mother decided to start talking with the troubled woman sitting next to her on the couch at a baby shower.

THE CHRISTIAN SOLDIER

I believe every Christian is called to be a soldier for Christ on the front lines; if he stays in the rear, he will be distracted, discouraged, and even defeated. To illustrate this, I use the "soldier and doughnut" principle: a marine is trained to be a soldier, not to sit around eating doughnuts. If he is assigned for long periods of time in the rear, he gets into fights, drinks too much, contracts venereal disease, and gets busted. This happens because marines are trained to stay in the battle. That's where their equipment works best, where their training is fulfilled, and where their lives are most useful.

The same is true of the Christian soldier. Our lives are best lived in the battle of winning and discipling businessmen—if that's our calling—or ministering to children, the aged, the infirm, or the imprisoned, if God directs that way. A marine away from the battlefield must constantly be reminded to keep his weapon clean, be instructed on the chain of command, and be counseled on the importance of teamwork and countless other aspects of soldiering. However, one flash of enemy fire calls the marine to war. All other problems are solved in a millisecond when he inhales the scent of battle.

A Christian man may argue with his wife on the way out the door to work, but she suddenly becomes a great blessing when he sits across the table from someone whose wife has just filed for divorce. I had an early morning argument with Susy by telephone just before I met with a friend whose wife had just moved in with his best friend. Somehow, the pettiness of my bickering instantly melted away, and I realized the gift God had given me in a woman who is faithful. By the same token, I have loved it over the years when Susy would come home after spending time with a woman she was discipling and comment, "Next to most women, I simply don't have a problem in the world." If we Christians would stop bickering over the color of the pew pads, we could get out into the battle and see what life is really all about. It's time we stop focusing our lives on success and begin to focus on significance.

Our modern culture is enamored with the concept of success, though most businessmen can't really define it. We all know men who are "successful," and we generally associate this with salary and perks, but if you ask one hundred men to define the word, chances are you'll get one hundred different definitions. To one guy, success means moving up the corporate ladder. To another, success is measured in the numbers of units sold. Webster's Dictionary defines success as "attaining a desired end," and the vagueness of that definition proves my point. We don't know exactly what success is, but we know how it feels. That's the reason I like this definition: success is the feeling you get when you reach your goals.

Reflect on that definition for a moment. You might earn a million dollars a year, but if your goal is two million, you don't feel successful. You might be the best salesman in your company's history, but if your goal is to move into management and you aren't offered the job, you don't feel successful. Our culture is in love with success. Our world system feeds on it. The accumulation of wealth and position and the trappings of "success" are of the greatest value to our fallen world. As Christians, the thing to remember is that we don't share the values of the world. Our values have been changed by the power of God.

Success is based on a feeling, and feelings come and go. That's why I can feel like a million bucks when I buy a new car, but a few months later, I find that my new car no longer gives me the same feeling of success and fulfillment. So I need to buy something else to prop up my fragile feelings of success. And not only are the feelings fragile, they are fleeting. During the NFL playoffs one year, one of the television announcers referred to a player, who was at the pinnacle of his profession and playing on one of the best teams in the league, by saying, "He stinks." That announcer didn't mention that the man was playing below his ability or that he was having a difficult day. He simply summed him up by telling the world he was a failure. Success is not only a feeling; it's a short-lived feeling.

One day I was having breakfast with a famous NASCAR racer who had a half dozen airplanes, hundreds of acres of land, a beautiful wife, cute children, and tons of money coming in every month from endorsements. But he had not won a race in ten months. He told me, "Phil, I'm only as good as my last race." That's the world's perspective on success. You've got to achieve, and you've got to keep achieving, or you're a loser.

So when you look across your driveway at the family next door that appears so "together" or you gaze across the conference table at the businessman who seemingly has the world by the tail, remember the message they often hear and will continue to

When Paul wrote from his jail cell in Rome to encourage the Christians at Philippi, he said, "Even if I am being poured out as a drink offering upon the sacrifice and service of your faith, I rejoice and share my joy with you all" (Phil. 2:17 NASB). Here, Paul refers to a Jewish sacrifice, equating his life with the drink offering that was poured out on the altar of God. When the cup was turned upside down, all the contents spilled out. There was nothing held back; it all belonged to the Lord.

That's what Paul's life was like. He was completely sold out to serving God. He gave everything to serve God by discipling men and women into maturity. Paul wasn't worried about meeting the world's standard of success. He was committed to making his life significant. He invested in the lives of people over time, and his investment changed our world forever.

Dan Sylvester, who operates a manufacturing company in the Midwest, built a multimillion-dollar enterprise from a basement project he started as a teenager. But along with becoming a manufacturer of auto parts, Sylvester devoted a few hours each week to discipling men in his growing company. He started with a delivery boy, who went on to become a college graduate and is now pastoring a church. His other Timothys have included his top two salesmen and a man who later became his director of operations. Other business leaders often ask Dan where he got such a fine Christian staff, and his response is always, "I invested in God's invention—people—and along the way, I was investing in my business." Sylvester won't admit to how many men he has impacted, but his friends say it must be thousands when you consider the third and fourth generations of faithfulness passed on from man to man over the years. He's never been much of a traveler, and he shies away from big religious events, but Dan Sylvester has truly impacted the world by influencing many people for Christ.

Brother, you are the pivotal factor in someone's eternal destiny. God can use you to bring others to him and to help them grow into maturity. Your life-to-life example, sharing your life with that of a spiritual brother, is imperative if you are going to help others grow up in Jesus Christ. Your story, your struggles, and the simple act of accompanying another on his spiritual journey will make all the difference in the world. If you demonstrate a willingness to give something of yourself so others can have a part in the riches of God's kingdom, you can change your world for the cause of Christ. As you get involved in the adventure of helping others discover God's love and grow into maturity, you'll find power you never thought possible. You will also be drawn closer to God and will experience the wonderful adventure that comes from serving him.

FROM SUCCESS TO SIGNIFICANCE

If you want to become a man of significance, consider the meaning of your life. If you want to squander your life on temporal things, you can join the hordes who are looking for meaning through success. But if you want to spend your life on eternal things, you can decide to be different by investing in another man. Remember, God doesn't judge us at the end of life but at the end of time. If you look at the book of Revelation, you'll see that men are not judged for their lives at the moment of death. Instead, the Lord waits until the very end of time, when this world is destroyed and all mankind is facing eternity. Why? Because a man is judged not simply by what he does but by whom he influences.

Adolf Hitler hasn't been fully judged yet, because his evil practices are still influencing people today. His ideas are still in print, still poisoning the minds of men. God is waiting until the end of this world to judge Hitler, for it is only then that the full extent of his life's meaning will be evident. By the same token, the ministry of the apostle John is still impacting the lives of men around the world. His words, forceful yet full of love, are still influencing lives. John will be judged at the end of time for the impact his life has had on history. So will you. You can begin right now to leave a legacy. You can choose to lead a life of significance, pour yourself into the life of another, and become a "spiritual grandfather."

Invest in the life of a new Christian. Forget about making a big splash through success. Commit to significance. Become a spiritual parent by discipling someone into maturity, and you will experience the joy of being a part of God's plan to change the world.

For more information on discipleship, contact us at PhilDowner@DNA ministries.org.

PART FIVE

CREATING
THE STRUCTURE

22

TRAINING MEN FOR SIGNIFICANCE

| *Chuck Brewster* |

H ave you ever heard of Clint Hill? Nick Zarvos? Larry Buendorf? Bob Aamon?
Tim McCarthy? All of these men were United States Secret Service agents
who reacted according to their training and were considered heroes as a result.

In 1963, Clint Hill jumped onto a speeding limousine in Dallas after President
Kennedy was shot and kept Jacqueline Kennedy from falling out the rear of the vehicle. Immediately after the shots were fired, the president's car accelerated sharply, just
as Mrs. Kennedy was reaching for her husband. She would have toppled out of the
vehicle if Agent Hill had not caught her.

In 1972, Nick Zarvos was the detail supervisor for the Secret Service team
assigned to protect Alabama governor George Wallace during a presidential campaign appearance in Laurel, Maryland. Agent Zarvos took a bullet to the throat when
gunman Arthur Bremmer shot Governor Wallace.

In 1976, Agent Larry Buendorf seized the gun from Squeaky Fromme when she
attempted to shoot President Gerald Ford in Sacramento, California. Buendorf grabbed
the automatic pistol in such a way that it couldn't fire, even though Fromme was squeezing the trigger with all her strength. At the time, President Ford was eight feet away.

Also in 1976, Bob Aamon was on duty when Sarah Jane Moore shot at
President Ford in San Francisco. Agent Aamon helped to subdue Moore and carried

her across the street to the Saint Francis Hotel. President Ford, unharmed, was whisked away in his armored car to the airport.

Agent Tim McCarthy was shot in the stomach on March 30, 1981, during John Hinckley's assassination attempt on President Reagan at the Hilton Hotel in Washington, D.C., McCarthy was shot because he reacted in the way that he'd been trained. When he heard the first shot, he "made himself large," shielding the president from further harm. The normal reaction for most people when shots are fired is to duck down, shrink away, and make themselves less of a target, but Secret Service agents are trained to shield and protect—immediately and without thinking.

Each of the men I've named responded normally for a Secret Service agent. If they were heroes, it was because they had been trained to react in a certain way. There was more heroism in their diligent training than in their brief, self-sacrificing moments in the line of fire. If they hadn't been prepared through training, they would have failed to respond at the moment of crisis.

During my twenty-three-year career as a special agent with the United States Secret Service, I spent countless hours on the firing range and in teamwork training and "assault on the principal" exercises. In fact, most of my time in the Secret Service was not spent standing guard over the president, other U.S. government officials, or foreign dignitaries but in training—training for the unexpected.

In preparation for my service to Presidents Jimmy Carter, Ronald Reagan, and Bill Clinton, to Vice Presidents Walter Mondale, George Bush, and Dan Quayle, and to many foreign dignitaries, I invested large amounts of time training to overcome things that might go wrong and to be ready to react properly in any given situation.

Many people believe that Secret Service agents are heroes because they think that only a hero would be willing to take a bullet for another person. But a Secret Service agent doesn't rationalize his responsibility or think about the consequences when shots are fired. He doesn't have time to think about his family or debate the relative merits of the person he's assigned to protect. Instead, he trains and trains and trains so that when trouble comes suddenly, he will react according to his training, which is to say, contrary to human nature. His training prepares him to sacrifice himself for another.

TRAINING FOR DISCIPLESHIP

Today, after my retirement from the Secret Service, as I travel and speak across the country, I share examples from my experience to emphasize the importance of training in our daily lives as disciples of the Lord. Jesus trained for thirty years to prepare for three years of ministry. He knew that eventually he would be called upon to be obedient unto death, even death on a cross. Jesus trained to make himself large and to sacrifice himself on our behalf—even though we didn't deserve it. He was obedient to the Father, because the Father was in him. What was inside of our Lord displayed itself in his behavior. Because Jesus had the Father, the Holy Spirit, and the Word of God within him, he reacted the way the Father wanted him to react, even though he was aware that he would soon be crucified.

If we desire to be like Christ, the Father must be within us and we must be trained to react the way God wants us to. We must be

full of the Holy Spirit.

available to teach and be taught.

willing to work for his goals, not our own.

obedient unto death.

willing to stretch beyond our own strength so that God can be our strength.

living pure lives and making holiness a priority.

We must empty ourselves of the things of this world so God can fill us with the things of his world. This fallen world is full of sin. We must be pure in order to impact others and be a light in the darkness.

How do we accomplish our purpose? God has provided us with a training manual—the living Word of God—so that we can discipline ourselves and condition our behavior. A vital role of our ministry to men, and to the church at large, is to continually train ourselves and our men to be obedient to God's calling in our lives. In the spiritual realm, just as in law enforcement, proper training and discipline are the difference between life and death.

Careful, meaningful study of the Bible gives us discipline and equips us for every situation. Being obedient in everything opens doors in our walk with Jesus. Psalm 119:1–16 shows us how embedding the Word of God in our lives will keep us steadfast in our obedience and our commitment to purity.

How blessed are those whose way is blameless,
Who walk in the law of the Lord.
How blessed are those who observe His testimonies,
Who seek Him with all their heart.
They also do no unrighteousness;
They walk in His ways.
You have ordained Your precepts,
That we should keep them diligently.
Oh that my ways may be established
To keep Your statutes!
Then I shall not be ashamed
When I look upon all Your commandments.
I shall give thanks to You with uprightness of heart,

When I learn Your righteous judgments.
I shall keep Your statutes;
Do not forsake me utterly!
How can a young man keep his way pure?
By keeping it according to Your word.
With all my heart I have sought You;
Do not let me wander from Your commandments.
Your word I have treasured in my heart,
That I may not sin against You.
Blessed are You, O LORD;
Teach me Your statutes.
With my lips I have told of
All the ordinances of Your mouth.
I have rejoiced in the way of Your testimonies,
As much as in all riches.
I will meditate on Your precepts
And regard Your ways.
I shall delight in Your statutes;
I shall not forget Your word.

—Psalm 119:1–16 NASB

The Word of God contains everything a man needs to know to seek God with all of his heart. We need to be obedient when God calls us, regardless of how we perceive the task. When we are obedient, God will use us.

In Acts 9:10–19, God asks Ananias to go to a certain house on Straight Street and lay hands on Saul and pray. Ananias is hesitant and questions God because Saul has a reputation for killing believers. In the natural realm, Ananias is nervous, but with God's urging that Saul is his chosen instrument, Ananias is obedient. This reference shows how one man's obedience to God helped shape the Christian world. In like fashion, our witness and obedience can impact others. All we need to do is be sensitive to God's urging and obey. Ananias was reluctant at first, but he obeyed. The result was Paul the apostle.

PROPER TRAINING IN OBEDIENCE

We must be obedient in all things. The only way to gain obedience is by proper training. Proper training means devoting ourselves to prayer, time in the Word, repentance, and holiness. That is how we truly serve God and walk in his light.

In Matthew 7:24, Jesus tells us that when we hear his words and put them into practice, it is like a wise man who built his house on a rock. Jesus further states that if we hear his words and do not act upon them, we are like the foolish man who built his house on a foundation of sand (v. 26).

When I was growing up, I remember being told that if I wanted to do something right, I would have to practice, because "practice makes perfect." A friend later pointed out that if we practice the wrong things, we'll end up perfectly wrong. He amended the axiom to read "practice makes permanent." Any way you say it, "practice" sounds like the same thing as "training" to me. So if we are to be obedient to God and react the way he wants us to react in times of crisis, we must train ourselves to react according to God's Word.

Luke 2:41–49 records the story of the time when Joseph and Mary began their journey home from the Passover feast in Jerusalem without realizing they had left twelve-year-old Jesus behind. Jesus didn't leave them; they left Jesus. Joseph and Mary searched for him for three days before they found him in the temple.

Today we find ourselves looking everywhere for Jesus. We need to realize that he is still in his Father's house. He never leaves; we're the ones who wander off. We need to discipline ourselves to stay with him in every situation and in every encounter.

Sensing God's presence in our lives is easier at some times than at others. We feel near to God when he miraculously heals someone close to us or blesses us in an extraordinary and visible manner. Also when we are at a low point, we might cry out to God in despair, recognizing his ability to lift us up. But in those day-to-day moments, when we're simply going about our business, it's easy to forget about Jesus, just as Joseph and Mary did. We need to focus on him constantly so he can train us for significance. God is calling men to press in closer to him. We need to obey his call.

We must pray and fill ourselves daily with the Word of God so that we will react according to his Word—not according to the world—in every situation. If Tim McCarthy had taken time to think about or intellectualize his decision before he moved to protect President Reagan, self-preservation might have overshadowed his commitment to duty and endangered the life of the president. Instead, Agent McCarthy reacted according to his training and discipline, and the president's life was spared.

Our training in the Word and the discipline of our minds and bodies prepare us to react in our offices and homes according to godly principles. We need to be filled with the Holy Spirit and covered with the full armor of God so that we can fend off the daily darts of the enemy. We must dwell in the shelter of the Most High. We must be ready to react. Are you ready?

Solid Rocks in Hard Places

I gleaned the following excerpt from a devotional in *Our Daily Bread*.

Has God called you to live as a rock in a hard place?

In the first century, Titus was drafted by the apostle Paul to live in a hard place called Crete. The people on this island were known throughout the region as lazy workers and dishonest merchants. . . . Morally and spiritually, Crete was a hard place to live . . . yet Paul established a church there and asked Titus to organize it and appoint leaders. Titus had to be a rock in a hard place. By his teaching, he was to expose error and proclaim truth; by his way of life he was to be an example of what it means to live for Christ.

If we are going to train the men in our congregations to be "rocks in hard places," we must teach them how to stand on the Rock of Ages, Jesus Christ. Whether it's preparing for the United States Secret Service or for the service of our Lord, training and obedience are the keys to success. If we want the lives of our men to be significant, we must train them to reach our lost and dying world for Christ. And we must model a godly obedience every day of our lives if we want to make a difference.

23

BECOMING IRRESISTIBLE HUSBANDS

| *Ed Cole* |

Divorce. The very word brings terror to my heart, sends shudders of fear down my spine far more than even the word cancer does. I cannot conceive of another man holding my wife in a loving embrace and touching her lips, soft, tender, and sweet, with loving passion. Or to think of someone else putting his hand on the places sacred to our marriage.

It is utterly horrible to imagine another man sitting at the breakfast table with my children, listening to them tell with childish enthusiasm their plans for that day. Missing the looks on their faces, shining with the drowsy delight of waking to another day filled with the mercies of God.

I cannot bear the thought of another man having the pleasure of watching my wife prepare for bedtime. Or the sight and sound of her daily miracles: preparing a meal, talking to the children, watching television, and talking on the phone all at the same time.

If you haven't told your wife often enough that you love her, haven't done enough to prove it, or haven't given enough of yourself to her, then please ask her to forgive you. If you have been engrossed in what you were doing and failed to pay attention to your precious wife, then repent of every selfish moment of your life with her.

I am frightened at the prospect of being single. Of not knowing how to take care of myself after my wife has done it with such caring for so long. I'm not sure I could make that adjustment, and I know I won't be able to make wise decisions without her advice and counsel.

The thought of dating is anathema to me. It seems so vulgar somehow and a violation of my very nature to attempt to find someone else to love. No! There is no place to go where I could find another precious and priceless jewel like the one I already have. There will never be a replacement for her—never. She is the original; all others would simply be an attempt to copy what I once enjoyed.

AN ABUSE OF GRACE

Every man is limited by three things: the knowledge in his mind, the strength of his character, and the principles upon which he builds his life. In our ministry to men, we must work to increase knowledge, build strength of character, and cement godly principles into the lives of the men we serve. And then we must walk alongside our brothers to keep each other on the straight and narrow pathway.

In his book *What's So Amazing about Grace*, Philip Yancey tells the story of a minister friend who told him he was divorcing his wife and marrying a younger woman because she "made him feel so good." The minister had become an idolater, making his feelings into an idol. Philip asked him, "What about your wife? What about God? What about your ministry?"

His friend replied, "I'm leaving the ministry, and when I get ready, I'll come back." What effrontery! By his actions, he was calling God a liar. "The one who believes in the Son of God has the testimony in himself; the one who does not believe God has made Him a liar, because he has not believed in the testimony that God has given concerning His Son" (1 John 5:10 NASB).

When Philip saw him again years later, the man was working at a secular company and had no thoughts about God or returning to the ministry. Because he had sought to abuse grace, he had desecrated God's gifting in his life and had defiled his wife. Like Esau, he will suffer the consequences for an eternity.

In our ministry to men, we must consistently teach the full counsel of God and hold men accountable for their actions. Through loving confrontation, we must draw near to the men in our fellowship and help them to see the consequences of their choices and actions the way God sees them.

At the same time, as we seek to help men become irresistible husbands and loving fathers, we must create a climate that offers mercy, eliminates judgment, provides forgiveness, erases anger, and focuses on service. The church should be a place of reconciliation, understanding, and love manifested in grace.

How do we balance duty and obligation with liberty and freedom? It was Jesus Christ who brought grace and truth into a world devoid of either. He showed us that truth is the foundation for the way we live and the life we have. He also showed us that grace is our only means of salvation, whether it is the salvation of our souls from sin or the salvation of marital, parental, and professional relationships that are precious to us. The challenge before us as ministers to men is to offer compassion without compromise. But it takes grace!

Scripture tells us that the early church had "abundant grace" (Acts 4:33 NASB), which was manifest in the way they gave of their earthly possessions and shared with others. Grace is the art of giving. The church at Corinth, on the other hand, had cheapened grace. They allowed known sinners into membership and good standing. Incest was tolerated in the life of a couple and the life of the congregation. During communion, the members of the congregation ate and drank to excess, not discerning the Lord's body, and as a result, many were sick and some died. Again, we must teach our men the truth, especially about the consequences of their actions. It is a dreadful thing to fall into the hands of an angry God.

RESTORATION THROUGH GRACE AND LOVE

Charles was a church member, deacon, and pornographer. His office was his sanctuary, his computer his altar, and triple-X videos were his obsession. Though a churchman, he was an idolater.

His marriage and his business suffered. Myrtle, his wife, was distraught and didn't know what to do to change the situation, their marriage, and especially him. He had learned his lifestyle from his father and had never known any other way. Most of his friends either knew nothing about his secret vice or thought nothing about it because they indulged on occasion also.

When I first met this couple, Myrtle was nervous and depressed. Charles was a bluff showoff. Their fights were monumental, even their bedroom was a battleground, and their children were sullen and withdrawn.

Myrtle wanted change. She thought about divorce but rejected it as wrong. Then change came. It didn't start with Charles but with Myrtle. She began to show him grace, loving him in spite of himself. Loving him when she felt as though it was wrong and dirty, knowing what his mind was engaged in.

Charles began to change. He became a staunch believer in Christ. Today this couple is a great success story in every way. But notice: it was not Myrtle's resentment of Charles, her accusations against him, or her nagging that brought about the answer to her prayers. It happened when she offered him grace for grit and blessing for cursing that he became her irresistible husband. In our ministry to men, we're called to the same level of grace. God's grace.

If you met them today, you would never guess what they were like previously. The entire family enjoys each other, and Charles dotes on Myrtle. Sometimes when I see them, I think, *Maybe it won't last,* but it is real and eternal.

We have nothing to give anyone other than the grace of God that is in Christ Jesus our Lord. How many times did Myrtle want to quit, forget it all, and start over without Charles? But she read about Jesus, and it changed her mind: "For consider Him who has endured such hostility by sinners against Himself, so that you will not grow weary and lose heart. You have not yet resisted to the point of shedding blood in your striving against sin" (Heb. 12:3–4 NASB).

BRINGING GLORY TO OUR WIVES

How can a woman be the glory of a man unless the man is becoming the glory of God by being conformed to the image of Christ?

For nine years, Pat and Kim had what could be called a good marriage, a comfortable living, and all the amenities that beget happiness. Then things began to go wrong with the business, stress settled into their marriage, and after a year, they began to talk about divorce. Neither one was happy with anything in their lives.

Then Kim heard a radio announcement about a meeting and encouraged Pat to go with her. At this meeting, they heard truths they had never heard before and met people who sat up until the wee hours of the morning ministering to them. And when they left to go home, divorce was out of the picture, and they were determined to make the marriage and business work.

Months later, they sat across the table from me and recounted their journey in marriage and faith. The culmination of their story had occurred just two weeks before we met together. Pat said, "I went into Kim and confessed everything to her. Told her about my addiction to pornography, my affinity toward another woman, and my unhappiness with her attitudes, and it just crushed her. She didn't know what to do then, and I didn't either. We were talking about divorce when we went to that meeting and met David and Toni, who ministered to us. They prayed with us the prayer of forgiveness, and Kim forgave me.

"We began to read the Bible together, pray, and talk to each other without rancor. Then I read about foot washing. So one night, a week ago, I knelt in front of Kim and washed her feet. I told her how much I loved her and how grateful I was to be married to her. Then she washed my feet. We took communion over our bed, in front of the television and the VCR, and when we went to bed, it was as if we had just been married for the first time."

When Pat finished, Kim told her side of the story.

"You cannot believe the way I love him now. It's just as if I have a new husband who genuinely and truly loves me. Always before, there was something missing. I knew it and could do nothing about it. At least I didn't know what to do. But when he knelt to wash my feet, it seemed the Holy Spirit was washing my mind, healing my spirit, and giving me a new heart. Neither of us has any shame or guilt now, and it is just wonderful."

The irresistible husband is an honest man. Honest with God, with himself, and with his wife. Repentance is necessary to the saving of a soul or a marriage. God doesn't want apologies, putting Band-Aids on wounds of the heart; he wants genuine repentance.

Repent is the first word of the gospel message, and it is the basis for being an irresistible husband. Repentance rids us of deceit and guilt and cleanses our hearts and our relationships. Repentance brings grace into action. It leads to reconciliation, restoration, and restitution.

God's favor is a manifestation of his grace. "You are their strength. What glory! Our power is based on your favor!" (Ps. 89:17 LB). It is God's favor that enables us to make choices that determine our conduct, character, and destiny. Three of the most powerful motives in human life are hate, fear, and greed. There is one motive, however, that is more powerful than all the other three; that is love. God's love! Love is composed of our choices and constructed by our words.

RESTITUTION FOLLOWS REPENTANCE

When Zaccheus, a publican and a tax collector, heard that Jesus was passing by, he climbed up into a tree to see him. When Jesus called him down because he wanted to dine at his house, Zaccheus responded to the Lord's grace with repentance.

"Zaccheus stopped and said to the Lord, 'Behold, Lord, half of my possessions I will give to the poor, and if I have defrauded anyone of anything, I will give back four times as much.' And Jesus said to him, 'Today salvation has come to this house, because he, too, is a son of Abraham. For the Son of Man has come to seek and to save that which was lost'" (Luke 19:8–10 NASB).

Restitution is an element of faith that follows repentance. Jesus didn't offer Zaccheus condemnation for his chicanery or judgment for his deceit; Jesus offered him grace, and it changed his life. Grace is "the power to do what is right for the sake of Jesus Christ and his kingdom, not the grace that grants me the right to do what I want or feel in pursuit of happiness and peace." Grace marks the life of the irresistible husband. Both love and grace change people. But grace is the essence of love. It is impossible to say you love if there is no grace.

Making Marriages Stronger

There are many good books and video packages your church can use to help men improve their marriages. Some of the best books for this include *The Five Love Languages* by Gary Chapman, *His Needs/Her Needs* by Willard Harley, and several books by Bill and Pam Farrel, including *Marriage in the Whirlwind*, *Let Her Know You Love Her*, and *Love, Honor, and Forgive*. For an interesting study time, use Dave and Claudia Arp's video series *Ten Great Dates to Revitalize Your Marriage*.

One of the best things to try in a men's ministry is to interview a happily married couple. Simply asking the couple some questions on a particular strength of their relationship can prove tremendously helpful to other married couples.

Questions to Explore

Encourage your men to think through some basic marriage questions.

1. Who modeled marriage for you? Who modeled it for your wife?
2. How have the models in your life shaped your marriage relationship?
3. What do you and your wife fight about most often? What two things would help to resolve this difference?
4. What values will your marriage pass along to your children?
5. What ministry would you like to try doing with your wife?

24

FATHERS
AND SONS

| *Steve Farrar* |

A group of appreciative tourists watched a demonstration put on by the Royal Artillery of the Queen. The six-man team worked with flawless precision. Actually, only five of them worked with precision. The sixth soldier positioned himself about twenty-five yards away from the cannon and stood at attention during the entire exhibition, doing nothing. After the exhibition, one of the tourists asked the staff officer to explain the duty of the man standing off to the side.

"He's number six," came the reply.

"Yes, but what does he do?"

"He stands at attention."

"Yes, I know, but why does he stand at attention?" No one knew. The commanding officer didn't know. Even the soldier himself didn't know.

After many hours of searching through old training manuals, it became clear what number six was to do: he was to hold the horses. Only problem was, the Royal Artillery hadn't used horses for nearly a century.

Why was soldier number six standing at attention? Because he was appointed to do so. Did he have any idea what his role was supposed to be? No. I'm afraid there are too many husbands and fathers today who are in the same situation. When it comes to their families, they're simply standing there. Motionless. Like the sixth man in the Royal Artillery, they're making about as much difference in their homes as a sprig of parsley on a plate of guacamole. The sixth man had no idea that he was supposed to be holding the horses. And too many men today have no idea that their job is to save their boys.

"If I could offer a single prescription for the survival of America, and particularly black America," writes William Raspberry, a columnist with the *Washington Post*, "it would be to restore the family. And if you asked me how to do it, my answer—no doubt oversimplified—would be: save the boys." Tragically, the black family in modern America has largely lost its boys. The enemy has effectively removed black males from their God-appointed positions of leadership and responsibility, and he has the same goal in mind for the rest of America. He may use different methods to achieve his goal, but his strategy is the same: destroy the boys by neutralizing the fathers.

Don Lewis, director of the Nehemiah Project, in testimony before the United States House of Representatives, summarized the crisis: "Through decades of social policy ... the federal government has gutted and plundered the black community of its husbands and fathers. The result is that boys learn that drugs and larceny are the fastest ways of making lots of cash. They simply don't have fathers who can teach and demonstrate the virtues of a healthy work ethic, the importance of sexual discipline and responsibility, the benefits of education, and the beauty of transcendent values." So the cycle repeats itself, generation after generation. Millions of boys don't know what it's like to have a father. That's why I believe William Raspberry was right; we must save the boys. And the local church should be helping us. It is our job as men to provide a model that will equip youngsters to confidently take on the responsibilities of life and marriage. Our children are going to need godly spouses with whom they can raise the next generation for Christ. If the boys in our churches are not equipped to lead families, then the families of the next generation will not have leaders. And that will become a vicious epidemic, multiplying with each generation.

THE CHANGING CULTURE FOR SAVING BOYS

From eternity, God instituted a divine plan for the family. It was to be followed by each generation. It has been noted by sociologists that the family is the only institution present in every tribe, every village, and every nation throughout history. One prominent researcher called the family "the rearing device for our species."

God's plan has always been for families to raise children, so that they may become competent to raise their own children. In other words, children learn from their parents' example how to raise the next generation. But when the chain is broken, when a man abandons his wife and leaves his children to fend for themselves, a boy cannot learn to be a man, for there are no men to learn from.

Dave Simmons, who trains fathers through his excellent "Dad, the Family Shepherd" seminars, has noted that God's plan for developing men is a hands-on, master-to-apprentice relationship, with Dad as the instructor. The task of the father is to equip child-raisers, who will in turn equip their own children. For literally thousands of years, this is how men have functioned. Men raised their boys, and as a result, there was stability in the family. Men didn't have identity crises; they knew who they were and what they were supposed to do, because they had seen a model.

Too few men today raise their sons in this way. Satan's strategy to counteract God's plan is to lure a man away from his God-given responsibilities. And that's exactly what happened during the Industrial Revolution.

Prior to the Industrial Revolution, life was built around the home. Four out of five Americans were farmers. Men worked at home, women worked at home, and so did the children. The pattern remained the same for centuries. The mother raised the children until they were somewhere between five and seven, then the boys would work with their fathers and the girls with their mothers. The men who weren't farmers were silversmiths, blacksmiths, skilled craftsmen, and merchants. The same pattern applied to them; when a boy reached the age of seven, he would go to work with his dad and learn the trade. Most of the time, "going to work" meant simply going from one room to another. Fathers raised their sons, and they were together nearly every waking hour. A child's education came primarily through the tutelage of the parents.

As the Industrial Revolution took hold, things changed. Factories popped up, and men were hired to operate machines. They exchanged work at home for work away from home—work that often required them to be away for long periods of time. Time spent away from the home diminished the father's ability to influence the son. The formula is simple: less time = less influence.

Almost overnight, men stopped doing what they had done for thousands of years. They unknowingly brought a halt to the accumulated momentum of generations. Work now separated fathers from sons; no longer were they in a master-apprentice relationship. Men stopped raising their boys, because they weren't present to lead them. As the years have gone by, that all-important male role model has eroded even further. So it was over two hundred years ago that the seeds were planted that removed men from their God-appointed role of raising boys. In our generation, those seeds are bearing fruit, and the fruit is killing us.

THE INFLUENCE OF A FATHER

Harvard psychologist Samuel Osherson has noted that a boy learns to be a man by watching his father. If the father is not there to provide a model, the boy is left vulnerable. We save our boys by giving them a role model to follow. When boys have a clear model, they know how to function when the time comes to assume the responsibility of marriage and parenting.

In our generation, too many boys have no idea what it means to be a man. It is my God-appointed task to ensure that my sons will be ready to lead their families. I must equip them to that end. Little boys are the hope of the next generation. They are the fathers of tomorrow. They must know who they are and what they are to do. They must see their role model in action. That's how they will know what it means to be a man. This puts the ball in my court, and in yours. It means we must ask ourselves the question, What do I need to do to train my sons to become leaders of their families? And if the church is to help, it means our men's ministries must ask the question, What must the church be doing to equip men to train their sons? I have five goals for saving my own boys. It is my job as their father to model for them the importance of

knowing and obeying Jesus Christ

knowing and displaying godly character

knowing and loving my wife

knowing and loving my children

knowing my gifts and abilities so I can contribute to the lives of others

A friend of mine who enjoys archery notes that error increases with distance. When I'm close to the target, I'm an excellent archer. When I move farther away, my effectiveness drops dramatically. And what's true in archery is true in fathering: error increases with distance.

If I'm going to be the family leader that God has called me to be, then I must be there, on site, close to my boys, consistently. I must be there physically—an area in which we have a real disadvantage to the pre–Industrial Revolution generation. Most of us get up in the morning and leave for work. Our kids get up and travel to school, and we probably won't see them until dinner. We've lost a significant amount of time with our sons because the demands of our culture have taken the time away.

To begin to turn the tide back in favor of our boys, we as Christian men must realize the necessity of being in the home. When we deduct commuting and work time from our waking hours, we may have, at best, only two or three hours a day that can be spent with our children. That time must be used wisely if we're going to influence them.

One friend of mine said he wished he could spend more time with his sons, but he was too busy working. He wanted to give them all the things he'd never had as a boy, and in doing so, he failed to spend time with them. Before he knew it, his boys were in school. He missed their games because he had business meetings. Though he wanted to have time to talk with them, most days he came home late, and his boys were already in bed. The next thing he knew, they were teenagers. He missed their first dates, their concerts, their school assemblies, and their proms. Now his boys are grown and out of the house. They have their own interests, their own lives. The odd thing is, my friend now says he has time for his boys. Unfortunately, they don't have any time for him.

God has granted each of us a limited amount of time to spend with our children. How much time do you have left?

EMOTIONAL DISTANCE

Saving our boys requires more than just our physical presence in the home. Emotional distance is an even greater danger for our boys than a father's absence from the home. I once read an article that claimed "the curse of fatherhood is distance." Good fathers work to overcome that distance. They work to be with their boys emotionally and to be in tune with what is going on in their kids' lives. Unfortunately, many of the men in my generation had fathers who were present physically but absent emotionally. Research bears this out. Dr. Samuel Osherson, in his book *Finding Our Fathers*, studied 370 men who graduated from Harvard in the mid-1960s. They were the successes of society, the guys who "made it." Armed with degrees, they went into their respective vocational battlefields and won big. Yet many of them had been wounded by fathers who were not there for them emotionally as they were growing up. Osherson concluded his research by noting that the psychological absence of fathers is "one of the great underestimated tragedies of our times."

If you look around, you'll see evidence of the tragedy. Our churches are full of men who feel that their fathers were not there for them. One study of successful businessmen, scientists, and scholars found that the vast majority believed that their fathers were either absent or a negative influence in their lives. Another study showed that 85 percent of the participants had fathers who were physically absent, emotionally absent, or abusive.

We may have had fathers who were absent or distant, but we dare not pass that trait on to our children. We need to create new links in the chain, so that our sons do not have to deal with the emotional wounds so many men carry. We must save our boys so we can save our families. One thing the local church can do is to help men know how to be strong, loving husbands and fathers. A church can partner experienced dads with inexperienced dads to help the younger men make wise choices about raising their children. It can create mentoring programs and offer training to new husbands so that they know how to lead their homes with wisdom and loving concern for their wives. It can encourage leaders to model both physical and emotional closeness to their families and can in this way reshape the church. In fact, if the pastor or the leaders of the men's ministry will set the example for the other men, we will soon start to see changes in the church.

One man can make a difference. Churchill saved England. Lombardi turned the Packers from doormats into legends. Namath convinced the Jets they could win the Super Bowl. Iacocca turned Chrysler around. It happens all the time. One man can make a difference.

Jonathan Edwards was one man who made a difference. Born in 1703, he was perhaps the most brilliant intellectual America has ever produced. A pastor, writer, and later president of Princeton, he and his wife had eleven children. Of his known male descendants

more than 300 became pastors, missionaries, or theological professors

120 were professors at various universities

110 became attorneys

60 were prominent authors

30 were judges

14 served as presidents of universities and colleges

3 served in the U.S. Congress

1 became the Vice President of the United States

Jonathan Edwards made a difference because he saved his boys. And his boys saved their boys. And those boys grew up to save their boys. Generation after generation, the boys were saved. He was just one man, but he positively affected hundreds and even thousands of his descendants after his death. Although Edwards was known for his daily regimen of thirteen hours in the study and his busy schedule of teaching, writing, and pastoring, he made it a habit to come home and spend one hour each day with his children. Edwards was one of the great minds of history, yet this world-class scholar had his priorities right. He not only made sure he made it home for dinner, but he got in at least one hour of family time every night. It's my guess that Edwards made a difference in generation after generation because he understood his God-appointed role as husband and father.

As you look toward the future, what will your legacy look like? Will there be a chain linking generation after generation of godly men, who in turn produce other godly men? Or will it be one generation after another of confused leadership from men who have no clear-cut role model? The destiny of those future generations is in your hands. The choices you make with your family today will determine the quality of life in your family tree for generations to come. Likewise, the priorities you set in your men's ministry to create an instructive and supportive network for the husbands and fathers in your congregation will influence your entire community for generations. One man can make a difference, and a group of committed men working together can multiply that positive difference exponentially. And if we save our boys, it will be the greatest and most fulfilling accomplishment of our lives.

25

LIFE-CHANGING
SHORT-TERM
MISSIONS

| *Warren Hardig* |

The testimony of an eyewitness carries a powerful impact in a court of law. It can sway the jury's decision and determine the outcome of an entire case. In fact, eyewitness testimony can spell the difference between life and death for the accused. Our legal system recognizes the power of a firsthand report.

In much the same way, God's system for reclaiming his lost world depends on the powerful testimony of his witnesses. God has ordained that witnesses will be on the front lines of the battle for people's minds and hearts. Jesus commissioned his disciples (which includes us) to be his "witnesses both in Jerusalem [your home town], and in all Judea [nearby areas with the same culture] and Samaria [nearby areas with a different culture], and even to the remotest part of the earth [which could be anywhere]" (Acts 1:8 NASB).

Throughout the Bible, God uses common, ordinary people (like you)—shepherds and fishermen, carpenters and tax collectors, farmers and physicians—to be his witnesses communicating the message of God's love and mercy for everyone who will repent and believe.

Through all types of situations and circumstances, God uses men who are willing to be used by him. The secret of their success is directly related to their relationship with Jesus Christ. Look at Acts, chapter 4, for example. When Peter and John are brought before the Sanhedrin after healing the lame beggar at the gate of the temple, God uses Peter to preach salvation to the leaders of the Jews (vv. 5–8). In verse 13 it says, "Now as they observed the confidence of Peter and John, and understood that they were uneducated and untrained men, they were marveling, and began to recognize them as having been with Jesus" (NASB).

The same phenomenon is happening all around the world today as God uses laymen from all walks of life to reach the world through short-term missions—not in their own power but with God's help—by sharing their talents and testimonies on a one- or two-week overseas ministry team.

PANCAKES IN PANAMA

Serving together on a short-term mission will do more to cement the bond between the men in your church than a thousand pancake breakfasts. Pancake breakfasts and other such social gatherings have their place in your men's ministry, but don't stop short of stretching yourselves into missions and outreach.

Going on a missions trip will do many things in the lives of your men as they allow themselves to be used by God. God will expand their vision for a lost world, both overseas and at home. Many men are locked into pea-size boxes in their thinking. A short-term missions trip will open their eyes to the experience of being a missionary and break their hearts in compassion for the lost.

They can witness firsthand the power struggle with Satan in the voodoo culture of Haiti and what the Haitian people face every day. They can learn about the struggles of the Russian people with their government, which has lied to and cheated and killed their own people, their struggles with alcohol, and the aftereffects of being told for many years that there is no God besides communism.

"JUST SEND THE MONEY"

Some people just won't believe the benefits a missions trip can bring until they experience it. One pastor, who had five men from his church going to Ecuador, said to me, "For what it's costing to send these guys to South America, the money would probably be better spent by just sending it to Ecuador and hiring the workers to build the church there." But a few months after the men returned from their two-week missions trip, the pastor was singing a different tune. He had observed a change in the lives of those men that money couldn't buy.

They came home more committed to Christ. They knew how to pray more specifically for Ecuador and other foreign missions, because they had been there. They had experienced the life of a missionary firsthand. They had felt it, smelled it, and dealt with it. Missions was no longer just a slide-show presentation on Sunday night. The pastor said, "They knew how to give better because they had seen where their money was going and how it was helping. But most of all, it made them better laymen in our church. They became more committed in their Christian walk and more committed to the ministry of our local body."

One of the men who went on that trip later became a youth leader and eventually went into missionary service full-time. Another man became very involved with the missions board and its activities, and the other men became leaders in the children's ministry in the church. Not only that, but the men began witnessing to people in their community. No dollar amount can be placed on how short-term missions can change a person's heart for our lost world.

Stretching and Growing

A short-term missions trip will stretch you beyond your capabilities and cause your faith to grow by leaps and bounds. You learn to trust God when you're in over your head. As men, we all have a tendency to try plans A, B, and C before we turn to God for help and for his plan. Many men share their testimonies in front of other people for the first time on the missions field, and it is then that they learn to lean on God and not on themselves.

I tell people that half the fun of going on a missions trip is seeing how God works before you leave. Maybe it's getting time off you didn't think you could get or seeing God supply all the money for the trip. One man told me that he felt the Lord leading him to help out at a youth camp. At the time, his wife was nine months pregnant, his mom was dying of cancer, and he had a smoking habit. Still, he felt the Lord wanted him to go. Despite the circumstances, his family was supportive; so he went.

He quit smoking before he left, had a great time serving the kids at the camp, and watched God work in his heart. Shortly after he got back, his wife had the baby; a week later, his mom died of cancer. Through it all, his walk with the Lord became real, and he knew that he had done what the Lord had wanted him to do.

The Gift of Your Testimony

Going on a missions trip lets you use your talents and testimony to reach people across the lines of race and culture. Everybody has a testimony, and no one can dispute your eyewitness account of what God has done in your life. We took a group of men to Mexico, where they worked alongside a particular Mexican man each day. As they worked together, our men shared their testimonies with him and prayed for him. Right before we left, the man accepted Christ as we shared the plan of salvation with him. Just showing him Christ's love in action helped him to accept Jesus as his Savior.

Every man has life experiences that God can use to reach someone who is going through the same thing or someone who has the same interests. Everybody has a talent that God can use, whether it is laying blocks, mixing cement, or doing electrical work or medical work. God can use every gift to further his kingdom.

Dale Larrance, a farmer from central Illinois, struggled with the pressures of life. He attended church, but it was more out of habit than desire. Then one day, at the age of forty-five, Dale found deliverance and forgiveness of sin. He then attended church because he wanted to, and he began to become more involved. I'll let him tell his own story about missions.

In the course of time, I attended a Men For Missions (MFM) banquet sponsored by our church. Max Edwards, the speaker, interested me because he had been a farmer, like me. Even though he was now a missionary in Brazil, I knew I could identify with another man of the soil.

We ate the usual hotel banquet room meal—starchy potatoes, greasy chicken, and cold peas—but listening to Max made it all worthwhile. He began by showing slides of the work OMS has accomplished in Brazil. He told us about a chapel that he wanted to build at the youth camp where he worked. He was forming a ministry team to go down and build it. He needed two more men.

At that moment, I heard the voice of the Holy Spirit. I was to go. Me, a dirt farmer from central Illinois, going all the way to South America to build a chapel for Christ. What a change of events. I couldn't wait to tell Betty.

But Betty already knew that something big was brewing. The Holy Spirit had influenced her as well. When I gave her my news, she was thoroughly delighted. I found no difficulty in meeting the second part of MFM's three-point pledge: to go wherever God asked me to go.

Although the ministry team was scheduled to leave in only two weeks, I managed to obtain a copy of my birth certificate. I could never have opened those bureaucratic doors that quickly without God's help. There were twenty men on this ministry team. It was hot and the work was hard, but I was so excited about being a part of God's cause, I hardly noticed the discomfort. I carried block, mixed cement, and learned the skills of a brick mason "overnight."

As our team worked together, a bond of fellowship developed. We exchanged testimonies. I told the other men how my son Bobby's birth had affected me and how Betty's response had been part of God's plan to bring me to salvation. They related their own experiences and I saw God's sovereignty in their lives, too. We had devotions every morning, shared our faith during the day, and prayed together in the evening. We were no longer individuals but a unified instrument of God, sharply focused on a single objective: saving souls.

The walls of the chapel rose daily. First two feet, then four feet. Obscure openings became functional windows and doors. Finally, the walls were completed, an event which occurred simultaneously with the end of the trip. The roof would have to wait. Before we left, we gathered in the chapel. As I sat there, the moon and stars never seemed more beautiful. In song and prayer, we worshipped God from the depths of our hearts. Then I heard a petition I will never forget:

"O God, we have toiled to build this chapel so others might come to worship You. We have love in our hearts, and our hands have worked with the strength You provide. Each brick has been placed to honor You and bring salvation to the lost. Lord, we pray that for each brick laid, one soul will be saved. The walls contain 3,800 bricks. We ask that the fruit of our labor would bring 3,800 lost souls to heaven's gates."

My last night in Brazil was bittersweet. I was not ready to leave. I had discovered new relationships with other Christians, and more important, with God, a bonding I had never before experienced. I returned to Betty in Illinois as a changed man. I now realized that God could use me, a simple farmer. I also learned that he could use me at home. In fact, there was much to do. I accepted a responsible office in our church, prayed regularly for missionaries and gave them financial support, and joined the local Men for Missions council.

God gave me a burning, intense desire to give personal obedience to the Great Commission: "'Go into all the world and preach the gospel to all creation" (Mark 16:15 NASB). Not only did I have the desire, but Romans 10:14–15 challenged me with the practical reasons to do so: "How then will they call on Him in whom they have not believed? How will they believe in Him whom they have not heard? And how will they hear without a preacher? How will they preach unless they are sent? Just as it is written, 'How beautiful are the feet of those who bring good news of good things!'" (NASB).

God has allowed me to satisfy my new desire by sharing the good news on more than twenty-five Men for Missions ministry teams. Most of my work for Christ—building, witnessing, and praying—has been in Brazil, but I've also served in Colombia, Ecuador, and Spain. My life has been greatly enriched by the experiences in each of these countries. On one of these excursions, I saw a new video on Brazil. It spoke of missionaries and exciting new programs and projects. Then, as I watched, God touched my heart in a most unexpected way. A missionary told how MFMers built a chapel ten years ago. He mentioned the long hours, the hard work, and the heat. He also told about our prayer—a soul to be saved for each of the chapel's 3,800 bricks. Then, smiling broadly, he announced: "Records now indicate that over 3,800 men, women, and young adults have found Christ within the chapel's walls." Tears furrowed my cheeks as God put a love in my heart, which will last forever.

I am so unworthy to be part of such a great movement. I can only thank my wife, Betty, for her spiritual guidance, Men For Missions for the opportunity to serve, and Jesus Christ for His love and forgiving grace. I intend to serve Him faithfully each day of my life.

As of today, more than 15,000 people have accepted Christ in that chapel.

GOD'S WORK IN YOUR HEART

Rich and Joan Ring are in Russia above the Arctic Circle. They are starting their third year of teaching Bible studies and being grandparents to a number of the youth in the city where they live. Rich Ring started his ministry involvement years ago by going to Colombia, South America, on a work team. He came home and found that as he was going about his daily labors, tears came to his eyes whenever he thought about the sights, scenes, and friends he had made in Colombia. Rich will tell you that the most important thing that happens on a missions trip is what God does down deep in your heart. That is what matters more than anything else. Rich continued to work in the business world for the next several years. He was in a business that he loved and was very dedicated to, and he was quite successful.

A few years ago, at a missions conference, he was challenged to go to Russia to work as a part of the Co-Mission, teaching Christian ethics and biology. After a long struggle, Rich and his wife, Joan, made the decision to go to Russia for one year. But while they were overseas, they were so captivated by the Russian people that on the way home, they told their son, "Sell the remainder of the business. We are not going back into that."

Rich and Joan are now back in Russia for their third year and are having an effective ministry. They are sharing with their Russian neighbors what Christ has done in their lives, and they are seeing lives changed.

Is there a place for short-term missions in the life of your men's ministry? Only if there's room for building friendships, working side by side with others, and touching the lives of other people with the love of God.

Planning a Short-Term Missions Trip

12 months before your trip

1. *Get the big picture.* Review your purpose, create a checklist, prepare a budget.
2. *Establish a leadership committee.* Determine who must give input, who will be best for the tasks of planning the trip, create responsibility sheets, explain roles, appoint or invite participation in leadership, set dates of committee meetings.
3. *Review past plans and evaluations.* If your group has done this before, what was praised, what was panned, what was recommended?

10 months before your trip

4. *Think and pray through the event.* What does God want to have happen? Ideally, who do you want to participate? What needs do they have? What will motivate them? What do you want your men to leave thinking, knowing, doing, and experiencing? What outside help will you need to make it successful?
5. *Consider the essentials.* What are the best dates and times? What calendar conflicts exist? What potential resource people can you rely on? What will your primary focus be? What special activities will you include? What facilities will be required? What travel arrangements will be required? What food requirements will you have, and who will buy and prepare it? What insurance needs will you have? What international requirements will have to be met?
6. *Consider the promotional possibilities.* How can we best communicate this event?

8 months before your trip

7. *Make decisions about your budget and financial policies.* What are your projected expenses? What is your expected income? What will it cost per man? What financial assistance will you offer? What will happen with profits or debt? What conditions will determine whether you decide not to go? Who will handle the money?
8. *Make decisions about your schedule.* Create a day-by-day activity schedule and distribute it to everyone in leadership. Review your planning timetable and determine deadlines for confirmations. Determine your registration procedures, including refundablity of money, phone calls, mail, roommates, and separate traveling arrangements.

9. *Make decisions about emergencies.* How will medical emergencies be handled? Who will be the contact person with the families, the local authorities, the local medical staff? How will personal insurance coverage and liability insurance needs be resolved?

6 months before your trip

10. *Confirm your plans.* Agree on your in-country travel and activities. Get travel arrangements in writing, confirm costs, decide on deposits and deadlines, and determine the flexibility of your contracts.

11. *Confirm your leadership and contacts.* Did you clearly communicate the purpose to your people? Are you open to suggestions? Are financial, equipment, deadline, and activity expectations clear to all?

12. *Confirm your food, transportation, and insurance decisions.*

4 months before your trip

13. *Prepare your promotion.* Send mailings, brochures, and posters. Make phone calls. Provide information through the church and all group events. Make registration, cost, and expectations clear.

14. *Provide information.* Begin trip training by offering information on the country, the people, the project, and the purpose of the trip. Offer complete printed information that will answer men's questions regarding short-term missions.

15. *Coordinate registration.* Who will collect the money? Who will keep track of registration? Who will check to make sure that the size of the group fits with the budget, facilities, activities, and transportation?

2 months before your trip

16. *Review everything.* Are your plans still on target? Are your deadlines being met? Who needs help? What decisions need to be made? Is the purpose being fulfilled? Are registrations on target? Is the budget still accurate? Do your in-country contacts need anything? Do you have confirmation on travel and activities?

17. *Make modifications.* Do you need to change the budget, food, travel, activities, or facilities? Are there special tools, equipment, or resources you will need to take? Go through your entire checklist to see what information is missing.

18. *Prepare your people.* Arrange for weekly training sessions. Pray together as a team. Make sure everyone has a passport and a medical exam, if needed. Tell them what to take and what not to take. Answer everyone's questions about the trip.

The month of your trip

19. *Make phone calls*. Reconnect with everyone involved in the trip. Make sure participants know where and when they will leave, what to bring, and how to pack it. Assign a "special problems" person to handle last-minute changes and emergencies. Get reports from people, make decisions, and encourage everyone. Make your collections, pay the travel companies, and purchase equipment and food. Keep a servant perspective. Pray hard.

20. *Maintain good records*. Keep financial records and the reports of each coordinator. Make note of things that could be done differently next time.

21. *Evaluate the trip*. Get feedback on the trip, asking your men what they liked and disliked. Ask for suggestions concerning future trips. Send notes of thanks to everyone involved.

26

SUCCESSFUL MEN'S RETREATS

Larry Kreider

More can be accomplished at a weekend men's retreat than in a year's worth of other men's events. With so much at stake, the enemy seeks to prevent or destroy our efforts to make a lasting impact in the lives of men. That's why great retreats are so hard to pull off. Unless you're willing to jump through all the hoops, you're better off not even planning a retreat. When your committee convenes for the first time, count the cost in terms of time and effort before you decide to go ahead.

Despite all the challenges, however, if you pray fervently, plan meticulously, and execute diligently, you can put on a life-changing retreat, one that they'll be talking about for years to come.

CHOOSING YOUR RETREAT COMMITTEE

The most important factor in planning a successful retreat is the leadership team you assemble. Recruit men based on their skills, savvy, and the value they can add to the event. Just because a man loves Jesus and is a good ol' boy, doesn't mean he'll be an asset to your team. You need to recruit guys who are willing to work tirelessly and creatively to plan the best event possible. You need men who are gifted planners, recruiters, organizers, and implementers. Even the best-laid plans will fall apart if you don't have guys who can follow through.

The key to every successful team is the captain or leader. He must initiate action and remain in constant communication with the rest of the committee. The captain cannot be expected to do all the work himself. He must recruit committee members who are dependable and capable. In the words of President Reagan, the operative principle when delegating responsibility is "trust . . . but verify."

The planning process will usually commence six to nine months before the event. In some cases, you may need to secure your retreat facility as much as one year in advance to ensure availability. The essential elements of the planning process are as follows.

- Establish your retreat theme.
- Develop a marketing strategy.
- Book your site.
- Select and solicit your speaker.
- Outline your retreat program.
- Arrange for necessary equipment.
- Establish your budget.

Let's elaborate on each of these important elements.

ESTABLISH YOUR RETREAT THEME

The theme of your retreat will be determined by the spiritual goals you want to accomplish or by the speaker you want to invite. It should be catchy enough to grab men's attention. If you have a specific speaker in mind who favors certain topics, then go with his strengths. The theme will be worked into the graphic presentation of your promotional campaign, the workshops or breakout sessions, and the music or worship. You may even decide to print the theme on T-shirts or other promotional items.

Know your target audience. If you have a lot of young believers in your congregation, you might want to use a theme like "Moving beyond Belief." Other ideas include

Courageous Christianity

From Success to Significance

Bold Faith, Tender Heart

A Man and His Faith

A Man and His Family

A Man and His Leadership

DEVELOP A MARKETING STRATEGY

A successful marketing strategy will push forward on two fronts: information and recruitment. Printed materials, such as brochures and bulletin inserts, will create an image of your retreat in the minds of men and will communicate important information. Printed materials will not recruit guys to attend the retreat. The only way that men will sign up for the retreat is if you organize a concerted recruitment effort and plan for men to personally invite other men.

When you're designing your printed materials, remember this: if the image isn't right, men won't read the information. You don't need to print a four-color glossy brochure, but don't settle for a bland, typewritten page, either. Hire a graphics professional or recruit a talented artist within the church to capture the desired feel of the event, and keep the information short, punchy, and to the point. Make a big splash and grab the guys' attention. Remember: the purpose of your printed materials is information, not recruitment. Cover the essentials.

- When is the retreat?
- Where is the retreat?
- Who is speaking?
- What is the theme or focus?
- What is the itinerary?
- How much does it cost?
- Are scholarships available for hardship cases?
- How do men sign up?
- When is the sign-up deadline?
- Who can the men call for more information?

Effective recruiting is accomplished hand to hand and man to man. Each member of your retreat committee should be assigned a list of men to invite and should be prepared to follow up until a decision is made. Communicate enthusiasm and encourage each man in your congregation to spread the net by inviting friends and neighbors to attend. Remember, just because a guy says yes, doesn't mean he's going. A yes is not a yes until you have a deposit check in hand!

BOOK YOUR SITE

Don't leave this important step for last, or you may find your preferred location is unavailable. As soon as you nail down the dates for your retreat, choose your site and get it booked.

Factors in determining the best location and facility for your retreat include cost, the type of men you are recruiting, and the distance from your church. Great retreats have been held at church retreat centers and also at expensive golf course inns. If you decide to go the more pricey route, establish a scholarship fund to assist men who want to attend but cannot afford it. Another important consideration is whether the location enhances or detracts from the image of your ministry.

An ideal retreat site will be close enough to home to make it convenient for men to drive in on Friday night after work but far enough away to provide a break from everyday concerns. Part of what makes a retreat an effective ministry tool is that it liberates men from their routines and focuses their attention on relationship building and studying God's Word.

SELECT AND SOLICIT YOUR SPEAKER

Your cousin's Sunday school teacher is probably not the best choice for your speaker, unless he happens to have a proven track record for speaking at men's retreats. Even good preachers don't necessarily make good retreat speakers.

At a men's retreat, the speaker must have great content, humor, and the ability to connect with men regarding the key issues of their lives. Contact the National Coalition of Men's Ministries for a list of recommended speakers.

Once you have selected a speaker, communicate thoroughly with him regarding your expectations as well as his. He needs to know how many times he'll be expected to speak, when, and for how long. He needs to know about compensation, travel arrangements, and accommodations at the retreat facility. If you've selected your theme, let him know what it is or work out a theme together based on his strengths as a speaker or on a particular topic that is mutually agreeable. Don't leave the speaker hanging, and don't leave the topic to chance. The more organized and precise you are in your agreement with the speaker, the better your retreat experience will be.

OUTLINE YOUR RETREAT PROGRAM

The elements of a good program include a capable master of ceremonies, appropriate music, well-executed skits, and prepared speakers. Depending on the needs of your men and the size of your church, you may also want to plan for breakout sessions and small groups.

Master of ceremonies. This man's job is to lighten up the audience, make everyone feel comfortable, make transitions from one segment to the next, and explain the details of the weekend. He is not the speaker. Stay away from men who only want the limelight or who insist on gabbing. The timeline of the overall schedule is ultimately in the hands of the MC.

Music. Depending on the style and resources of your congregation, your retreat music can be as simple as one man with a guitar leading praise choruses or as elaborate as a full-blown worship band with drum kit, bongos, and synthesizers. Decide on and recruit your musicians well before the retreat. Take into consideration the acoustics and other amenities of the main meeting room and plan your music accordingly. It is imperative that you have a good sound system and that you set it up—and test it!—beforehand. Put the words to the songs on an overhead projector. Most men will sing if the choruses are familiar, the words are available, and the band leads the way.

Remind your songleader that his purpose is to draw the men into worship, not to stand up front and talk. Spontaneity is great, but don't take anything for granted. Agree on how many songs, and which songs, you're going to sing, and stick to the program. Know your songleader and how he intends to lead. A well-done praise and worship time can set the tone for the entire retreat. The same is true for a lackluster performance, so plan well and pick your musicians carefully.

Skits. Skits can inject fun and humor and truth into a meeting, but they can also be risky. A good skit can send your program over the top; a lame one can be a real wet blanket. Skits should fit the theme of your retreat and should be performed by men who know what they're doing. For amateurs, the biggest challenge is finding adequate time to rehearse. If your skit is not rehearsed and well-timed, don't do it. Audition all participants in front of people who understand the criteria of a successful skit. It's better to turn a guy down than to watch him bomb during the meeting. Keep your props simple and small, but don't shortcut the visual elements of your skit.

Speakers. Once your speaker is on site, keep him comfortable, focused, and on schedule.

Small groups. If appropriate, small groups can be an excellent forum for reinforcing the speaker's messages and allowing men to go deeper in their fellowship and application of truth.

Free time and recreation. Time to relax and play is an essential ingredient of a successful retreat. Free time allows men to build friendships and to get some exercise. Activities will vary depending on your retreat location, but make a list of available resources and disseminate this information to your men. Depending on the composi-

---

Planning Effective Small Groups

To plan effective small groups, three questions must be answered.

1. How should your small groups be formed? Usually, the best way is to assign men to a group before the retreat commences.
2. When and where should your small groups meet? The best time for small groups is immediately after a plenary session. To avoid confusion and to keep things moving smoothly, it's best to assign meeting locations somewhere on the premises. Make sure that each room has the necessary amenities, such as coffee and snacks (if appropriate), sound and projection equipment (if necessary), and whiteboard, easel, or other writing equipment. To save time, have your meeting rooms set up in advance.
3. What should your small groups discuss? The speaker should give you a list of discussion questions for each session, or you can designate members of your leadership committee to design and implement your breakout sessions.

tion of your group, you may want to organize games or other activities or just turn the men loose to find their own recreation. If you are planning a golf tournament or another organized activity, such as river rafting, tennis, or hiking, let your men know in advance so they can pack the necessary equipment or clothing. Allow enough free time for the men to comfortably complete their activities without having to rush or play hooky from your other sessions. If you are planning a golf tournament in conjunction with your retreat, establish a separate committee to organize this activity.

Here is a sample retreat agenda that can be adjusted to fit your situation.

Friday Evening

5:30–6:30 P.M.	Arrival and check-in
6:30–7:30 P.M.	Buffet dinner
7:45–9:30 P.M.	Icebreakers
	Music and worship
	Session 1
	Small group discussion

Saturday

7:30–8:30 A.M.	Continental breakfast
8:45–10:15 A.M.	Music and worship
	Session 2
	Small group discussion
10:15–10:30 A.M.	Break
10:30 A.M.–12:00 P.M.	Music and worship
	Session 3
	Small group discussion
12:15–1:00 P.M.	Box luncheon
1:00–6:00 P.M.	Free time and recreational activities
6:30–7:30 P.M.	Dinner
7:30–9:15 P.M.	Music and worship
	Session 4
	Small group discussion
9:15 P.M.	Dessert and fellowship

Sunday

8:00–8:45 A.M.	Breakfast buffet
9:00–10:30 A.M.	Music and worship
	Session 5
	Small group discussion
10:30–11:00 A.M.	Break to check out
11:00 A.M.–12:00 P.M.	Worship and communion

ARRANGE FOR NECESSARY EQUIPMENT

Plan for what you will need in the way of sound equipment, overhead projectors, screens, and musical instruments. Put someone in charge of acquiring, transporting, setting up, and operating this equipment for the retreat. Find out what resources are available at your retreat site and remember to plan for the equipment and supplies you will need for your breakout sessions and other activities.

ESTABLISH YOUR BUDGET

Setting a budget is always tough. It has to be large enough to pay the bills but small enough to be affordable. Find out how much of your budget will be underwritten by your men's ministry or the church's general fund and how much you will need to charge attendees to make up the difference. Keep the following elements in mind when determining your costs.

- Cost of promotion (brochures, mailings, etc.)
- Cost of retreat facilities
- Meals
- Snacks
- Golf tournament or other organized activities
- Music and worship team expenses
- Equipment (sound systems, overhead projectors, screens)
- Speaker expenses (travel, honorarium, room)
- Incidental expenses

WRAPPING IT ALL UP

Don't underestimate the amount of time and energy it will take to plan a successful retreat. If the work falls on too few shoulders, you are primed for disappointment and burnout. It is best to have the next year's retreat chairman serve on this year's committee so that he will go into his year of leadership responsibilities with his eyes wide open. Here are some tips to help you make the most of your retreat experience in planning for future retreats.

- Keep good records of your expenses and plans. Don't re-create the wheel every year. Include retreat expenses in your overall men's ministry planning. Remember, a well-done retreat could be the most significant men's ministry activity you do all year.
- Solicit feedback from the men who attend the retreat. Ask them to be candid about what worked and what didn't. Focus on improving each year.

Retreat Budget Worksheet

Income	This Year	Last Year
Registrations: Number of people ____ @ $____	$____	$____
Sales: Books	$____	$____
Materials	$____	$____
Underwriting by church:	$____	$____
Total	$____	$____

Expenditures	This Year	Last Year
Facilities	$____	$____
Speaker honorarium	$____	$____
Music expenses	$____	$____
Entertainment	$____	$____
Staff	$____	$____
Nurse	$____	$____
Security	$____	$____
Program materials	$____	$____
Staging/decorations	$____	$____
Equipment rental	$____	$____
Promotions	$____	$____
Postage	$____	$____
Advertising	$____	$____
Food	$____	$____
Transportation	$____	$____
Insurance	$____	$____
Set-up costs	$____	$____
Cleaning costs	$____	$____
Subtotal	$____	$____
Miscellaneous (an additional 10% of subtotal)	$____	$____
Total	$____	$____
Net profit or loss	$____	$____

- Conduct a debriefing session with your leadership team after the retreat to review feedback, learn from your experience, and make course corrections for next year.

Planning a men's retreat is well worth the effort, but only if the leadership team commits to doing it right! Men will deal with life-changing issues at a retreat in ways that they won't in other environments and circumstances. Make the most of your opportunity. Make your decisions and set your plans months before the event. Don't wait until the last minute if you want to have a successful and meaningful retreat experience.

DOING TOGETHER WHAT WE CAN'T DO APART

Willie Richardson

But many who heard the message believed,
and the number of men grew to about five thousand.

Acts 4:4

More than one reason exists to establish or strengthen a men's ministry in the church, but the most important reason is to rescue men from the kingdom of darkness and see them translated into the kingdom of Christ. The mission of the church is to reach people for Christ and then to edify them. We should aim not only to help men to be obedient to the Great Commission but also to strengthen families by winning unsaved husbands and fathers. We also need to increase the ranks of single men in the church, something we've done a poor job of recently. To do that, we need to develop specific ministries to men.

We are challenged by Acts 4:4. In spite of opposition, God blessed the ministry of the first church leaders with men who believed in Christ when they heard the gospel, and the church grew by five thousand men. Today we have a generation of men who have never even been inside a church. Thousands of men do not own a Bible nor have they ever read one. Many men are members of a church but do not have a vibrant relationship with Jesus Christ as Lord and Savior. These men have to be developed through the power of the Holy Spirit into committed, reproducing believers. We have to make disciples.

Receive a Fresh Vision from God

In 1 Chronicles 12, men continued to come to support David's kingship: "Day after day men came to help David, until he had a great army, like the army of God" (1 Chron. 12:22). We need an army of Christian men who are committed to making Jesus king in the lives of men. We need you. We cannot spare a man.

Brother, you must ask yourself what the Spirit of God has been saying to you as you have read this book. It does not matter whether you are a pastor, a leader, or a layman; you can contribute to the cause of Christ by ministering to men. We need *you*.

Perhaps your vision has been broadened or you now know that you need a vision. To have a vision is to see things not as they are but as they can become. God trained Abraham to have vision. In Genesis 13, God has Abraham looking at land that belonged to others as if it belonged to him. God shows him dust grains and tells him to imagine, to *believe*, the promise that a people will come from his loins that cannot be numbered. In Genesis 15, God has him counting stars, an impossibility that challenged Abraham with the idea that masses of people would come from him and become a nation.

What is it that God is challenging you to believe and imagine he can do through you? What is it that you would like to see changed among men by the power of God? Dream a dream. Believe God for vision!

What You Can Do As an Individual

Christian, you can commit yourself to being a channel through which God can bless other men. He is always looking for men who want to be used for his glory. You can become a prayer warrior for men. You can commit to discover the needs of men. This book is a source of unlimited trails that you can investigate. Knowing the needs and issues of your men will deepen your burden for them and broaden your vision.

Every believer is commanded by the Great Commission to spread the gospel of Jesus Christ. You can become a soul winner and a personal discipler of men. I know a fellow who works at the Philadelphia International Airport, and over the last twenty years while going about his daily duties, he has led hundreds of people to Christ. His evangelism is not a part of his church's ministry; it is a personal commitment to the Lord that motivates him. His church benefits from his ministry because of all the converts who have joined the church.

The only way most people will ever be introduced to Christ is through another believer. You can be that man. All of us have a personal circle of influence—our relatives, coworkers, neighbors, and people we do business with. We can share our faith with the people in our circle who do not know Christ. Some of the men in your circle of influence will be eternally indebted to you for leading them to Christ.

What You Can Do As a Ministry Leader

I think parachurch leaders and denominational leaders serve a very special need in the kingdom of our Lord. They are similar to specialists in the medical field; they are experts at what they do. As a ministry leader, you serve as a consultant to pastors and churches. You are a researcher who studies the trends in the kingdom of Christ and lets us know what God is doing in the churches. You help us to see our weaknesses in ministry and how to correct them, and you save pastors a lot of time by helping people work together.

In the 1970s, two Campus Crusade staff people came to give me assistance in our church evangelism ministry. Our church's continual growth over the last thirty years is due largely to the expertise of those two men. One of them taught me the principles of discipling people and how to continue to identify and build leaders. The other man, a statistical and analytical expert, took our church directory and placed each member's location on a wall map, quietly letting me see that we had not reached our Jerusalem. We have continued to use their ideas in our evangelism ministry to invade and rescue sinners from the kingdom of darkness. We just recently discovered that we are not simply a local church but a regional church with members in three states. This calls for a new strategy.

Pastors, as you have already read in this book, you are the key to the success of the men's ministry in your church. Even if you do not take a hands-on role, the part you play will be crucial. It has always been clear to me as a pastor that God intended for us to do ministry through other people in the church (Eph. 4:11–12). He has called every believer to do the work of the ministry. The Holy Spirit has blessed everyone with spiritual gifts, and the nature of the gifts each person possesses determines what they should be doing in the way of ministry.

This book is a great resource for pastors and church leaders in many different ways. We have had an official men's ministry in our church for the last twenty-five years, yet this book has taught me some things and has given me many fresh ideas on how to improve the men's ministry we already have.

DOING TOGETHER WHAT WE CAN'T DO APART

This book serves as a reminder that we can do some things together that we cannot do apart. We need leaders of the same mind-set and heartbeat, men who have a passion for ministering to other men. I'm excited about the possibilities of what we can do together. As believers, we need to thank God for Pat Morley and Phil Downer, the men who brought us together because of their God-given vision. We also need to pray for Dan Erickson and the leaders of the NCMM, who have undertaken the challenging task of bringing Christian men together across denominational, ethnic, racial, and cultural lines to be the body of Christ in ministering to men. We must knit hearts and lock arms as we minister together to improve the lives of men in the world.

CONTRIBUTORS

Gary G. Bateman is the founder of ProActive Resources, which provides assessment and support resources to local churches attempting to create successful men's ministries. A Denver Seminary graduate, Gary also directs the Institute for Church Development, a nonprofit consulting organization that helps congregations and denominations become more effective in ministry. With his background in sales, Christian education, and organizational leadership, Gary provides assistance to the Evangelical Free Church of America's National Council for Men. You can write to him at growgo2@aol.com.

Chuck Brewster is the national coordinator of HonorBound: Men of Promise. For twenty-three years, Chuck served with the United States Secret Service, where his duties ranged from protecting the president to coordinating security for the 1984 Los Angeles Olympic Games. A Vietnam veteran, Chuck is dedicated to helping men grow in their commitments to God and their families. You can contact Chuck at www.honorbound.org.

Ed Cole is the founder and president of the Christian Men's Network and is generally recognized as "the father of men's ministries." With thirty-eight international offices serving more than 120 countries, CMN ministers to tens of thousands of men via books, tapes, and conferences. His books have sold over two million copies and have been translated into more than forty languages. A former pastor, evangelist, missionary, and business executive, Ed Cole continues serving the Lord by "majoring in men." You can find out more about his ministry at www.edcole.org.

Rod Cooper serves as the director of the Masters of Leadership Program at Denver Seminary. The former national director of educational ministries for Promise Keepers, Rod is one of the most sought-after speakers to Christian men today and the author of *We Stand Together: Reconciling Men of Color; Double Bind: Escaping the Contradictory Demands of Manhood;* and *Shoulder to Shoulder: The Journey from Isolation to Brotherhood.* A counselor and business consultant on conflict resolution, he has worked with numerous national organizations to encourage achievement and create successful organizational environments. You can contact Rod at www.denverseminary.org.

Haman Cross is the senior pastor at Rosedale Park Church in Detroit, Michigan. The author of several books, including *Man to Man, Cross Colors,* and *Have You Got Good Religion?* Haman is a regular contributor to several magazines and has been a guest on nearly every Christian radio and television program, including *Focus on the Family.* An electrifying preacher, he speaks regularly in Europe, Africa, and across the Americas. For more information, write to Haman at RosedaleParkCh@cs.com.

Vince D'Acchioli is the founder and president of On Target Ministries in Colorado Springs, offering management, leadership, and relational assistance to churches and other organizations. A former business executive, Vince served as the executive vice president of a worldwide missions ministry for several years and is a sought-after speaker and consultant. A frequent guest on radio and television programs, his humorous and dynamic presentations have put him at the forefront of those speaking on men's issues. Vince can be reached at www.otm.org.

Phil Downer serves as president of Discipleship Network of America (DNA). DNA is a nationwide network of people committed to following Christ's example of reaching people with the gospel, making disciples by modeling deep one-on-one relationships with men, women, couples, and families, and encouraging and training them to engage in spiritual reproduction. He is also on the steering committee of the National Coalition of Men's Ministries and a member of CBMC.

A graduate of Southern Methodist University and the Emory University School of Law, Phil was a successful lawyer before being led to Christ and discipled by fellow professionals. After leaving the position of a senior managing partner of a fifty-person law firm, he served as president of the Christian Business Men's Committee (CMBC) for a decade.

A popular speaker at men's events—and at couples' events with his wife of thirty years, Susy—he is the author of *Eternal Impact: Investing in the Lives of Men; A Father's Reward;* and *Brave, Strong, and Tender,* a book that details how this Vietnam veteran learned to transfer his leadership from the battlefield to his home, his law practice, and eventually to running a nationwide ministry. He and Susy are also coauthors with David and Theresa Ferguson of *Unlimited Partnership: Building Intimacy and Teamwork into Your Marriage.*

Phil and Susy have six children. You can get in touch with Phil by e-mail (PhilDowner@DNAministries.org) or by phone (423-886-6DNA [362]). His address is DNA Ministries, 100 Downers Grove, Signal Mountain, TN 37377.

Gordon England is the executive director of prayer and evangelism for Promise Keepers, a well-known ministry dedicated to helping men know and serve Jesus Christ. Prior to that, he served as a missionary in the Philippines, taught at two seminaries, and spent fourteen years pastoring an Evangelical Free Church. Recognized as an effective evangelist and motivational speaker, Gordon's years of cross-cultural work and his commitment to relevant ministry have formed the basis of his service to men. You may contact Gordon via www.promisekeepers.org.

Dan Erickson is the executive director for the National Coalition of Men's Ministries, a coalition of more than fifty parachurch organizations sharing the primary focus of helping the local church develop healthy men's ministries. The former director of denominational and parachurch relations for Promise Keepers, Dan uses his twenty years of pastoral experience to build relational bridges and to help Christians collaborate for the purpose of biblical unity, brotherhood, and co-mission. You can get in touch with Dan at www.ncmm.org.

Steve Farrar is the president of Men's Leadership Ministries in Dallas, Texas. One of the most popular men's speakers in America, he is the founder of Steve Farrar Men's Conferences, which equip men to be more effective spiritual leaders in their homes. His books include *Point Man: How a Man Can Lead His Family* and *Standing Tall: How a Man Can Protect His Family*. The chapter in this book titled "Working with Men Who Fail" is excerpted from his book *Finishing Strong: Finding the Power to Go the Distance* (© 1995, by Steve Farrar) and is reprinted with the kind permission of Multnomah Publishers, Inc. For more information on his ministry, you can call Steve at 1-800-MEN-LEAD. The chapter "Fathers and Sons" is excerpted from his book *Point Man: How a Man Can Lead His Family* (© 1990, by Steve Farrar), and is reprinted with the kind permission of Multnomah Publishers.

Thomas Fritz is the director of intercultural resources for Campus Crusade for Christ. Author of *Fight Like a Man* and *The Man Behind the X*, he has pioneered ministries on historically black college campuses, has founded the Impact Movement, and ministers to ethnic staff members through CCC. Tom serves on the steering committee of the National Coalition of Men's Ministries. You can contact him at ThomasGFritz@cs.com.

Geoff Gorsuch is the director of men's ministry for the Navigators. A popular author and speaker to men, Geoff was formerly the deputy director of the Navigator's ministry in France until being "loaned" to Promise Keepers to help develop their men's ministry curriculum and teach it to thousands of men across North America. A graduate of the United States Air Force Academy, Geoff flew more than one hundred combat missions over Vietnam and was awarded the Silver Star as well as four Distinguished Flying Crosses. If you'd like to contact Geoff, you can reach him at www.navigators.com.

Warren Hardig is the international director of OMS International, coordinating a program titled Men for Missions International. Formerly an executive with Standard Oil, Warren became a Christian as an adult and was led by God to begin sharing the gospel to people in other cultures, which has allowed him the opportunity to minister in fifty-five different countries. Having assisted the CoMission in the training of more than 250 missionaries to Russia, Warren wrote *Iron Sharpens Iron*, a book that has been printed in several languages. You can write to Warren at www.omsinternational.org.

Jack Hayford is the senior pastor of the Church on the Way in Van Nuys, California. His ministry reaches around the world through television, radio, and the books and music he has written over the years. Some of his books include *The Heart of Praise; Built by the Spirit;* and *The Mary Miracle*. The information in this chapter is based on material from his best-selling book *Pastors of Promise* and is reprinted with the kind permission of Regal Books. For more information, contact him at www.livingway.org.

Rick Kingham is the senior pastor at Overlake Christian Church in Redmond, Washington. One of the largest churches in the Pacific Northwest, Overlake is a growing congregation with a strong focus on evangelism, discipleship, and worship. A former vice president of Promise Keepers, Rick was one of the original men who founded that ministry and served as the radio and television host as executive producer of Promise Keepers worship projects. You can reach Rick at www.occ.org.

Larry Kreider is the president of the Gathering/USA, which offers leadership training to Christian professionals. The author of *Bottom Line Faith*, Larry is the founder of the influential Greater Orlando Leadership Foundation, a training, consulting, and resource organization that has been copied and talked about by mentors all across the country. To find out more about Larry's work, check out www.thegathering.org.

Chip MacGregor is a former pastor and a longtime men's ministry director. A frequent consultant to Christian ministries, he earned a Ph.D. in organizational development from the University of Oregon and is the coauthor of numerous books, including *Family Times* (with his wife Patti), *Standing Together* (with Howard Hendricks), and *Eternal Impact: Investing in the Lives of Men* (with Phil Downer). Chip works as a literary agent with Alive Communications in Colorado Springs and can be reached at cmacgregor@alivecom.com.

Pat Morley is one of America's most respected authorities on the unique challenges and opportunities facing men. After a successful career in business, he wrote *The Man in the Mirror*, a landmark book for Christian men that launched Pat into a speaking and writing ministry. He currently helps conduct church-sponsored men's events nationwide and chairs the steering committee for the National Coalition of Men's Ministries. For more information, you can reach Pat at www.maninthemirror.com.

Willie Richardson is founder and senior pastor of Christian Stronghold Baptist Church in Philadelphia. Under his ministry, the church has grown from six people to a thriving congregation of more than 4,000. Willie is also the president of Christian Research and Development, researching needs and methods for family training and church ministry development. He is the author of *Reclaiming the Urban Family*. You can contact him at 4701 Lancaster Avenue, Philadelphia, PA 19131-4620.

Stacy T. Rinehart is the chief executive officer of MentorLink.org, whose goal is to accelerate the mobilization and development of mentoring leaders in the body of Christ. Prior to his ministry at MentorLink, he served in numerous capacities with the Navigators. Stacy lives in Raleigh, North Carolina, and can be reached at www.MentorLink.org.

Dan Schaffer is the founder of Building Brothers, a ministry dedicated to serving the church by helping to equip men in their pursuit of God. One of the cofounders of Promise Keepers, Dan has been committed to relational discipleship since 1972 and has spoken extensively on the subject in churches across North and South America, Europe, Australia, and New Zealand. His popular book, *Brothers*, was published by NavPress. You can reach Dan at www.buildingbrothers.org.

Dale Schlafer is the founder and president of the Center for World Revival and Awakening, a ministry that works through pastors and leaders to awaken the lost and promote revival in the church. A longtime pastor and former vice president of Promise Keepers, Dale was instrumental in the success of the Fan into Flame clergy conference in Atlanta in 1996 and served as the director of Stand in the Gap in 1997 on the mall in Washington D.C.—two of the seminal events in the modern Christian men's movement. You can get in touch with him at LREVTOGO@aol.com.

Robert Sena is the National Hispanic Missionary for the North American Mission Board of the Southern Baptist Convention. He assists in the evaluation, planning, and implementation of the Hispanic Church Planting Unit and serves as a strategic resource to churches and associations, offering training to church planters and assisting in the development of strategies, services, and materials to enhance Hispanic church plants. You can reach Bobby via www.sbc.net.

Steve Sonderman is an associate pastor at Elmbrook Church in Brookfield, Wisconsin. One of only a handful of full-time men's pastors in the country, Steve regularly consults and leads seminars for churches and denominations. He founded Top Gun Ministries to help local churches develop ministries focused on the unique needs of men, and his book, *How to Build a Life-Changing Men's Ministry*, is a wonderful resource guide for those needing assistance with the nuts and bolts of creating a men's program that works. You can contact Steve through the men's ministries icon at www.elmbrook.org.

Chuck Stecker is the president and founder of A Chosen Generation, which is a Christian ministry aimed at equipping parents, pastors, and leaders to recognize and affirm godly manhood for the next generation. A lieutenant colonel in the United States Army, Chuck served in the Rangers, Airborne, and Special Forces. After retiring in 1994, he was a field director for Promise Keepers, focusing on training godly leaders to reproduce themselves in future generations. You can get in touch with Chuck at www.achosengeneration.org.

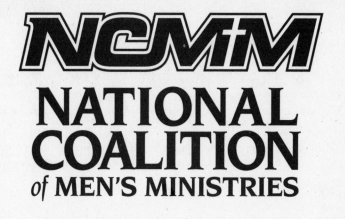

NATIONAL COALITION
of MEN'S MINISTRIES

THE MISSION OF THE NCMM

Together, we will help the local church present every man in America with a credible offer of the Gospel of Jesus Christ, encourage them to pursue God, and equip them for spiritual service in the home, church, workplace, community, and world.

THE VISION OF THE NCMM

"A disciple-making ministry to men in every willing church."

HISTORY

In January 1996, leaders of men's servant ministries (parachurch) assembled in Atlanta, Georgia, and asked the question, What can we do together that none of us could do alone? It was concluded that our calling and mission together would be to reach and equip every man in America for Jesus Christ. The National Coalition of Men's Ministries (NCMM) was formed.

In November 1997, a historic meeting of the National Coalition of Men's Ministries took place at the Billy Graham Training Center in Asheville, North Carolina, at which God supernaturally united the hearts and purposes of denominational men's ministry leaders and men's servant ministry leaders. It was concluded that God had opened a window to reach men for Jesus Christ that would last five more years, unless we, the leaders, would come together in a "one body, many parts" display of brotherhood, unity, and mission (1 Corinthians 12).

In February 1998, an equally historic meeting took place in Denver, Colorado, at which God supernaturally knit the hearts of Bill McCartney and representatives of the

NCMM together in a like manner. Because of the outcome of these two unprecedented meetings, we believe the power of God is at work among us in an extraordinary way.

THE GOALS OF THE NCMM

1. To increase the number and effectiveness of all men's ministries reaching out to men.
2. To provide an umbrella organization to unite efforts and create synergy in reaching men.
3. To increase the return on dollars invested in building more healthy families throughout the United States by building a stronger infrastructure of men's ministries.

THE TARGET MARKET OF THE NCMM

- 94 million men in America and their families
- 68 million men who do not profess the name of Christ
- 26 million men who profess the name of Christ
- 132 denominations, their pastors and leaders of men
- 320,000 churches in America, their pastors and leaders of men
- All parachurch ministries that minister to men

The National Coalition of Men's Ministries is a 501(c)(3), not-for-profit organization established in Denver, Colorado, in 1998 and is governed by a steering committee consisting of sixteen national men's leaders. Our geographic interest is primarily within the United States.

MEMBER ORGANIZATIONS

Adventures in Missions
American Baptist Men
Assemblies of God, HonorBound
Barrington Baptist Church
Bay Area Men's Ministry Alliance
Biblical Leadership for Excellence
Body Builders Ministries
Building Brothers
Career Impact Ministries, Intl.
Carolina Men of Integrity
Center for World Revival and Awakening
Center Peace Ministries
Character That Counts
Charleston Christian Men of Integrity

A Chosen Generation
Christian Men's Network
Christian Stronghold Baptist Church
Church of God Life Builders Men's Ministries
Church of God of Prophecy
Cornerstone Glory
Cross Beam Ministry
Crystal Cathedral Men's Ministries
Dad the Family Shepherd
Discipleship Network of America (DNA)
Encourage Men to Pray
Episcopal Men's Ministry Diocese of SW FL
Evangelical Free Church of America
Evangelical Presbyterian

Faith in the Family International
Family Foundation Fund
Fellowship Associates
First Baptist Church
Florida Men of Integrity
Focus on the Family Institute
Free Methodist Men's Ministry Int.
Fresh Word Ministries
The Gathering USA, Inc.
General Conference Mennonite Church
Georgia Men of Integrity
Great Dads
Hope Christian Community
Hydesville Community Church
Indiana Men of Integrity
Integrity Music Inc.
Intercultural Resources
Int'l Pentecostal Holiness Church
Jericho Ministries
Job Seekers U.S.A.
Joseph Resource Group
Kentucky Men of Integrity
Kingdom Builders
Legacy Event Mgmt, Inc.
Lehigh Valley Men of Faith
Lifeway Christian Resources
Man Adventures
Man in the Mirror
Medical Marriage and Family Ministries
Men for Missions International
Men's Life
Men's Ministry Network
MidAtlantic Christian Men of Integrity

The Missionary Church
Missions Ministries
NACCMS
National Coalition for the Protection of
    Children and Families
The Navigators
New England Men of Integrity
New Man Magazine
New York Christian Men of Integrity
North Atlanta Coalition of Men's Ministries
On Target Ministries
Priority Associates
ProActive Resources
Promise Keepers
Pure Life Ministries
Rhode Island Men of Hope
Rosedale Baptist Church
The Salvation Army
Shoulder to Shoulder
South Carolina Coalition of Men's Ministries
St. Ignatius Church
Strang Communications
Thomas Nelson Publishers
Top Gun Ministries
United Methodist Men
Valiant Brotherhood of God
Walk Thru the Bible
West Central Georgia Coalition
Wiconi International
Willow Creek Community Church
World Prayer Center
Young Business Leaders

TO CONTACT THE NCMM

Dr. Daniel L. Erickson, Executive Director
National Coalition of Men's Ministries
P. O. Box 1300
Lee's Summit, MO 64063
816-554-7009 voice mail
816-554-8186 fax
877-626-6266 toll-free
816-554-8169 home
E-mail: dexdirncmm@aol.com
Website: www.ncmm.org

We want to hear from you. Please send your comments about this book to us in care of the address below. Thank you.

ZONDERVAN™

GRAND RAPIDS, MICHIGAN 49530

www.zondervan.com